The Espresso Break

Tours and Nooks of Naples, Italy
and Beyond

Barbara Zaragoza

ISBN: 978-0-9835099-2-9

MERCHANT'S PRESS
P.O. Box 211322
Chula Vista, CA 91921
USA

CONTENTS

ACKNOWLEDGMENTS

First and foremost, I would like to thank my erudite Naples editor, Penny Ewles-Bergeron who went through this manuscript with a meticulous eye, checking for factual errors, translation errors, prose blunders, and adding extra tidbits. She also contributed extra knowledge, including the paragraph on the suburban baths for Herculaneum as well as the suburban bath photo *(p. 40)*, the research of "Pompeii yellow" for the Villa of the Mysteries *(p. 52)*, the paragraph about Paestum *(p. 36)*, the *presepe* at the Salerno Duomo *(p. 199)*, and she wrote two sub-chapters with accompanying pictures: **Le Fontanelle Cemetery** *(p. 90)* and **The Bourbon Tunnel** *(p. 92)*.

I would like to thank Don Gawlik, a wonderful sixth grade science teacher as well as an avid explorer of the region who wrote and provided the pictures for **And Beyond: San Bartolomeo** *(p. 96)* as well as **And Beyond: The Papermakers of Amalfi** *(p. 154)*. Thanks also to his wife, graphic designer and artist Leesa Zarinelli Gawlik, for providing the write-up of **The Paper Making Shop** *(p. 157)*.

Thanks to Tiziana Cirillo for giving me my first introduction to the city on a tour of downtown Naples. She also accompanied me on the interview to Café Kimbo *(p. 185)*, re-assured me of the safety of Naples, and wrote the English translation of the Neapolitan song **À Tazze 'E Caffè** *(p. 173)*. Thanks to Raffaele Iovine for showing me his work at the Santa Maria Maggiore Della Pietrasanta *(p. 84)* and, subsequent thanks goes to Luca Cuttitta, another spelunker who befriended me on Facebook and provided me with a wealth of articles on Neapolitan spelunking as well as the problems with trash and cavity collapses. Thanks to Lynn LaBenz for permission to print her post **Hospital Emergencies** *(p. 246)*. Thanks to Theresa Duran for creating the index and providing detailed formatting consultation for the entire book.

Thanks to Mauro S. for his warm hearted tour of his world famous glove factory *(p. 140)*. To Stephanie Dardanello for inviting me to visit her family's wine shop *(p. 94)*, introducing me to her wonderful in-laws, and also for taking me to the glove factory of Mauro S. To Signora Claudia di Paco and Dottoressa Marizia Rubino for their tour of the Café do Brasil factory *(p. 185)*, their wealth of information about Neapolitan caffè, and their generosity in agreeing to my visit even as the company generally keeps their doors closed due to the proprietary nature of coffee roasting. A subsequent thanks goes to Signora di Paco for providing me with the Café Kimbo pictures. Thanks also to Professor Riccardo Dalisi and friends for allowing me to interview him and take pictures of his workshop *(p. 238)*. Thanks to Teresa Massa for permission to use the picture of the Bourbon Tunnel *(p. 92)*.

A thanks to the many Neapolitan museum, library, and church employees who work very hard under severe budgetary constraints and long hours to preserve the artifacts of the city and answer questions to travel writers who just come off the streets. They are too many to name individually over my three years roaming the region, but I am grateful to so many for such warm heartedness.

Then there were those who accompanied me to my destinations, including a thanks to Laura Hitchcock who came to the Roman Cistern *(p. 24)* and searched for the Mystery Tower with me *(p. 215)*, to Cynthia Gracianette Fuerst and Bernd Fuerst for rushing over to Pausilypon with me to see the stunning sight *(p. 30)*, to Sarah Hogan for coming along on the underground tour at Caffè Gambrinus *(p. 77)* and keeping my daughter company so that it wouldn't seem soooo boring, to Wojciech Zalewski for accompanying me along the Etruscan Tour *(p. 66)*, for touring the National Library with me *(p. 61)*, and for taking the photo of the papyri *(p. 62)* for that sub-chapter, to Mary Ann Leynes for trekking down to Via Bagnoli to see the graffiti art *(p. 224)*, and to Tricia Reynolds for introducing me to the English-language ex-pat community in downtown Naples and for giving me the information about the charity work done at the Missionarie della Carita *(p. 209)*.

To Kathy Wonderly who inspired me to start a blog, which led to this book; our day-trip to Vomero for shopping and coffee began this wonderful journey. She also provided me with the tip about asking at the Capua amphitheater to get the key to the Mithras Sanctuary and lent me the Capua guidebook *(p. 200)*. Thanks also to her husband, Mike Wonderly, who subsequently provided me with the citation for that work.

To Jennifer Medveckis Marzo, my friend from our days as students at Stanford University and then pen-pals for over twenty years, who has read near everything I have ever written, provided critiques and constant support, and who I have consulted throughout the creation of this work.

Thanks goes especially to my husband, Robert Zaragoza, for the many tours we took together, in particular our many day-dates to Pompeii, where we wandered the nooks and crannies together until we could recite the streets by heart. He also helped me with the Soccer in Naples *(see p. 222)* and kissing *(see p. 236)* sub-chapters.

And finally, a thank you to my three young daughters, Nadia, Sofia, and Mimi who trekked along many of these tours, in rain or humid sunshine, in the back seat of long car rides when I thought I was interminably lost and unable to answer "Are we there yet?" For trudging through so many museums and archeological sites, despite tired feet, to see "just a bunch of old stones" – girls, you have truly earned your year-long passes to Disneyland.

INTRODUCTION

Welcome to one of the oldest cities in the Western world – Naples, Italy. This insider's guide is a compilation of three years researching and traveling throughout the Campania region and a little beyond. Founded by Greek colonists perhaps as far back as the 8th century B.C., today Naples, like southern Italy in general, tends to be less explored and even feared. Yet the Campania region boasts the best-preserved and largest collection of ancient ruins in the world at Pompeii and Herculaneum as well as a rich collection of artifacts on display at the National Archeological Museum. What's more, the powerful Kingdom of Naples was for centuries without

geopolitical rival. As the seat of the monarchy, the city employed thousands of architects, artists, writers, cooks, construction workers and more. Only when Italy unified in the late 1800's and Rome became the capital did Naples lose out. In many ways, the city sights today offer a rich and colorful record of a once illustrious capital on the Mediterranean shore. To walk down the narrow streets of the *Centro Storico* (or Historical District) of Naples is to travel back to ancient, medieval, Spanish, and Bourbon times with crumbling *palazzi*, gold-laden churches, and even sometimes trash-strewn cobblestone alleys just the way they used to be two hundred or two thousand years ago.

OLD IS BETTER

The most important part of Neapolitan culture is the attitude that *old is better*. Visit Pompeii to see the wood brick ovens and then go to a pizza restaurant afterwards or even to a friend's house to see the same wood brick oven two millennia later. The glove maker, Mauro S. *(see p. 140)*, insists that his employees use Singer sewing machines from the early 1900's. The modern artist, Riccardo Dalisi *(see p. 238)*, creates Roman masks from junk yard metals.

This guidebook tries to re-create this cultural feel of the city, using both tours and nooks to go deeper into the ancient ruins, bubbling upwards into the medieval Kingdom of Naples and shining (or darkening) into the modern twists of Neapolitan espresso. What this guide tries not to do is drone on about historical facts that are usually more like best guesses anyway. If you ask the locals about particular ruins or artifacts, notice that their answers will blend myth, legend, and historical fact.

I'd like to propose that the sights in the following pages and their stories are mostly myth, juicy folklore, and creative archeological license that allow *you* to create your own narrative. The tours are meant to be self-guided and allow for less time following the stick of a guide and more time imagining and immersing yourself in your own picture of what's important about these stones and relics. I also provide ample book, movie, and food recommendations to broaden your experience.

GO WITH THE FLOW

This guidebook is written for those who want either to drive and use an updated GPS, for those who will MapQuest their destinations before departure, or for those who will pick up a public transportation map at one of the many tourist offices around the center of Naples *(see 249)*. This travel book does not provide comprehensive directions, bus routes, or hours of operations.

Googling any one of the sights will provide an updated listing. More importantly, hours of operation are not provided because in Campania, they are utterly unreliable. Museums and archeological sites tend to shut down at all hours for all sorts of reasons. Often places close indefinitely due to budget problems or renovations and it's anybody's guess when they will re-open. And yet, remember too that often asking nicely will get you into a place before or after hours anyway. See, for example, Villa Pignatelli *(p. 215)* where I suggest that you try to make friends with the office staff so that they will give you a tour of the Carriage Museum, which has been closed to the public for twenty-odd years. Have a friendly conversation with a security guard in Pompeii and he might just take out a key and show your entire group the houses closed to the public. These are extremely important points in Naples because if you make a plan and intend to stick to it, you're likely to be very disappointed. This is a city where *going with the flow* is essential.

My **Getting There** reflects the chaos of the city, providing as much or as little information as my personal experience has proven necessary beyond Googling the sight to get the pragmatic updated information. I also use the metric system when describing distances because traffic signs and the locals will be familiar only with kilometers and meters (rather than miles and feet).

IS IT DANGEROUS?

Travelers regularly ask me if the city is dangerous, so it seems essential to answer this question first and foremost. My response: well, absolutely *no* and perhaps, *yes*, a little.

The absolutely *no* is that Italy, in terms of violent crime, is one of the safest countries in Europe and according to Neapolitan locals, so is the city of Naples. Surprised? Natives and even some expats sometimes argue it's precisely the existence of the Camorra (mafia) – whose hold has been strong here since the 1700's – that makes Naples so safe. Some locals further say that the Camorra leaves tourists completely alone because they bring money into the economy. You'll never stare eye-to-eye with a gun-toting mafia type, in spite of what the movies show, unless you have a strategic plan to buy or sell drugs and weapons. My statement: DON'T. As for the locals, if they commit a crime, the punishment might not only be in the hands of the *carabinieri*, but also the Camorra who take care of it more swiftly, which adds an extra deterrent for criminals. This, at any rate, is what a number of locals and long-time expats argued to me in order to put my anxieties to rest.

I won't give an opinion about the above reasoning behind why the violent crime rate is so low and why the Camorra stays invisible to tourists – other than bite my tongue – and if you haven't lived in the city for a very long time, I suggest you do the same. Political arguments in these parts can get heated quickly. But rest assured: Naples is safe.

So what's the *yes*, Naples is a little dangerous? First, pickpockets and thieves are rampant, which unfortunately, is not an exclusively Neapolitan problem, but seems to apply to all of Italy. I have known many people who were robbed in Naples. I, personally, never had a dime stolen from me in Naples or even in the Campania region, but my cameras, purses, and backpacks were stolen from me in Rome, Florence, and on a train to Venice. If, for example, you leave your personal belongings on a chair while paying your bill at the counter, they will be gone – I almost guarantee it. Keep your belongings close, keep expensive items out of your cars, and keep your doors locked.

Second, Naples traffic is intense. Traffic signals are merely a suggestion, the flow of cars is chaotic, and close calls are common. Auto insurance for locals is the most expensive in Europe due to the high risk of traffic accidents. Driving takes vigilance, defensiveness rather than offensiveness, and a *go with the flow* attitude *(see p. 243)*.

WHAT'S INSIDE THIS GUIDE?

For expats and the large number of military personnel living here, nine tours and thirty nooks can be enjoyed on the weekends, so that you can see the city again and again, each time in a new light. For short-term visitors, I recommend selecting only one tour and a few nooks in the city itself, allowing for ample time to find the sights.

In addition to my tours and nooks, I've added travel tips and a few essays on perennial problems faced by the city (such as trash) that are often considered controversial. You can also find my "top picks" of places  to stay, eat, pray, and shop. Because food plays such an essential role in Neapolitan life, food tidbits pepper the entire book.

While visiting sights are a fine way to experience the city, nothing compares to meeting and talking with the locals. With one million people inhabiting the city proper, the diversity of voices are essential to an appreciation of what it means to be Neapolitan. Three **Faces of Naples** are tucked in amongst the tours. In my view they represent the finest of Neapolitan history and culture.

At the end of the book, a quick reference of ten overlooked sights for Naples and all of Italy provide ideas on unusual travel. An additional five sections scattered throughout the book are what I call **"And Beyond"** that give details of off-the-beaten-track jaunts expats can enjoy for a weekend trip or travelers can easily add to a Naples vacation.

All this material (and more) can be viewed on my blog for free at **http://theespressobreak.blogspot.com**, which I wrote for almost two years. This guidebook is for those who like hard copies to carry with them along their journey or for those who still enjoy the old fashioned feel of paper. The organization of the book and much of the information is a bit different from the blog, so take a look at the table of contents in both and see what suits you.

I'd like to thank the city of Naples for hosting me with such warmth for three years and I hope your stay of any length will be as fulfilling as mine.

Enjoy!
Barbara

THE PHLEGRAEAN FIELDS TOUR

Charon ferried souls across the river Styx and sibyls uttered their trance-induced predictions – all within an eight square mile area west of Naples that today lies mostly under water. The Phlegraean Fields, also known as the Campi Flegrei or *Fields of Fire*, consist of twenty-four volcanoes and craters, many still bubbling with seismic activity.

The Greeks first settled here on the hilltop of Cuma (also written as Cumae) and centuries later, the Romans, who revered Greek culture, preserved their hilltop acropolis and built opulent getaways replete with villas, bathhouses, and domed temples nearby.

The poet Virgil (70 B.C.– 19 B.C.) is the starting point within this region from which a web of myth and history spins outwards. He spent the last ten years of his life in Naples writing *The Aeneid* whose protagonist Aeneas leaves Troy and lands on these shores. Virgil roamed this region alongside the rich and famous, describing locations that can still be visited today.

Since most short-term visitors opt to see Pompeii, these gems tend to remain quiet – desolate even. *The Espresso Break* tour starts here precisely because the sights are more accessible by car, the traffic is less intense, and a GPS brings you to the destinations easily.

Book Recommendation: A comprehensive travel guide specifically for this region is *Campi Flegrei: A Guide of Discovery to the Lands of Fire* by Massimo D'Antonio. The book is available for purchase in the bookstores at most of these locations.

A 3-DAY TOUR

Day 1:

Start in the morning at
the **Pozzuoli** port where
cafés, markets, and
restaurants line the water.
Boats depart for the
islands of Procida and
Ischia and along this way,
you'll see the **Temple of
Serapis**, which lies thirty
feet below ground level.
Drive up the hill and
you'll find the **Flavian
Amphitheater**, the third

largest next to the Roman Coliseum. Then follow the road signs to
find the **Temple of Neptune** and a few ruins of a **Necropoli
Romana**, both tucked out of the way. Head to the active crater of
Solfatara. Finish the day at **Cuma**, the oldest settlement of the
Greeks.

Day 2:

Begin the day walking around **Lago Averno**, stopping at the
Temple of Apollo and then pass the boarded up **Grotta di
Cocceio**. Make your way around the lake to the **Grotta della Sibilla**
where the Cimmerian Sibyl may have uttered her oracles in Homeric
times. Leave the lake by car and pass **Lago Lucrino**, then drive up
the mountain from the lake to find the **Archeological Park of
Baia**, a large complex that still baffles archeologists today.

Head further along the mountain to visit the **Baia Castle**. Now
drive toward Monte di Procida, park your car, and take a walk to a

private home where a lady with keys will escort you to **Piscina Mirabilis**, the grand Roman water cistern. Thereafter, you can drive to **Casina Vanvitelliana**, surrounded by a quiet park.

Next, take windy roads up, up, up a mountain as far as you can until you spill into the outlook point of **Capo Miseno** where the Roman Imperial Navy was once stationed. There's a hiking trail that leads to a **Roman Milestone**. Head back down the hill and end the day at the **Tomb of Agrippina**. This is a great place to stroll by the port, get some gelato from the outdoor vendors, or have dinner at one of the restaurants.

Day 3:

Make an appointment to visit **Pausilypon**, also known as the Villa di Pollione, located in Bacoli. A block away is the **Children's Science Center** (Città della Scienza at Via Coroglio 104, Naples). A stone's throw away is the island of **Nisida**. Next, make your way into central Naples to find **Virgil's Tomb** and peek into the mammoth **Crypta Neapoletana**. Finish the day at **Parco Virgiliano** in Posillipo for a stroll high above the city overlooking the sea.

Book Recommendations: Virgil's *Book Six* of *The Aeneid* describes, with uncanny accuracy, the sights that you can still visit today.

Although these ruins and natural features date back hundreds and thousands of years, archeologists have best preserved the structures from between the 1st century B.C. and the 1st century A.D. Therefore, I highly recommend reading the titillating descriptions of the first six Caesars, most of whom spent time here, in Suetonius' *The Twelve Caesars*.

THE FISHING TOWN OF POZZUOLI

The bustling port town of Pozzuoli thrived during Roman times when it was known as Puteoli (or "little wells"). Drive along the road by the water and you can see how archeologists have excavated the Macellum of Pozzuoli, also known as the **Temple of Serapis**. Eighteenth century excavations uncovered a statue of the god Serapis; however, these ruins were later identified as those of a two-story market first built in the late 1st century A.D.

The Romans worshipped hundreds, perhaps even thousands, of gods and Serapis was the god of the underworld, but also of the sun, healing, and fertility. Ptolemy I of Egypt created Serapis as an Egyptian-Greek god that would unite the two cultures. The Romans subsequently adopted his cult.

The market lies thirty-feet below street level due to bradyseism: the rise and fall of ground due to the ebb and flow of magma chambers deep within the earth, a phenomenon common throughout the Phlegraean Fields.

Next to the Macellum, the port blends the contemporary with the ancient world. Like their Roman forebears, fishermen still work their nets in boats. They bring plastic buckets to the banks with all kinds of live fish, shellfish, and octopi. The port is brimful with seafood restaurants along with cafés and gelaterias. Pozzuoli is also where ferries depart to the islands of **Ischia** and **Procida**. Day trips to the islands are inexpensive and easy to take *(see 'Getting There' of The Blue Grotto on p. 73-4)*.

Signs along the Pozzuoli roads point to a number of other Roman ruins. The **Temple of Neptune** overlooks the sea with its mammoth dome peeking out from the dirt. Other signs lead through a narrow tunnel and then along a road next to the **Necropoli Romana**. Hidden behind overgrown weeds, the locals walk by this ancient cemetery as though the ghosts inside are simply amicable neighbors.

The **Flavian Amphitheater** sits further up the hill in Pozzuoli and is the third largest in Italy next to the Roman Coliseum and the Capua amphitheater. This amphitheater once held up to 20,000 spectators during the first century A.D. Beneath the stadium, the visitor can see thick brick walls, fallen marble columns, and dark inlets which once housed caged wild animals and elaborate props.

While wandering around the Pozzuoli area, don't forget that the Roman senator and writer Cicero owned a villa nearby, St. Paul docked at Pozzuoli on his way to Rome, and Sophia Loren lived in the vicinity with her grandmother when bombs rained down during World War II.

Getting There: The Flavian Amphitheater is at Via Terracciano 75, Pozzuoli. From there, signs are adequately posted, making the sights easy to find if one person drives and another searches for the ruins.

Also, when in doubt – ask, ask, ask the locals. Roads accommodate the ruins, not traffic, so directions can get very confusing. Even natives stop at every block to ask for directions.

SOLFATARA

Virgil likely found his inspiration for Hades at the Solfatara crater, which continues to smolder on endlessly today. Located a few meters from the sea, an entrance leads down a tree lined path to a sandy plain. Curls of smoke puff on the slopes all around. The rotten egg smell is inescapable and, depending on the direction of the wind, wafts all the way to the city of Naples or gets carried to the city center in the trains. Two fumaroles vent their steam at somewhere around 160 degrees Celsius and turn the rocks into a copper-gold color. The Italians call these vents **La Bocca Grande** or **The Big Mouth**. Behind their plume and hiss, a green algae grows that's considered a biological rarity seen only when high temperatures and high acidity combine together.

At another end of the crater, **La Fangaia** or the boiling mud lake sizzles at temperatures between 170-250 degrees Celsius. The mud contains a cocktail of gases and minerals that the Romans harnessed for their hydrothermal spas. A few arched bricks left by the Romans still wisp with sulfurous smoke that visitors are welcome to inhale for its healthful properties.

The Romans believed that Vulcan, the god of fire, worked beneath this ground hammering and shaping his armor for the gods. Take a stick and dig a little hole into the soil, then put your finger inside to feel the intense heat. Next, throw a large rock on the ground to hear the hollow cavities underneath you.

For those who like science, four **corner reflectors** dot the sandy terrain. They work with two satellites of the European Space Agency (ESA) to reflect their signals and map

the volcano's ground deformations. The park also offers campgrounds for those who'd like to sleep for a night breathing in sulfurous fumes.

Getting There: Use a GPS or MapQuest and you'll easily find this address at Via Solfatara 161, Pozzuoli.

Book & Movie Recommendation: Modern-day Naples is known for its pollution and bad odor, but perhaps the city's seedy reputation began in ancient times when the sulfurous smell wafted from Solfatara into the city, reminding inhabitants that hell wasn't far away. Today, the hell of Naples can be found inside the world of the Neapolitan mafia. The Camorra is blamed for, among other things, the garbage collection problem *(see p. 249)* and the toxic mozzarella crisis of 2008.

A book that is essential to understanding this aspect of Naples is *Gomorrah: A Personal Journey into the Violent International Empire of Naples' Organized Crime System* by Roberto Saviano, translated by Virginia Jewiss. A movie, directed by Matteo Garrone, *Gomorra*, won the Cannes Film Festival in 2008.

THE SIBYL'S ORACLE AT CUMA

The first stop on any tour of Naples should be the acropolis of Cuma (or Cumae), first founded in the 8th century B.C. by Euboean Greeks. Virgil's account of the Sibyl's cave in *Book Six* of *The Aeneid* describes the sight as it can be seen today, giving the impression that the author must have wandered along these stones. Perhaps he strolled here with his friend Emperor Augustus who commissioned the book. Virgil left it unfinished at his death, but Augustus insisted that the work be published anyway and the epic became an instant success.

Here is how Virgil describes Aeneas' first meeting with the Cumaean Sibyl:

> This rocky citadel had been colonized by Chalcidians from Euboea, and one side of it had been hollowed out to form a vast cavern into which led a hundred broad shafts, a hundred mouths, from which streamed as many voices giving the responses of the Sibyl.[1]

The ticket office leads down a tree-lined path to a trapezoidal shaft. Known as the **Antro della Sibilla**, this is where the Cumaean Sibyl may have written down her oracles on oak leaves that then blew away. When they did so, she refused to help reassemble her messages.

Archeologists, however, ruin the mystique, claiming this was merely a Roman military tunnel and that if the Sibyl ever existed, her temple is lost to time. By Virgil's day the sibyls had already disappeared, so his own account of the woman is purely fictional.

Virgil also describes the temples at Cuma, which you can find by climbing up a flight of steps and past an overlook to the sea. Stop and take in the Bay of Naples where both the mythical Aeneas and the real-life Roman Imperial Navy could have sailed. A little further up a hill, the **Temple of Apollo** is nothing more than flattened stones, likely with philosopher spirits holding out their hands for a little money. While many young Roman students went to study in Athens, Greeks also came to this region to found their schools. It

---

1 Virgil, *The Aeneid*, trans. David West (London: Penguin Books, 2003) 116.

was the Epicurean School in Naples that first brought Virgil to the city in 48 B.C.

Another path leads to a second terrace where the **Temple of Jupiter** has more of its structure intact, but that's not saying much. The temple's stones were later used to erect a paleo-Christian basilica, a common practice after the Roman Empire banned paganism in the 300's A.D.

Returning to the ticket office, an entire city spreads out below the parking lot. The vast complex includes the **Tomb of the Sibyl**, a Greek agora (that became a **Samnite forum**), **thermal baths**, pieces of original marble  strewn everywhere, and a **necropolis** that once extended three kilometers. This area used to be a sprawling city that sat along the water, inhabited first by the Greeks and then by the Samnites – a people who, among other things, battled the Romans and spoke the Oscan language.

Walking over these stones gives the impression of a city deeply layered in cultural diversity and sophistication with much still to explore: an entire amphitheater across the street remains in situ.

Getting There: Fairly easy to find using MapQuest, the address is Via Acropoli 39, Cuma.

LAGO AVERNO

Virgil's fictional character Aeneas wandered down to Lago Averno with the Sibyl, determined to travel to Hades and consult his dead father. The name of the lake, as Book Six of *The Aeneid* tells us, comes from the Greek word *aernos* meaning *the place without birds*. In Virgil's time, the sulfurous steam from the bubbling vents of Solfatara very likely wafted to this lake, giving it a rotten smell, which made all the birds flee.

Today, Lago Averno is a water-filled crater dotted with ducks and geese. Discos and restaurants line the lake, which is popular with teenagers who find this an excellent spot to display their open affections.

A footpath circles the entire lake, punctuated with nature huts that give descriptions of the unique animals and plants inhabiting the crater. On one end of the trail, the ancient **Grotta di Cocceio** once was a Roman military tunnel that connected the lake with Cuma, but it's now closed due to structural problems.

On the other side of the lake, vineyards testify to the rich volcanic soils that make everything grow here, including excellent grapes for wine. Next to the vineyards, a **Temple of Apollo** juts out from the dirt. During the equinoxes and solstices, a group of earth lovers gather inside the temple for a festival *(see p. 193)*.

Due to bradyseism, about thirty feet of dirt buries the temple, actually believed to have been a bathing complex that harnessed underground hydrothermal activity. Only the dome can be seen, but its massive proportions show that this building once towered several stories high and probably had a technologically advanced hydraulics system.

Getting There: From Naples, take the Tangenziale in the direction of Pozzuoli. Exit at n. 14 Pozzuoli - Arco Felice. Follow signs for Napoli-Pozzuoli, Baia, and Bacoli. When you arrive at Arco Felice, turn right. Drive down the road and when you see the Bay of Naples on the left and Lago Lucrino in front of you, turn right. Go down a narrow road until you reach the lake.

Book Recommendation: *The Inferno* by Dante Alighieri. Written in the 14th century, it recounts how Dante selects the poet Virgil to take him down to hell. Lago Averno is often referred to as Dante's gate of hell.

GROTTA DELLA SIBILLA

Along the road of Lake Averno, an easily missed sign **Grotta della Sibilla** leads to a dirt path overarched with trees. The path curves and ends at a cave. Here Aeneas, with the Sibyl at his side, embarked on a journey into Hades. Nowadays instead, a charming guide, Carlo Santillo, gives tours by reservation, handing visitors candles and oil lamps.

This, archeologists say, was once a Roman military tunnel that connected Lake Averno to Lake Lucrino where fish used to be abundant until the 1538 volcanic eruption which killed them off and created a whole new mountain nearby called **Monte Nuovo**.

Inside the tunnel, carved out holes above show that during Roman times oil lamps perched in the crevices to light the way. This

also means that the space would have been filled with noxious fumes.

The cave has many corridors of what once was a sophisticated circuitry of stairs and passageways. Now they are no longer connected, but instead end in dirt or water.

One stairwell in the middle of the cave, Carlo insists, leads to the beginning of the **River Styx**. At the bottom of the stairwell lie limpid water pools, past which there is only blackness.

Going back down the main tunnel, at the very end a vast staircase leads to another cavern. This may have been a Roman restaurant, bathhouse, or – Carlo maintains – the cave of the Cimmerian Sibyl who uttered her oracles in Homeric times.

A body of water has a wooden plank where visitors cross to see the caverns in which the Sibyl bathed and uttered her predictions *(see also p. 106)*.

In truth, because of bradyseism it's difficult to tell what exactly existed here two thousand years ago; most of the grotto is under thirty to sixty feet of dirt, but when the candles go out, the pitch blackness of the cavern gives the impression of being in a place where Hades himself still roams.

Getting There: Located inside Lago Averno, the Grotta della Sibilla is privately owned and a visit is by reservation only. Call Carlo Santillo at 333 632 0642.

THE ARCHEOLOGICAL PARK OF BAIA (OR TERME ROMANE)

Virgil puttered about in this spa town and playground for rich and debauched Romans. So did other renowned Roman writers, including Horace and Cicero. Today, the villas of Baia lie mostly under water, but the Roman ruins that remain inspire the imagination due to their vast scale. The huge complex at the Archeological Park encompasses three terraces of labyrinth-like structures.

Perhaps the Romans harnessed the hydrothermal activity for their baths, or wealthy patricians built summer villas, or perhaps this was the Imperial Villa for the Emperors. Layers of ancient construction spanning four centuries baffle inquiry, but we can guess that these ruins once sparkled with skyscraper-like temples and buildings made of marble, their domes and floors tiled in mosaics and their façades splashed with deep colored frescoes.

Spaghetti alle Vongole

The port of Pozzuoli and Lago Lucrino once teemed with all sorts of fish and shellfish. The Grotto della Sibilla may also have been an upscale fish restaurant for wealthy Romans.

Today, the most common Neapolitan dish is Spaghetti alle Vongole. With its endless variations, it's simple, light, and cooks up in about ten minutes.

Here's my personal recipe:

- ½ kilogram (or 1lb.) of vermicelli
- 1 kilogram (or about 2 lbs.) of clams
- 2-3 tbsp. olive oil
- 3 cloves of garlic
- a splash of white wine
- 3 pinches of salt
- 1 fist full of chopped parsley

Cook the vermicelli in boiling water and add a liberal amount of salt. (Salt gives the pasta its flavor.) In a large pan, heat the olive oil. Add 3 cloves of chopped garlic and cook for three minutes. Add a splash of white wine. Place the clams in the pan, turn heat to low, then cover and simmer until the shells open. Drain vermicelli and add to the pan of clams. Mix the pasta and shellfish together. Top with parsley and serve immediately.

The ruins haven't been very well preserved, but while wandering through them, look for a **Statue of Hermes** that still stands in an alcove. An arched corridor leads to a grassy field named after the goddess **Sosandra**.

Three temples also display some forgotten majesty: the **Temple of Venus** overlooking the port of Baia, only its mammoth dome peeking out from the dirt; the muddy half-shell of the **Temple of Diana** sitting against a hill; and the **Temple of Mercury** (or Temple of Echoes, so named by travelers in the 18th century) has a wooden walkway over a pool of algae-green water. High-pitched yelling inside this dome makes sounds bounce in wonderful echoes.

Getting There: Although the entrance seems to be across the street from the port of Baia, the gates and entrance box are locked and abandoned. Instead, drive up the hill from the port a little ways and look for the entrance overlooking the sea. The small plaque outside reads *Terme Romana* (or "Roman Baths"), but tourist guidebooks call it "The Archeological Park of Baia." The parking lot is small, but there aren't many tourists who come this way, so it's not difficult to find a space. The address is Via Fusaro 37, Bacoli.

Book & Movie Recommendation: *The Satyricon* by Gaius Petronius is a Roman work about Encolpius and his many gay lovers. Although the book has survived only in fragments, it provides a glimpse into the life of the Romans.

The Italian film-director, Federico Fellini, made a movie in 1969 called *Satyricon* based on this Roman work. The filmmaker brought not only the dress styles and daily life of the Romans onto the screen, but also captured the foreignness of Roman cultural mores. Modern day viewers might think this film a bit bizarre.

Underwater Archeological Tours: Since much of the splendor of Baia lies under water, archeological tours are available through diving centers. **Centro Sub Campi Flegrei** at Via Napoli 1, Pozzuoli (www.centrosubcampiflegrei.it) offers dives, but you need to be a certified diver or stay longer in Naples in order to take the classes when they are offered.

JULIUS CAESAR'S SUMMER VILLA (OR BAIA CASTLE)

Perched on a steep cliff, Baia Castle, as it is known, was thought to be the summer residence of Julius Caesar. Archeologists, however, theorize that the villa actually belonged to Emperor Nero. Whatever the truth, by the late 15th century the Aragonese built a castle above the ancient Roman ruins and the fortress became an outlook point designed to scare pirates away from the shores.

During the 16th century, Barbary Pirates seized ships throughout the Mediterranean, but even during Roman times (ca. 70 B.C.) powerful Cicilian and Cretan pirates circled waters around Puteoli. They wanted, most of

all, to capture slaves and bring them to the Delos market for sale. Because policing the waters proved difficult for the Romans, the owners constructed this fortress on a cliff with sheer walls that couldn't be climbed. When the Romans did capture pirates, they weren't taken as slaves, but were settled in deserted places of the empire. Virgil, in the *Georgics*, wrote about one pirate who became a gardener in Cicilia and was renowned for his early blooms.

The outside terraces of Baia castle tout stunning views of the sea. Inside, the **Archeological Museum of Campi Flegrei** has a long stretch of rooms displaying marble statues and a multitude of other ancient artifacts found in this area.

Don't miss two important sights: The **Domitian-Nerva** is the only equestrian bronze statue to survive from ancient times. The **Nymphaeum Triclinium of Claudius** depicts a Roman dining room as it might have looked during the reign of Emperor Claudius, with marble

statues in alcoves. The front niche depicts Odysseus offering black wine to a Cyclops as told in Homer's *Odyssey*. Baio (or Bajos) stands on the opposite side of Odysseus, squeezing a wineskin. Baio was said to have been Odysseus' navigator who died and was buried somewhere in Baia – hence how the city gets its name.

Getting There: Easy to find, especially since you can see it on the cliff, Baia Castle is at Via Castello 39, Baia-Bacoli.

THE ROMAN CISTERN (OR PISCINA MIRABILIS)

Piscina Mirabilis is the largest Roman cistern still in existence today and provides a detailed glimpse into their advanced technology. Here, the Romans collected water brought by an aqueduct from the Serino River, but scholars disagree about who used this water tank. The cistern may have supplied water to the navy fleet stationed at

Miseno about one kilometer away or it might have provided water to the nearby villas.

In order to visit, you must first call a number and make an appointment. Then go to the cistern at the agreed upon time, walk down a nearby block, and call out asking the locals: "*Piscina Mirabilis?*" They will point. Follow the fingers until you reach an apartment complex where a woman comes out with her toddler – and a key in hand.

The woman walks with you to the cistern and opens the doors, but she refuses to go inside. Instead, she waits at the top while you explore on your own, trekking down steep metal steps and into a mossy cavern.

Constructed in the Augustan period, the cistern measures 70 meters long, 25.5 meters wide, and 15 meters tall. Dug into the tuff rock, it has two entrances. The first

is by way of the metal stairs. The second is on the opposite end, but the tuff stairs currently lead only to dirt. A middle nave lies one meter below the rest of the structure and once served as a decantation pool for periodic cleansing and emptying of the cistern. A thick layer of waterproof *cocciopesto* or signinum once covered the cistern walls. They were made of broken tiles mixed with mortar. The water capacity could reach 12,600 cubic meters and the Romans created hydraulic machines on the roof terrace that pumped the water.

Added to the cistern during the first and second century A.D., twelve small rooms covered by barrel vaults increased the power of the hydraulic system. These rooms can still be seen along the outside wall of the cistern.

As hollow cracks and clicks echo through this underground cavern, one wonders: if archeologists preserved this kind of impressive knowledge, did the Romans have even more innovative technology that remains lost to us moderns?

Getting There: The address is Via Piscina Mirabile, Bacoli. Call to make an appointment at 081 523 3199.

THE ROMAN IMPERIAL NAVY AT MISENUM

Capo Miseno or Misenum in Latin comes from Misenus, a character in Virgil's *The Aeneid* who drowned off the coast nearby after a trumpet competition with the sea-god Triton. It's a tough place to find; try some adventurous exploring by car and when the signs disappear, continue up, up, up through the steep and curvy road, trying to get to the peak of the mountain. When (or if) you come to a one-lane tunnel, you'll spill out on the other end into a beautiful

Vista Point overlooking the Gulf of Pozzuoli. Mt. Vesuvius and the city of Naples glimmer through the haze.

On one side of the vista, the mountain of Miseno has a walking trail, the hike leading to a **Roman Milestone**. On the other side, a gate bars access to a modern military area.

The largest Roman naval base was first established here in 27 B.C. during Emperor Augustus' rule. When Vesuvius erupted in 79 A.D., Pliny the Elder was in charge of the naval fleet and went by ship from here toward the destruction to help rescue people, but he ended up reaching Stabia where he died. His nephew, Pliny the Younger, was a resident of Misenum at the time and much later wrote an account of the eruption as he watched from this very mountain.

The Roman Caesars also used Misenum as a remote place to exile their enemies, including Agrippina the Younger.

Getting There: Getting to the vista point of Capo Miseno takes patience and the will to be an explorer through winding narrow streets. Start in Bacoli and drive up the mountain, grasping at signs wherever possible. That's the only recommendation.

Casina Vanvitelliana

After a visit to the cistern, stop by Casina Vanvitelliana at Via Fusaro 162, Baia. (See www.parcovanvitelliana for more information). A hunting lodge during Bourbon times, emperors, tsars, and famous notables rested here during their visits to the Phlegraean Fields.

THE TOMB OF AGRIPPINA

The truth about Agrippina, her death, and her remains are as difficult to find as the location itself. Signs for her tomb appear and then vanish throughout the twisting Campi Flegrei roads, but plug **Piazza Guglielmo Marconi** into a GPS and you'll see the "Via Agrippina" sign that leads down to a port. Park your car and make your way along crumbling buildings and a walkway by the sea. Another sign marks the tomb, whose bricks today are overgrown with weeds. A fence bars visitors as though making clear that the owners haven't paid their rent in years.

It's unknown if the people who called these stones the **Tomb of Agrippina** meant Agrippina the Elder or Agrippina the Younger – the story of each woman full of intrigue.

Agrippina the Elder was the granddaughter of Augustus, mother of Caligula, and grandmother of Nero. She had nine children and also accompanied her husband, Germanicus, on military campaigns, earning high respect from the Roman citizens who saw her as a heroic woman, wife, and mother. But after the death of her husband, the Emperor Tiberius banished her to an island off the coast of the Campania region. When she died, so the story goes, Caligula brought her ashes back to Rome.

Agrippina the Younger was the daughter of Agrippina the Elder and also the mother of Emperor Nero. She was renowned, above all, for her sexual escapades and ruthless will to power. While her brother Caligula was still Emperor, it is said that he would hold lavish banquets and commit incest with his sisters, including Agrippina herself. Then, Agrippina, her sister Livilla and their maternal cousin Lepidus – who were all lovers – tried to kill Caligula. For that, Agrippina was exiled.

When Caligula was murdered in 41 A.D., the new Emperor Claudius brought Agrippina the Younger back to Rome. She quickly married a second husband, Crispus. (Her first husband, Domitius, was the father of Nero. She married Domitius at the age of thirteen by the order of Tiberius.) When Crispus died, rumors held that she'd poisoned her own husband to gain his estate. And indeed, she became very wealthy. Thereafter, she became mistress to one of Emperor Claudius' advisers and through him arranged to get herself married to the Emperor himself. Her motive: to put her son Nero on the throne.

A crafty woman, Agrippina succeeded. Once married to Emperor Claudius, she schemed and ordered murders to get rid of many political rivals. Then, after Claudius adopted Nero as his son, the Emperor died and rumors abounded that Agrippina poisoned him too.

Nero took the throne and Agrippina tried to control her son and the empire, but Nero had other plans and expelled his mother to Misenum. Thereafter, he tried to kill his mother several times – but failed. Nero tried to drown Agrippina in a collapsible boat; he failed to poison her three times; he failed to crush her by a mechanical ceiling over her bed; but then he finally succeeded when he sent assassins to stab her. The Roman historian Tacitus famously wrote that just before the assassins succeeded in killing her, Agrippina shouted, "Smite my womb!"

After reading a bit about these women, the ruins resonate with ancient events. The bricks leave you waiting for Agrippina's ghost – the one Nero claimed plagued him after his mother died. Perhaps she walks through the hallway inside and travelers can be thankful that the fence limits her range.

Archeologists, however, once again ruin the myth and lore, saying that these stones were simply part of a Roman odeon (theater).

Getting There: When you reach **Piazza Guglielmo Marconi** in Bacoli, turn down onto Via Agrippina. Drive all the way to the port. The tomb is off to the left along the pedestrian walkway.

Today, moored boats bob in the port of Bacoli. A lido called **Ritorno Quintilio** (Via Spiaggia 13) overlooks the water adjacent to the tomb and two restaurants – **Da Garibaldi** and the lavish **Rock Bar** – offer epicurean delights.

Book Recommendation: For a comprehensive history of Agrippina the Younger, see *Agrippina: Sex, Power and Politics in the Early Empire* by Anthony Barrett.

THE CRUEL EQUESTRIAN KNIGHT: PAUSILYPON

When his slave broke a crystal cup, Publius Vedius Pollio condemned him to death, insisting that he be dropped into a pool of moray eels. Pollio's friend, Emperor Augustus, told the self-made ga-gillionaire to spare the slave's life. Augustus then ordered all Pollio's expensive drinking vessels smashed and his pool filled in.

Pollio was described as a cruel Roman knight of the equestrian order. He was also so wealthy that he owned a private grotto 770 meters long. People and horses could pass through the tunnel by invitation only, which led to his villa perched on a cliff. Inside, he had his own amphitheater for gladiator fights as well as an odeon for theater spectacles. After Pollio's death, the notorious minister of Tiberius, Sejanus, bought the villa. Hence, today the long tunnel is known as the **Grotta di Seiano**.

While walking down the grotto, three corridors provide ventilation. One corridor has a hallway of old toilets that people used during WWII when this tunnel was used as a temporary bomb shelter. The main tunnel ends at a pathway filled with vegetation that curves over to a massive villa, known as Pausilypon, which means a respite from toil or pain in Greek.

Publius Vedius Pollio's **amphitheater** and **odeon** are well-preserved. Broad steps take visitors up to what could have been a suite of **bedrooms** overlooking the sea. The **kitchen** downstairs still displays the original slabs of red marble against the walls. While the villa sits on a cliff, it can't be seen from any angle within the city or by boat – its construction craftily tucked into the mountain.

Behind the villa, another pathway meanders to an outlook point where three small islands dot the water. On one island, an eighteenth century villa sits abandoned. Legend has it that the owners left during the twentieth century because it was haunted by ghosts. Other folklore says that a woman lived there in complete solitude for many years until her death and the villa remained uninhabited thereafter.

Getting There: The Villa di Pollione (also called Pausilypon) with its Grotta di Seiano, is at Discesa Coroglio 36, Naples. Parking is available along the sidewalk.

When is it open? Answer: Unclear. The men at the front say they are at the desk Monday through Saturday from 9 a.m. to 1 p.m. and their tours are free. You must only call this number: 081 230 1030, which after three rings goes to a fax machine. Another number to call is: 081 575 4465, which goes to someone who gives private tours for an unknown fee. In truth, someone answers both these numbers only sporadically. My advice: be persistent and get someone on the phone to find out when the gates are open. Getting someone on the phone is the trick: it may take months and when they answer and give you a date – run over as fast as you can. It's worth the trip!

Book Recommendation: The famous Roman historian Tacitus is an amazing primary source. In *The Complete Works of Tacitus*, he describes, often in gossipy political commentator detail, the shenanigans of Sejanus as well as many others who figure prominently in Campania, including the Caesars, Agrippina, and Poppaea.

VIRGIL'S TOMB

After a decade of writing *The Aeneid* while living in Naples, Virgil traveled to Athens in 19 B.C. where he met his friend and patron, Emperor Augustus. During the trip, he caught a fever and he eventually died in the Brundisium harbor. Augustus ordered Virgil's remains sent back to Naples and today a park with a sign off the congested road between the districts of Mergellina and Fuorigrotta announces "Virgil's Tomb."

Park your car on the sidewalk to the rear of **Santa Maria di Piedigrotta Church** and then stroll through unassuming gates and a small visitor center, presumably where tickets can be purchased, but it's abandoned. Instead, the park is free to the public. A concrete path leads to an alcove with a bust of Virgil. The path turns steep after that and **plaques** in the grass identify the lush Mediterranean vegetation. Whoever takes care of this park nurtures the very plants mentioned in Virgil's works, including strawberries, myrtle, and ivy.

The path winds up to a trapezoidal **Grotta Vecchia**, also called the **Crypta Neapoletana**. It's a mammoth tunnel cut into the tuff-stone, measuring about 700 meters long by 16 meters wide that the Romans constructed during the first century B.C. A locked fence bars visitors from entering. Up high on the ceiling, there's a well-preserved, brightly colored 14th century fresco of the Madonna and Child.

The early Renaissance humanist, Petrarch, wrote that a chapel was built here in an attempt to curb pilgrims during the early Middle Ages from gathering for all-night parties and orgies in honor of the god Mithras. The Church then absorbed these gatherings into its own tradition, creating a celebration at this location for the Madonna of Piedigrotta.

As the Church increasingly pressured paganism out of existence from 330 A.D. onwards, emperors and clergy alike had a difficult time convincing people to convert fully to Christianity. As a consequence, pagan festivals were turned into Christian festivals and the Church replaced the many gods and goddesses with a variety of male and female saints. If you wander through this region long enough, you'll observe the seamless blend of pagan and Christian traditions, which no longer harbor any contradictions.

To the right of the Grotta Vecchia, steps lead to a **Roman aqueduct** that used to carry water along a one-hundred kilometer route. Additional steps lead up and across the top of the Grotta Vecchia to a **sanctuary**. Inside, a tripod burner originally dedicated to Apollo sits in a hollow space. This may have been the place where Virgil's ashes once rested.

Virgil is said to have foretold the coming of Christ in his *Eclogues*, so myths grew during medieval times about how he had possessed magical powers during his lifetime and how he even hid a magical egg inside Castel dell'Ovo *(see p. 146)*. Pilgrims, including Petrarch and Dante, continued to come to this sanctuary and pay homage to the poet for many centuries. His remains, of course, are lost to time, but from the shrine, you can admire the mystical view of downtown Naples and Mt. Vesuvius.

Getting There: The address is Via Salita della Grotta 1, Naples. You can take the Line 2 Metropolitana to the Mergellina stop and ask directions – it's only two blocks away. The park entrance lies right before a road tunnel and behind **Santa Maria di Piedigrotta Church**. It's easy to miss and there's no parking except on the sidewalk. To get there, you'll also have to wade through the Naples traffic, so the metro might be an excellent choice.

AND BEYOND: VELIA AND PAESTUM

Impecunious Greek philosophers wandered not only around the agora in Athens, but likely expounded their theories throughout today's Italian peninsula. Some of the earliest Greek philosophers, the Eleatics, lived in an area about three hours south of Naples.

Parmenides was the founder of the Eleatic School and a citizen of Elea (today Velia). Born towards the end of the sixth century B.C., at the age of sixty-five he met Socrates in Athens. He also drew up laws at Elea and his main belief was, simply stated: *All is One.*

A disciple of Parmenides, Zeno of Elea was born in 489 B.C. and he created some witty arguments to prove the impossibility of motion. His most famous argument – the paradox of the arrow in flight – explains that for any one instant in time, an arrow in flight must either move to where it is or move to where it is not. Since it can't move to where it is not, because this is a single instant and by the same token, it can't move to where it is because it's already there, logically an arrow in flight can never move in any single instant.

The Eleatics lived in a city that is located about three hours' drive south of Naples in the Cilento and Vallo di Diano National Park. Italians call the ruins Velia, but it was originally named Hyele by the Greeks who founded the city in 535 B.C. Off-the-beaten-track, these ruins contain a complex of structures, including an old marketplace at the bottom of the hill by the entrance. You can walk up a cobblestone road, taking a small detour down an overgrown path to a crumbled villa. The pathway then becomes steep and leads first to an amphitheater and then to a medieval watchtower built next to an ancient temple. A one-room museum stands off to the side with sculptures that archeologists found at the site.

Nearby, don't miss visiting the **Grotto dell'Angelo** *(see p. 74).*

Another must-see are the Greek temples at **Paestum**. Paestum dates back to 600 B.C. when it was part of Magna Graecia and the Greeks called it Poseidonia (after the god of the sea). At that time Greek colonists settled parts of the peninsula; these three temples – one to the warrior goddess Athena, two to Hera, goddess of women and marriage – remind us of their rich and sophisticated culture.

The Romans added a forum and an amphitheater to the site, but it's the temples that are so visually striking. A springtime visit means you wander through flower-strewn meadows to see the ruins. While you walk, consider the arresting fact that the malarial swamps once surrounded the temples, which is why these stones were not robbed out for use in other buildings.

Not far away, a small museum displays the many finds from the site and has some well-preserved frescoes from tombs, including the iconic image of a lone young man diving into a stream.

Getting To Velia: You won't find directions on-line and a GPS won't get you there either. I found Velia through trial and error and I share the insider's scoop here: Take the A3 Salerno-Reggio Calabria autostrada until you see the signs for Cilento. Exit at the Cilento SS road 267 that follows the coast from Agropoli to Velia. Follow the signs and ask a lot of people along the way. You'll find many places to eat, wonderful beaches, and very few tourists at the actual ruins.

Getting To Paestum: Easy to find, from the A3 heading south take the SS18 all the way into Paestum. See also www.paestumsites.it.

THE ANCIENT ROMAN TOUR

For travelers whose stay is short, Pompeii and the National Archeological Museum are the top two sights of the city. Guided tours are available everywhere, but for those who would rather wander on their own, this chapter provides self-guided tours, the top *must-see* items at the National Archeological Museum, and also describes some well-preserved villas and artifacts of the Roman world from before the eruption of Mt. Vesuvius in 79 A.D. You can find more information about many of these sights, including hours of operation and short term exhibits at this excellent website: www.pompeiisites.org.

HERCULANEUM: A SELF-GUIDED TOUR

Herculaneum, as the myth goes, was founded by Hercules. The town does have Greek origins, the city having come into existence sometime in the 6th century B.C. The Romans had conquered Herculaneum by 89 B.C. and soon the city became a high-class resort with many wealthy Roman residences. The eruption of Mt. Vesuvius, however, plunged the city into a huge river of boiling mud and debris twenty meters deep. The population probably had time to reach the sea, but they perished in the first of a series of pyroclastic

surges of ash and hot gases, as evidenced by the human remains found lying next to boats.

In 1709 an Austrian General, Prince d'Elboeuf, hearing of treasures being unearthed near his estate at Portici, bought the land and engaged workers to begin to dig. They discovered part of Herculaneum's theater and in 1738 the **Villa of the Papyri** – an area still not open to the public – was found with a library consisting of about 2,000 papyrus scrolls. Today, the scrolls are housed in the Naples National Library and the artifacts found in the villa are located downtown at the National Archeological Museum.

After you leave the ticket office, a long bridge curves above the entire ancient city, giving a bird's eye view of its streets and buildings. Some say that visitors who have scant time should choose Herculaneum over Pompeii because the city is better preserved, and most impressively, the structures include original wood materials that normally would have decayed if the city hadn't been covered by volcanic ash.

Make sure to pick up a map and a small brochure at the ticket office, then follow this path.

What To See:

Walking along the bridge, you enter the ruins of a long cobblestone street. Go all the way down this street and take a right turn at the very end. Here you come to the **Welder's Shop** with a smelting crucible and terracotta vats used to cool forged pieces of metal.

Next to this house is a preserved lead pipe – evidence that the city once had a highly developed plumbing system.

Take a right down another street and you immediately come to the **House of Nero's Living Room**. This villa shows the opulence and grandeur of villas through its large atrium and faded frescoes.

A little further along this road is the most impressive villa of the entire site – the **House of the Neptune and Amphitrite**. At the back of this house, a wall mosaic sparkles with blues, reds, and coral pink.

Then along the same street the **Trellis House** preserves the original wood and reed laths. This used to be a lower class multi-family dwelling – effectively a boarding house.

Go down to the end of this street and turn left and left again. You enter the **House of the Stags** where excavators found round marble tables and sculptures of stags and dogs. This villa once had a view to the sea.

Leave the villa and turn left up the street to the **Gymnasium**. To your right, a vast area was once dedicated to sporting activities and a tunnel inside the gymnasium once led to an indoor pool. Now, a large hydra replica adorns the hollow space.

Return back toward the House of the Stags and follow the stairs until you reach the **Ancient Beach** where archeologists found the skeletons of more than three hundred people who tried to escape in boats. You can see the arches of former boathouses and, looking at the cliff above, appreciate the level to which the city was covered by volcanic debris. A nine-meter long ship was also discovered here.

Just above the port area are the sumptuous **Suburban Baths**, built around 40 A.D. The elegant marble decoration indicates an up-market clientele for this bath complex. When the hot mud poured in, a labrum, or tub, was torn from its stand and the impression of it remains in the solidified lava.

From here a bridge passes over the port area and into a tunnel where stairs take you back to the entrance. Along the way back to the ticket office, an exhibition space houses a re-creation of a Roman ship.

Getting There: Herculaneum sits below the present day town of Ercolano. It's fairly simple to get there using a GPS and taking the autostrada is a welcome break from the bumper to hood traffic of downtown Naples. A large paid parking lot is right outside the gates of Herculaneum. The address is Traversa Via Alveo, Ercolano. Alternatively take the Circumvesuviana train line to Ercolano Scavi station and the ruins are a ten minute walk away.

For a full day-trip, after your visit to Herculaneum walk to the **Portici villas and the royal palace** *(see p. 217),* then shop at the **Resina Via Pugliano** market in the modern-day city of Ercolano *(see p. 268).*

POMPEII: A SELF-GUIDED TOUR

Pompeii, the most visited attraction in the Campania region, is swamped by tourists most of the year. Because archeologists have re-created a veritable Disneyland of the ancient world, nowhere else can you find the wealth and expansive feel of walking back in time. To beat the crowds, try to visit on a weekday in the middle of winter – that's when you'll get the city almost all to yourself.

Mary Beard's *Pompeii: The Life of a Roman Town* describes the smells, sounds, and important individuals of this frozen city. The culture comes alive with chapters that describe how the Romans worshipped, dined, and entertained themselves. The prose is accessible and I have used the book to describe some of the sights in the following self-guided tour. I recommend reading the book beforehand, so that you can recognize and fill in the following summarized descriptions as you walk along the streets. For a fictional account of the last days of Pompeii, Robert Harris' book *Pompeii* is also a gripping and fun read.

Pompeii was founded around the 6th century B.C., so by the time Mt. Vesuvius erupted on August 24, 79 A.D. the city already had several hundred years of history. However, most of what you see today is how the inhabitants lived and died on that fatal day in 79 A.D.

The decorating style of Pompeiians at this frozen moment is worth noting. They adored Greek art and culture, which for them was as far back as the Renaissance is for us. They also admired Egyptian art and religion, building temples to Egyptian deities and decorating their homes with Egyptian motifs. Again,  the world of the Pharaohs for Pompeiians was as distant to them as the Roman world is to us.

Okay – so gear up for a day at Pompeii. When you buy a ticket at the entrance, go to the information desk and get yourself a map and a small descriptive booklet. Then, using the map, see the following places in this order. This self-guided tour can take anywhere from three to five hours depending on how fast you walk.

What To See:

The Forum: Walk from the entrance through the Sea Gate, an inclined cobblestone pathway that goes under an arched tunnel.

(Remember, Pompeii was once a port town and the sea was close to where you are walking.) You then spill into the center of the city – the Forum. Take a look at Mt. Vesuvius in the distance and imagine that day when pumice spewed from the sky. The Forum itself is surrounded by public buildings, including the Temple of Jupiter, the Temple of Apollo, a storehouse with pottery and plaster casts of Pompeiians, and a market where the woolen cloth guilds once sold their wares. The Temple of Apollo is the oldest in Pompeii, dating back to the 6th century B.C. The largest edifice in the Forum, the Building of Eumachia, was sponsored by a wealthy female priestess of Venus.

Via dell'Abbondanza: The liveliest street in Pompeii, the name was made up by archeologists along with every other street name in the city because we don't actually know what the Romans called these roads.

Follow this street to see the *dolia* (terracotta receptacles) in shops that sold all manner of food. Pompeii was most famous for its *garum*, or fish sauce. Some of these places were stores and others were bars. Tour guides will tell you the citizens of Pompeii always ate lunch outside the home. Oil lamps within the restaurants and bars hint that they had customers all day and all night, which makes sense considering most people lived in cramped quarters, so they likely lived most of their lives either outside or in these establishments.

The streets had very high stone sidewalks because garbage collection always posed a problem, as it does today *(see p. 249)*.

They also were likely strewn with refuse dumped from chamber pots, animal dung, rotting vegetables, and even on occasion human body parts. The smells would have been pungent. Notice also there were no drains in the streets, so when it rained the roads would turn into torrents of water that, helpfully, washed away the trash[2]... best not to ask where.

The large blocks at the end of the streets barred wheeled transport from entering (particularly into the Forum). The streets were also one-way, which kept jingling carts from colliding.[3]

The Brothel: Situated on Brothel Lane, a narrow side-street off Via dell'Abbondanza, the brothel has a small hallway with several bedrooms to the right and left. Inside these bedrooms are broad slabs.

This was the largest brothel of the city, run by a woman (known as a *leonine*), but prostitutes in Pompeii were everywhere. Prices ranged from two to eight *sesterces* (a portion of wine cost one *sesterces*) and the earnings usually went to the *leonine*. It's believed that prostitutes weren't allowed to wear standard women's clothes, instead dressing in a male toga. Prostitutes could be slaves or free women. Their customers would have ranged from actors and gladiators, seamen from the port to wealthy Roman citizens.

Graffiti left by customers indicate that most Pompeiians were literate, but prostitutes wouldn't have necessarily known Latin or have known how to read and write. (Pompeii, interestingly, was a multi-lingual city with Oscan used just as often as Latin.) The frescoes show many different sexual positions and it's thought that perhaps a man would point to one of the pictures before entering a bedroom, letting the prostitute know what kind of service he would enjoy for the night.[4]

---

2 Mary Beard, *Pompeii: The Life of a Roman Town* (London: Profile Books, 2008) 55-7.

3 Ibid., 65-6.

4 Ibid., 233-40.

Along Via dell'Abbondanza are four "must-see" houses:

House of the Chaste Lovers: This house is named for a fresco depicting two couples reclining and dining. One couple steals a tender kiss. The front of this building was a bakery and behind it were a dining room and a living room. A mule carcass was found in situ, showing how the owners ran in haste during the eruption, leaving their animals behind. The mules lived in the house and drove the millstone for grinding wheat.

House of the Painters: A cadre of professional painters were in the middle of painting lavish frescoes in this home when Mt. Vesuvius erupted and they hopped up and left without their brushes and paints. From their abandoned paraphernalia we catch a glimpse of how painters created their frescoes.

Thermopolium of Vetutius Placidus: This thermopolium looked out onto the street and had benches as well as *dolia* containing food. Behind the restaurant is the owner's house with a *Rape of Europa* fresco located in the garden triclinium. (A triclinium was the place where Romans ate their meals, probably reclining on long couches.)

You can also take a side road off Via dell'Abbondanza right before the House of the Painters and visit the **House of the Ceii**. A political campaign message on the house's facade has the name L. Ceius Secundus. A large hunting scene with Egyptian themes is painted on the back wall of this house.

**Toward the end of the excavation area on
Via dell'Abbondanza are:**

House of Octavius Quartio: Two long pools have a temple in
the middle and frescoes on one end. This was once the outdoor
dining area for a wealthy family.

House of Venus: A Venus fresco was painted in the back of
the villa. During WWII bombs fell on Pompeii, destroying this villa,
but archeologists reconstructed it – showing how Pompeii is far
more of a tourist-friendly theme park than an accurate portrayal of
excavations. In fact, most of these re-created homes were thirty feet
underground and piece-by-piece brought to the surface and
reconstructed. It's always good to remember that much of what we
see today has been created with some form of artistic license by
archeologists *(see p. 252)*.

**Take a right turn at the end of the road and you'll see the
amphitheater up ahead. Remember, archeologists still haven't
excavated all of Pompeii. Only about thirty percent of the city
is available to visitors
today.**

The Amphitheater:
At the far end of Pompeii,
the earliest stone
amphitheater in the
ancient world could hold
up to 20,000 spectators.
Adjacent to it was the
training space for

Ancient Roman Recipes

Roman writers left numerous records on botany, agriculture, and food preparation. Virgil, for example, named many of the plants that existed during his time. Food recipes appear in the works of Marcus Porcius Cato, in the collection dedicated to Marcus Gavius Apicius and the writings of Lucius Junius Moderatus Columella.

Eugenia Salza Prina Ricotti has collected many ancient Roman recipes into a book called *Ricette Della Cucina Romana A Pompei* (or *Recipes of the Roman Kitchen in Pompeii*). The author is an archeologist who has written extensively on the Roman period.

Also, when you visit Pompeii look for the Botanical Gardens and the vineyards, where gardeners painstakingly re-create the vegetation that existed two thousand years ago.

gladiators, surrounded by porches, and a swimming pool in its center. Gladiators were often slaves or condemned criminals. A *lanista* or a troupe manager controlled when the gladiators performed. He also scouted for new recruits and acquired animals from distant parts of the empire.[5]

The gladiators themselves lived in the most basic of barracks where no traces of beds have been found. They kept bronze

---

5 Ibid., 269.

decorated helmets and an assortment of daggers in their rooms. Some fame came with the best fighters and it was said that they had enormous sex appeal for the women. However, considering most of the graffiti, such as "Celadus, heartthrob of the girls" was written in the gladiator barracks, these notes were likely written by the gladiators themselves who faced a short life in cramped quarters and never actually got a girl. The death rate among gladiators was about one in six for each show.[6]

The audio guide that you can purchase at the Information Office will also tell you about the Nocera protests that happened here. As with soccer fans today *(see p. 222)* the rival supporters from Nocera and Pompeii got a little out of hand. A fight began and turned wild in 59 A.D. and several people were killed. Thereafter, Pompeiians forbid Nocerans from stepping foot in their city for many years. The town of Nocera still exists not far away and, hopefully, relations between the two towns are better today.

Via dei Sepolcri: The main road leaving Pompeii was lined with tombs, poor graves side by side with wealthy sepulchers. Marble statues of families can still be seen above their tombs along with Latin inscriptions. The priestess Eumachia's tomb is the largest.

Nearby is a monument built by ex-slave Publius Vesonius Phileros. Three statues stand side by side with their heads missing. One is a statue of Marcus Orfellius Faustus, his erstwhile friend. Phileros added a plaque before he died that said:

---

6 Ibid., 272-4.

Publius Vesonius Phileros, freedman of a woman, Augustalis, built this monument for himself and his kin in his lifetime, for Vesonia, daughter of Publius, his patron and for Marcus Orfellius Faustus, son of Marcus, his friend. Stranger, stop a little while if it isn't too much trouble and learn what to avoid. This man that I had hoped was my friend – it was he who produced accusers against me and started a court case. I thank the gods and my innocence that I was freed from all this trouble. May neither the household gods nor the gods below receive the man who lied about our affairs.[7]

Many Pompeiians took this road as they fled the city, carrying their valuables with them. One man carried a sword, another woman carried a figurine of the goddess Fortuna. Children kept up with parents, but these people didn't make it past this road and succumbed to the ash.[8]

Check the map now and ask directions. This is where the walking tour can get a little confusing.

Garden of the Fugitives: A vast number of plaster casts lie next to these vineyards in a large glass case. Giuseppe Fiorelli, director of the Pompeii digs in the late 19th century, invented the plaster cast method. He poured liquid plaster into a cavity left in the bed of ashes by the gradual decomposition of the victim's body. As the plaster solidified, it reproduced the body's shape.

---

7 Ibid., 312.

8 Ibid., 1-2.

House of the Ship *Europa*: Excavators found seeds in twenty-eight terracotta vases as well as the remains of animals in the stalls at the back of the garden. The owners here may have once grown beans, onions, cabbage, grapes, and more. The front room displays a stone olive oil press.

Temple of Isis: The number of gods and goddesses in the ancient world likely numbered more than the living human population of Pompeii.[9] The debates Romans would have with each other over religion would revolve around whether they did actually take human form and when & why they intervened in human lives, but generally there were no tenets of belief. Instead, religious worship was active, most often centering around communal animal sacrifice.[10] Handouts of animal meat from the sacrifices were given to the rich, not the poor.[11] New gods could be recruited from among mortal men, in particular emperors.[12] The most prominent worship in Pompeii was of Isis and other Egyptian deities. Offering hope of life after death, initiates of Isis bathed themselves in water brought especially from the Nile.[13] The Isis temple here was built at the end of the 2nd century B.C. and two other Egyptian deities were honored within the niches.

The Great Theater and Small Theater are just up the way and to your left from the Temple of Isis. Pompeii was a theatrical town and by now you may have noticed that many houses were decorated with images from the stage. The pantomime was a major attraction in Pompeii and a portrait at the Temple of Isis as well as at the Building of Eumachia in the Forum commemorate Caius Norbanus Sorex, who was a mime actor.[14]

---

9 Ibid., 276.

10 Ibid., 278-9.

11 Ibid., 292.

12 Ibid., 299.

13 Ibid., 303-5.

14 Ibid., 256.

Return to Via dell'Abbondanza and enter the Forum. From there, go up toward the cafeteria and have a snack. A few steps from there, visit:

The Forum Baths: Wherever there is Roman culture, there is a Roman bath. Here, Pompeiians exercised, steamed, swam, gamed, or enjoyed barber services. The baths were a social leveler too, only the richest having their own private baths at home.

The Forum Baths, one of three bath complexes in Pompeii, are larger than the Forum itself. The construction of a male and female bath house dates back to about 80 B.C. Since most people didn't have indoor plumbing, this was where they came to wash. The baths had a changing room (*apodyterium*), a room for a cold bath (*frigidarium*), lukewarm bath (*tepidarium*), and a hot bath (*caldarium*). Today the visitor can still see stucco friezes and frescoes in these rooms. In the lukewarm bath, terracotta figures of Atlas support a frieze with entwining plant motifs. In the hot water bath, a large marble fountain adorns the front niche.

The Forum Baths are newly renovated and replace the Stabian Baths, which are closed to the public, but the fact that two large bathhouses existed only blocks apart tells of the prominence of this practice.

House of the Tragic Poet: Just across the street from the exit of the forum baths, this house has an impressive mosaic of a barking dog with the words *Cave Canum* – "Beware of Dog."

House of the Faun: The largest of all the villas and the most famous, this wealthy dwelling had airy rooms and some indications of indoor baths, toilets, and kitchen areas. Visitors can see an accurate copy of a 2nd century B.C. dancing faun in bronze. Most impressive is the mosaic – using somewhere between 1.5 and 5 million tiny stones or *tesserae* – depicting a battle between Alexander the Great and the Persian King Darius (the original now housed at the National Archeological Museum – *see p. 60)*. This house is also the oldest, built in the late 2nd century B.C.

From here, walk back to the House of the Tragic Poet and then pass it, coming to the end of the road. Turn right and amble along another street going downhill. Eventually, you come to what looks like a country road. You round a bend and enter the most impressive villa of all:

Villa of the Mysteries: Frescoes with deep red colors depict Dionysian or Orphic initiation rites. The images lead archeologists to believe that a priestess of the Dionysian cult owned this villa.

A final surprising thought about the famous Pompeiian red color: recent research at La Sapienza University in Rome has revealed that many of the reds we see in Pompeii and Herculaneum were once yellow and turned dark red as a result of exposure to hot gases during the eruption.

From here, you can exit and walk straight along the road until you reach the entrance again.

Getting There: You can either take the Circumvesuviana train to Pompeii Scavi station, which conveniently lets you out right next to the entrance gates, or you can drive. Pompeii is right off the autostrada and easy to find using MapQuest or a GPS. There are plenty of paid parking lots in the vicinity. The address is Via Sacra 1, Pompei.

THE VILLA OF POPPAEA IN OPLONTIS

An ancient map named this suburb city of Pompeii Oplontis. Today, the modern town is known as Torre Annunziata. What remains of the Roman suburb is a well-preserved villa ten meters below the modern street level where visitors can roam a massive residential complex that archeologists believe  once belonged to Nero's wife, Poppaea Sabina.

Buried during the eruption of Mt. Vesuvius in 79 A.D., the rooms still tell a compelling story about the daily lives of its former inhabitants. The first room at the entrance of the villa is the atrium, a grand sitting room with an opening in the roof and a corresponding tub in the center of the floor that collects rainwater. A brick oven looks as though it could still be fired up and the adjacent triclinium still boasts red frescoes. There are latrines with top slabs and a channel below. At the entrance to the bathroom, a tub once contained water used to clean out the channel. The bath rooms are particularly impressive, including a *caldarium* and *tepidarium* that once had an advanced system of hot and warm air flowing along the walls and under the floor. Roofless indoor gardens still depict lush vegetation on the walls and vast gardens are lined with marble sculptures. Archeologists have also created casts out of the roots of tall trees they found here, which are believed to have been sycamores.

Cassata Di Oplontis

Eugenia Salza Prina Ricotti in her book *Ricette Della Cucina Romana A Pompei* describes a dessert called "Cassata di Oplontis." The dessert mixes dried apricots, prunes, raisins, and caramelized walnuts into ricotta and places the soft mixture between marzipan dough. Neapolitans still make this dish, calling it Tutti-Frutti.

If you don't want to make it at home, visit **Il Principe Restaurant** at Piazza Bartolo Longo 8, Pompei (www.ilprincipe.com) located in the piazza of modern-day Pompei. This restaurant serves Cassata di Oplontis as well as dishes with ancient *garum* sauce. They also hold parties in ancient Roman style.

The villa truly comes alive with the history of Poppaea Sabina (30-65 A.D.). Apparently, she was cruel, bisexual, and enjoyed taking milk baths, especially with her female servants. Born in Pompeii and possibly living at what today is called the House of Menander, her mother committed suicide when Poppaea was seventeen. At the age of fourteen she had already married Rufrius Crispinus, a man of Egyptian origin and leader of the Praetorian Guard. (The military group that assisted emperors in campaigns and were known for their intrigues and assassinations.) But Poppaea divorced him and married Otho, a good friend of Emperor Nero. Then, Nero fell in love with her and she became his favorite mistress. Some sources, including Tacitus, claim that seeing her advantage, Poppaea convinced Nero to kill his mother, Agrippina. After Nero's mother was out of the way, she pressured Nero to divorce and later execute his wife, Claudia Octavia. Poppaea then became pregnant and bore Nero one daughter who died at four months of age. Two years later, while she was pregnant with their second child, Nero killed her.

Tacitus describes her death this way:

> Soon after the games Poppaea died. She was pregnant, and her husband, in a chance fit of anger, kicked her. Some writers record that she was poisoned; but this sounds malevolent rather than truthful, and I do not believe it – for Nero wanted children and loved his wife. She was buried in the Mausoleum of Augustus. Her body was not cremated in the Roman fashion, but was stuffed with spices and embalmed in the manner of foreign potentates. At the State funeral, Nero mounted the platform to praise her looks, her parenthood of an infant now deified, and her other lucky assets which could be interpreted as virtues.
>
> Publicly Poppaea's death was mourned. But those who remembered her immorality and cruelty welcomed it....[15]

Of course, archeologists debate whether Poppaea resided here at all. The villa was heavily damaged during the earthquake of 62 A.D. and left abandoned thereafter, so by the time ash from the Mt. Vesuvius eruption covered the villa, nobody inhabited these fresco-filled rooms.

Getting There: The address is Via Sepolcri 1, Torre Annunziata. Although you can get here by train and the villa is a short walk from Torre Annunziata, this town is considered somewhat seedy, so driving by car is a better option. While again, not dangerous in terms of violent crime, it's best to keep your purses and wallets close.

BOSCOREALE

Tucked away behind a complex of apartments, Boscoreale lies about two kilometers away from Pompeii. In Roman times, the area was part of a hunting reserve.

---

15 Publius Cornelius Tacitus, *The Annals of Imperial Rome*, trans. Michael Grant (London: Penguin Classics, 1977) 384.

This particular villa burned down during the eruption of Mt. Vesuvius, so there's not much to see. A grassy slope leads to the excavation site thirty feet below ground level. Only a few rooms remain, but the kitchen makes the visit worthwhile. Inside are rows of buried amphorae that must have held all sorts of delights.

Next to the villa, a small museum houses frescoes, marble statues, and other items, but there's no brochure and the collection is eclectic, not necessarily displaying what was found exclusively at this location.

Interestingly, a huge number of coins were hidden in a cistern at Boscoreale just before the eruption. They were re-discovered in the

late nineteenth century and museums throughout Europe, including the Louvre, snatched up the coins for their own collections. Fortunately, the National Archeological Museum in downtown Naples *(see p. 60)* also houses many frescoes and coins from Boscoreale.

Getting There: The address is Via Settetermini 15, Boscoreale.

Wine Recommendation: *Lacryma Christi* comes from this region. The name, meaning the *Tears of Christ*, derives from an old tale that when Christ wept over Lucifer's fall from heaven (and into the fiery pit of lava), his tears fell along the sides of the volcano. Christ's tears then made the soil along the lower slopes of Mt. Vesuvius extremely fertile, and indeed fruits, vegetables, and wine grapes grow here in abundance all year round.

STABIA

Pliny the Elder described the many luxury villas of Stabia, a popular resort for wealthy Romans. Pliny died here after setting sail from Misenum and crossing the Bay of Naples to rescue people during the 79 A.D. eruption. Stabia itself was destroyed by more than ten feet of volcanic ash.

Driving through small streets, you might go in circles for a while, passing town centers where vendors sell pizza and caffè. Stabia was once a resort town, which lies about five kilometers from Pompeii and on the way to Sorrento and the Amalfi Coast. You know you've found the ruins when you hit a long narrow road with signs leading to an empty parking lot. A trailer is wedged to the left of a gravel road. After you buy a ticket inside the trailer, a guide escorts you to a stunning edifice hovering over a dramatic view of Naples.

The **Villa of Arianna** stretches along a walkway overlooking Mt. Vesuvius much like the ancient Roman villas that once stood along this ridge overlooking the bay. This huge villa was once richly decorated with deep colored frescoes on every wall, detailed mosaics on every floor, and a complicated maze of rooms. The building grew gradually over 150 years, so it's hard to get a complete picture of what functions all the rooms had. A service quarter has a masonry hearth and a courtyard with a square pool, probably used as a hatchery for small fish. A thermal quarter with a *caldarium, tepidarium,*

and *frigidarium* preserve a lead water-duct that brought the water from a pool. A bronze cauldron also still exists that was used to heat the *caldarium*.

One other villa is also open to the public, located down the road from the Villa of Arianna: the **Villa San Marco**, which measures more than 11,000 square meters. On a stroll through this structure you will see a well-preserved atrium, triclinium, and kitchen. The villa also once had an extensive bath system. Along the walls are detailed frescoes and there's also a large *palestra* (gymnasium) inside.

Getting There: Use a GPS and plug in Via Passeggiata Archeologica, Castellammare di Stabia. The Circumvesuviana railway stops nearby, but to get to the ruins you'll have to take a taxi or drive on your own. Check www.stabiae.com for more information. From the Stabia Circumvesuviana stop, you can also take the funicular to **Monte Faito** *(see p. 232).*

MT. VESUVIUS

Mt. Vesuvius looms over every bit of the Naples region. The only active volcano on the mainland continent of Europe, Mt. Vesuvius is over twelve thousand years old. Its highest point is 1,270 meters high and records show that before 79 A.D. its slopes were probably covered by forest. At its foot the lush soil made cultivation of various crops easy, especially vines.

A visit to the volcano means driving up a narrow winding road with easy-to-follow signs, until you stop at the parking lot. Walk to a hut where you can purchase tickets and hike beyond a gate. From here, the trek to the peak takes about twenty minutes, souvenir shops and caffès available along the way. On a clear day the breathtaking view of Naples as well as the three islands of Capri, Ischia, and Procida make the steep climb very pleasurable.

Once at the top, the inside of the crater is filled with dirt – sorry, you can't see bubbling lava. However, the experience can feel a bit daring only because vulcanologists anticipate another eruption sometime soon. Interestingly, that doesn't prevent Neapolitans from building a sprawling metropolis around the skirts of this active volcano.

Getting There: By car, take the A3 Napoli-Salerno autostrada and exit at Ercolano. Follow the clearly marked *Vesuvio* signs for about thirteen kilometers until you reach the entrance gate at the bottom of Mt. Vesuvius. You can also ask outside the gates of Pompeii or take the Circumvesuviana line to Ercolano Scavi station and the locals will direct you to buses that shuttle you up to the volcano.

Art Recommendation: The modern artist Andy Warhol painted many images of the volcano. His original works of Mt. Vesuvius can be visited at both the **National Museum of Capodimonte** *(see p. 123)* and the modern art museum **MADRE** in downtown Naples *(see p. 228).*

THE NATIONAL ARCHEOLOGICAL MUSEUM: FIVE MUST-SEE'S

Boasting one of the largest collections of ancient Roman artifacts, the National Archeological Museum can and should be visited over and over again, but what to look for and not get overwhelmed? Here are my top five picks of what to see:

The **Villa of the Papyri** displays fantastic bronze sculptures (look for the Bust of Seneca) as well as a few papyrus scrolls. These items were discovered at Herculaneum in a villa believed to have been owned by the father-in-law of Julius Caesar. The largest part of the papyrus scroll collection can be found at the National Library, but here you'll see a few samples as well as the rudimentary gadgets initially used to unroll the scrolls.

The Secret Cabinet is an ongoing favorite. Displaying erotic statues such as Priapus and sexually explicit frescoes from Pompeii, the area is off-limits to children.

The Alexander Mosaic: The largest and oldest villa in Pompeii – the House of the Faun (see p. 51-2) – once had a mammoth floor mosaic displaying Alexander the Great's victory over the Persian emperor Darius III. The mosaic is now housed in the museum.

The **Farnese Hercules** is a Roman copy (3rd century A.D.) of a lost Greek sculpture made by the Greek master sculptor, Lysippus, in the 4th century B.C. The sculpture was famous in the ancient world.

Paquius Proculus and His Wife is the original 1st century A.D. painting from Pompeii that is most often seen in reproduction.

There's much more to explore, including any temporary exhibitions. The museum also has the third largest collection of Egyptian artifacts and re-creates the Temple of Isis. The Farnese collection includes the largest number of Roman copies of classical Greek sculptures – the only surviving indications of those lost works. And finally, if you take my Phlegraean Fields tour and this Ancient Roman tour, you'll then find a rich selection of artifacts from the aforementioned sights, including Baia, Boscoreale, Stabia, and Cuma.

Getting There: Take the metro to Piazza Cavour. When you exit the station, the museum is toward your right along Via Foria. The address is Piazza Museo Nazionale 19, Naples.

Before you go, consider heading to the Wine Shop (see p. 94) only a block away to get a little modern-day Pompei wine poured for you into a plastic cup from a spout.

THE NATIONAL LIBRARY

There was a time when an olfactory sensation went hand in hand with the visual pleasure of reading. Yes, books and libraries had smells, whether of paper or of leather, that can't be replicated in the on-line world.

To trek back into the past, you can take a free tour of the National Library in downtown Naples. Established within the Palazzo Reale in 1804 the library currently houses more than 1,775,588 volumes and prints.

On an interesting note, libraries in Europe differ from America in that they don't use the Dewey decimal system. At the National Library, they also don't organize their collection by subject matter. Instead, books are stored in a labyrinth of back rooms. Students, scholars, and the general public look up what they want in the card catalog or at the on-line computer catalogue and then request the materials from the librarians.

If you make an appointment with the public relations department, they hospitably offer free tours that take you inside these back rooms. You can walk through high ceiling hallways and past rooms bursting with materials mostly collected to preserve the art, history, and culture of Italy. At the very back of the library, scrolls from the **Villa of the Papyri** are on display.

The eruption of Mt. Vesuvius in 79 A.D. carbonized the collection of approximately 2,000 papyri scrolls that are believed to have belonged to the father-in-law of Julius Caesar. The ash turned them into what looked like burnt wood. For two centuries after their discovery, conservators attempted to open the scrolls and succeeded through different methods. By 1984 a Norwegian team used a glue composed of gelatin and acetic acid to separate many more.

Some papyri are, nevertheless, too damaged to read. But astonishingly others — when put under strong light — have writing that can be deciphered by even an untrained eye. Most of the papyri are written in Greek and are philosophical texts from the 3rd century B.C. to the 1st century A.D., many of them from Epicurus' *On Nature* (particularly significant for this region as Virgil initially came to Naples to study with the Epicureans). The librarians open the glass cabinets for visitors who can then bring their noses inches away from an original papyrus scroll.

The tour also includes a visit to the rare manuscripts department where a librarian puts on white gloves before bringing out several illuminated manuscripts, including an original handwritten book by St. Thomas Aquinas (who spent time in Naples – *see p. 207*) as well as a 500 A.D. Greek manuscript on pharmacology.

Best of all, the library is open to anyone who wishes to read in the sitting rooms. You're given a free locker at the entrance for storing your belongings and then, if you wish, you can inhale the smell of books, books, and more books.

Getting There: The address is Palazzo Reale, Piazza del Plebiscito 1, Naples. For tours contact the public relations department by email urp@bnnonline.it or call 081 781 9231/387.

VILLA OF TIBERIUS IN SPERLONGA

Driving north of Naples toward Formia and Gaeta, you come to sheer cliffs that overlook the sea at Sperlonga. Here, the Emperor Tiberius (42 B.C. – 37 A.D.) created a summer villa which included a grotto.

Suetonius has an other-worldly description of the Emperor:

Tiberius was strongly and heavily built, and above average height. His shoulders and chest were broad, and his body perfectly proportioned from top to toe. His left hand was more agile than the right, and so strong that he could poke a hole in a sound, newly plucked apple or wound the skull of a boy or young man with a flick of his finger. He had a handsome, fresh-complexioned face, though subject to occasional rashes of pimples. Letting his back hair grow down over the nape seems to have been a family habit of the Claudii. Tiberius' eyes were remarkably large and possessed the unusual power of seeing in the dark...[16]

Suetonius explains that as a young man, Tiberius distinguished himself in the military. He married Vipsania whom he loved, but Emperor Augustus forced him to divorce her and marry Julia the

---

16 Gaius Tranquillus Suetonius, *The Twelve Caesars*, trans. Robert Graves, intro. and notes J.B. Rives (London: Penguin Books, 2007) 140.

Elder, Augustus' daughter. Tiberius loathed Julia who was known to be very promiscuous.

When Augustus died and Tiberius was his only remaining heir, he at first ruled with equanimity, consulting his senators for every decision and remaining humble to the point of refusing to be considered a deity. He even remained prudish during this period, issuing an edict against promiscuous kissing.

After the death of his son Drusus at Rome and then of his adopted son Germanicus in Syria, Tiberius went to Campania, but he probably didn't stay here long. Sejanus won the Emperor's gratitude when the roof of the grotto at these Sperlonga ruins collapsed while Tiberius dined; Sejanus saved his life. Sejanus then persuaded the Emperor to live in Capri, leaving Sejanus to rule Rome as he wished. In **Capri**, Tiberius' life took a turn to the darker side (see p. 71).

The villa in Sperlonga lies along the shore of a public beach. Tiberius didn't worship any gods, believing that the world was ruled by fate, so it's interesting that this grotto was once filled with marble statues of the gods and also included a naked Polyphemus being speared. The impressive **Polyphemus statue** still exists in the accompanying **Archeological Museum** at the entrance to the complex.

Getting There: Drive north of Naples toward Formia and then follow the signs to Sperlonga. After that, signs are everywhere to the Tiberius Villa. Next to the ruins there's one of the few **public beaches** where you can swim in the Mediterranean or sit on the sand. While there, you can also visit the city of Formia that boasts, among other things, **Cicero's Tomb**. Nearby, the city of Gaeta has **Split Rock** where the rock is said to have split three-ways on the day that Jesus was crucified. You can also follow the signs to the **Grotte di Pastena** *(see p. 70)*.

AND BEYOND:
THE ETRUSCANS

The Etruscans once lived in the Umbria and Tuscany regions, some settling as far down the boot as Capua in Campania. Archeological remains set their beginnings at 1200 B.C. Through the centuries, they co-existed with the Greek colonizers and then with the Romans, trading and warring with them. Cross-cultural integration also occurred as exemplified through the three Etruscan Kings of Rome from 600-500 B.C. and the large number of Greek vases found in Etruscan tombs.

What made the Etruscans well-known throughout the ancient world was their technological savvy in mining metals. It seems that the Etruscans traded their metals thanks to an insatiable desire for gold, which they could only acquire through contact with the outside world.

Though the Etruscans left very few written documents – the most descriptive only a few lines long – we do know that they used a non-Indo-European language. Their art shows they were likely either heavily influenced by Eastern dress and artwork, or possibly came from the East themselves. As a consequence, questions persist as to whether they were indigenous or first settled the region from a faraway land.

We know of them predominantly through their richly-decorated cemeteries full of red and black painted vases, opulently sculpted sarcophagi, and the many multi-colored frescoes on the walls of their tombs.

Cerveteri has the largest necropolis in the world next to the Egyptian pyramids; the cemetery is layered with a thousand empty Etruscan tombs. What archeologists have found inside the tombs, they have preserved at the **Etruscan Museum** in downtown Cerveteri.

In **Tarquinia**, travelers can visit another twenty or so Etruscan tombs. They remain buried under several feet of dirt, thereby better preserving the paintings inside. The frescoes – in various conditions – depict dolphins jumping next to seamen and lavish banquets with their accompanying musicians. It seems that the above-ground urns kept the cremated remains of poor people, while the rich received the opulent tombs below.

Beyond the Tarquinia tombs, visitors can look out to the **Tyrrhenian Sea** where the Etruscans once sailed their ships. According to Roman writers, the Etruscans were notorious pirates. They also liked to send their dearly departed into the next world with an abundance of goodies. What remained in their tombs by the nineteenth century was taken out by the city of Tarquinia and placed in the city's own **Etruscan Museum**.

Orvieto is another once Etruscan city perched up on sheer cliffs. The **necropolis** still sits right under the cliff with a maze of stone tombs. Then, on the hilltop, Orvieto's **visitor information center** gives tours of the caverns hollowed deep inside the rock. During the Middle Ages monks created wine-cellar-like spaces to house pigeons bred for the table. The monks also used a stone olive oil press in this underground. Most impressive for the Etruscan tour is the **one-hundred meter deep well**. Archeologists are stumped as to what kind of technology the Etruscans had in order to build this well. They dug one-hundred meters down, carving footholds into the tuff stone, but how they were able to breathe by the time they got down to the bottom remains a question; no oxygen exists that deep, only carbon dioxide.

The Etruscans were wiped off the map when the Romans annexed their territory during the 1st century B.C. The Romans probably looted and burned most of their cities and ancient writers then recounted only stories about Etruscan ruthlessness in war and reckless piracy. Today, what little remains of the Etruscans still incites an intense curiosity and a desire to uncover their mysteries.

Places To See: Use a GPS and plug in these cities: Cerveteri and Tarquinia, which are located in Lazio. The towns are small and the Etruscan sights are easy to find. The **National Etruscan Museum in Rome** (Piazzale di Villa Giulia 9, Rome) is also a nice start or finish to an Etruscan tour.

The number of Etruscan artifacts preserved throughout Italian cities are large and the following website provides comprehensive information: www.mysteriousetruscans.com.

Book Recommendations: *The Etruscans* by Michael Grant and D.H. Lawrence's *Etruscan Places*.

THE GROTTO TOUR

The nature lover, the spelunker, or children who want to climb and jump far away from museums will enjoy a grotto tour. The porous tuff stone makes grottoes particularly abundant in this region. Geologists will tell you that a natural grotto is defined as a small cave near water that is liable to flood at high tide. The word comes from the vulgar Latin *grupta* meaning "crypt."

The history of grottoes predates the existence of human beings, their stalactites and stalagmites reaching back tens of thousands of years. In ancient times grottoes were considered the dwelling places of gods and goddesses. Perhaps Ovid got his inspiration for his

Metamorphoses here, describing nymphs, gods, goddesses, and humans bathing in these cool waters.

If you are driving from Rome going south, you will find the following nine caves described in this chapter, listed in order.

Book Recommendation: *Heavenly Caves: Reflections on the Garden Grotto* by Naomi Miller. This book traces the development of the grotto from antiquity to modern times.

Another useful source is the Roman writer Ovid. His *Metamorphoses* describes the many gods, goddesses, and nymphs who lived in these magical places.

GROTTE DI PASTENA

The impressive and yet out of the way Grotte di Pastena is about eighty-five kilometers north of Naples. If you drive to the city of Formia, signs for the grotto begin along the road, but beware: the signs don't mark the number of kilometers to the destination, taking you instead into endlessly winding and mountainous roads.

An hour's drive later amid beautiful views of valleys and lush vegetation, the signs lead to a gravel parking lot replete with a restaurant and souvenir shop. The entrance to the grotto is at the end of the parking lot and a concrete pathway leads down a hill to a rock opening with shades of copper and mossy green.

The grotto system measures 2,127 meters long and is actually a huge river cave. The river drains into the cave from the valley, creating a sinkhole.

The tour begins in a chamber, where you can see small blue lakes and water streams. Stalagmites rise from the floor and stalactites hang from the ceiling of caves, which form through the dripping of mineral-saturated water.

The echo of running water persists throughout the tour accompanied by the sound of squeaking bats. As you walk deeper and deeper into the cave, a path takes you to a sheer dark cliff on one side and turns down into another tunnel, leading into a dark grotto. Here, impressive stalagmites scatter up a hill until dirt meets the rock above. Bats fly all around and a large black mound of bat excrement towers in the middle, prompting most tourists to comment: "Eeew."

Getting There: Either follow the signs from Formia for the scenic route or drive along the A1 either from Rome or from Naples until you see the signs to the Grotte di Pastena. The address is Via Porta Napoli, Pastena.

VILLA OF TIBERIUS

(See page 63.)

GROTTA DELLA SIBILLA

(See page 17.)

GROTTA DI SEIANO

(See page 30.)

GROTTA VECCHIA

(See page 32.)

THE BLUE GROTTO (AND THE ISLAND OF CAPRI)

Capri is a resort island reached by boat from Naples. When you arrive, take the **funicular** to the piazzetta (little square) where *It Started In Naples* was filmed starring Sophia Loren and Clark Gable. From here, walk two kilometers along narrow roads lined with white washed buildings and where hotel carts zip past. You'll end at the eerie remains of Emperor Tiberius' villa, called the **Jovis Villa**.

The emperor's summer villa still exists in Sperlonga *(see p. 63)*, but Tiberius exiled himself to the Jovis Villa with its stunning views of the sea. He then left the day-to-day ruling of Rome to his ruthless praetorian guard Sejanus.

The two historians who documented Tiberius' life, Tacitus and Suetonius, claim that by the time he lived in Capri, he was a depraved man. Known by his subjects as "Biberius" for his hard drinking, Suetonius seemed to almost enjoy the detailed descriptions of Tiberius' time on the island. Suetonius wrote:

> Bevies of girls and toy boys, whom he had collected from all over as adepts in unnatural practices and who were known as *spintriae*, would perform before him in groups of three to excite his waning passions. A number of small rooms were furnished with the most indecent pictures and statuary obtainable, as well as the erotic manuals of Elephantis; the inmates of the establishment would know from these exactly what was expected of them. He furthermore devised little nooks of lechery in the woods and glades of the island, and had boys and girls dressed up as Pans and nymphs posted in front of caverns or grottoes, so that the island was now openly and generally called "Caprineum."[17]

Leaving the governance of Rome to the ruthless Sejanus, Tiberius was no less ruthless on his island. Suetonius also said:

> In Capreae they still talk about how the place at the cliff top where Tiberius used to watch his victims being thrown into the sea after prolonged and exquisite tortures. A party of marines was stationed below, and when the bodies came hurtling down they whacked at them with oars and boat hooks, to make sure that they were completely dead. An ingenious torture of Tiberius' devising was to trick men into drinking huge draughts of wine, and then suddenly to knot a cord tightly around their genitals, which not only cut into the flesh but prevented them from urinating.[18]

17 Suetonius, *op. cit.*, 127.

18 Suetonius, *op. cit.*, 137.

Tiberius became so ruthless while exiling himself on Capri that upon his death at the age of seventy-seven, he was denied the usual divine honors of a Caesar and mobs of people in the streets of Rome yelled "To the Tiber with Tiberius." They refused even to bury his body.

Today, beaches and quiet nature make this island beautiful. The **Blue Grotto** is the main tourist attraction, which would be a wonderful experience – if it wasn't also a real assault on the pocketbook.

You pay a fee at the harbor and a boat takes you along the sheer cliffs until you reach the opening of the grotto. Here, you're required to pay another fee to get into a row boat. The rower then tells you to lie down in the boat. He pulls at a chain strung through a small rock opening and the boat rushes inside. You enter a cavern where startling electric blue ambient light shines from the bottom of the water. The rower sings a song – often this is *O Sole Mio* but we got something from the Spanish group *Gypsy Kings* – his voice echoing throughout the cave along with the many other boatmen. He then asks for a tip before you leave his rowboat... and asks for an additional tip after that.

It's brief, has a measure of magic but is, above all, an expensive experience that may leave you with a Tiberius-like sense of fiduciary perversity.

Getting There: You can catch a fast hydrofoil (*aliscafo*) to Capri every hour of every day at the Molo Beverello port in downtown Naples across the street from Castel Nuovo. Slower ferries (whether a *nave* or *traghetto*) depart from the nearby Calata Porta di Massa port or from Pozzuoli. Check timetables (*orari*) at any tourist office *(see also p. 249)* or on-line at the ferry and jet services, including: www.caremar.it and www.snav.it.

GROTTA DELL'ANGELO DI PERTOSA

Near the Greek ruins of Velia, a ferryman escorts you into a boat and pulls you deep into the cave. Once you disembark, the tour goes through a grotto of impressive lights, pathways lined with moist rock formations, and ends with pictures of modern day men, such as Mussolini, who the grotto caretakers claim are likely living out eternity in Dante's description of *Inferno*.

A stage production of Dante's *Inferno* takes place in the grotto during the year. You can find more information about the production at www.grottedellangelo.sa.it/dante.asp. The address is: Località Muraglione 18/20, Pertosa (SA).

THE EMERALD GROTTO

Also known as the Grotta di Smeraldo, you can charter a boat that takes you to the bay in Conca dei Marini about three miles west of Amalfi. The name of the grotto comes from the green color of the water that reflects off the ceilings and floors. (Google the grotto name to find the companies, along with their telephone numbers and addresses, that give tours and provide boats.)

GROTTA PALAZZESE

A high-class restaurant located inside a grotto, many famous people come here to dine and stay at the expensive hotel. It's off the Adriatic Coast and their website offers a glimpse of the experience as well as more information at www.grottapalazzese.it.

THE NAPLES UNDERGROUND TOUR

Naples, in truth, is a tale of two cities. One, the narrow streets with seemingly no logic, full of bustling traffic. The other, more than 3,000 years old that curves, collapses, and hollows underground. Sixty percent of Neapolitan inhabitants live on top of more than seven hundred cavities underneath the city. These subterranean passageways include old Roman markets, theaters, grottoes, crypts, and former bomb shelters. Most of these undergrounds remain closed or barely discovered; many are even privately owned.

Neapolitan spelunkers dedicate themselves to the study of these cavities. Otherwise known as speleologists, they study the structure, physical properties, history, and life forms inside caves. They also study the processes by which caves form (speleogenesis) and how caves change over time (speleomorphology). The term speleology is also commonly known as caving, spelunking, or potholing.

For up-to-date information about Neapolitan spelunking activities, you can visit the English language website www.napoliunderground.org or the Italian language www.lamacchinadeltempo.info. Larry Ray also has a wonderful history of the Naples underground. You can find him at www.larryray.com/napolibelow.htm.

Although this chapter provides mostly guided tours of the underground, keep an eye out for speleologists throughout the city who might be willing to show you some non-tourist gems. For example, on a visit to the **Church of Santa Maria Maggiore Della Pietrasanta** in the historic center, I met Raffaele Iovine who gave me a tour of a Roman cistern underneath a church. I also visited a **wine shop** where Stephanie Dardanello and her family took me down to her family's cellar that was once part of a Roman road.

Spelunkers aren't the only ones interested in the Naples underground. Mafia clans purportedly have created drug labs in underground caverns near the Naples central train station and city officials also have had on-going debates about whether these cavities could serve as repositories for trash. Meanwhile, residents live above the cavities much like they do at the foot of their active volcano – for the moment. To illustrate the dangers, in September 2009 three chasms opened up in the middle of Naples; one hole was twenty meters deep and forced almost three hundred people to evacuate their homes *(see p. 254)*.

For curious travelers, however, the underground is also an exciting playground. An underground tour of places outside the city include: the **Grotto Tour** covered in the previous chapter, the **Grotta della Sibilla** *(see p. 17)*, **Piscina Mirabilis** *(see p. 24)*, and the **Sanctuary of Mithras** in Capua *(see p. 200)*.

This chapter covers underground visits available within the city of Naples proper. **Caffè Gambrinus** offers tours that include air raid shelters and narrow passageways (only in Italian). In the *Centro Storico*, **Napoli Sotterranea** provides daily tours in English. Across the street, you can visit **San Lorenzo Maggiore** with its old Roman market. A little further along these streets, you can tour an underground dedicated to the souls of **purgatory**. Near Capodimonte, you can find the **Catacombs of San Gennaro** and if you buy a ticket to these catacombs, you can also visit the **Catacombs of San Gaudioso**. **Le Fontanelle Cemetery** contains thousands of spooky skulls and **The Bourbon Tunnel** offers a glimpse of three key periods of Neapolitan history: the 1630's, 1850's, and 1940's.

Be aware that tours of the underground can get claustrophobic due to narrow spaces. Also, the underground tours open or close throughout the year depending on safety factors, lack of funds, or reasons that simply befuddle visitors. That said, this chapter is a starting point for exploring the many fascinating aspects of speleology in the city of Naples. Many newly explored cavities continue to open to visitors and if you bring a spirit of adventure, you might just return above ground with an itch to become a spelunker.

CAFFÈ GAMBRINUS

An underground tour at a cafè? Yep. Several times every week urban speleologist, Signor Quaranta, a slender Neapolitan with lots of energy and funny stories that are hard to understand due to his Neapolitan dialect, takes groups from Caffè Gambrinus up a narrow street and into a double door that says "Napoli Sotterranea."

You walk past a small room and continue on to a whitewashed hall. Suddenly, you descend 118 stairs that spiral down past a small chapel, then to an open space where plastic chairs are in rows.

Signor Quaranta begins by telling visitors that they are sitting in an ancient aqueduct. The Greeks first harnessed the springs from the foot of Mt. Vesuvius and channeled the water into these underground cisterns, some as deep as eighty meters. Neapolitans used the cisterns as drinking water all the way up until the 1800's.

At some point in the history of Naples, most residential buildings (*palazzi*) had wells in their courtyards and even well-spouts in every room. The *pozzari* (or well attendants – from *pozzo* for "well") worked in these cisterns, scuffling through narrowly built holes, cleaning sinks and siphons, and making sure the cistern water ran clear. Palazzo owners regularly gave the *pozzari* money for their services, but the *pozzari* would additionally trick wealthy landowners into paying them to re-clean the wells. One *pozzaro*, for example, put a dead cat in the cistern so as to ensure himself more work.

There is also a wealth of folklore about the *munacielli*, or Neapolitan house goblins, that played tricks on those who lived in their homes. It's said that one goblin was a sickly boy who was raised in a convent where nuns hid his deformity by dressing him as a monk (hence the diminutive *munaciello*). When he died under mysterious circumstances, Neapolitans began to experience sightings of him. They conferred magical powers on the dead boy and said that he carried the lucky numbers necessary to win the lottery. Other folklore maintained that the goblins were the *pozzari* themselves who would get into homes through the channels used to lower the buckets.

After Signor Quaranta's talk, you walk through some of the fifteen kilometers of underground made of porous tuff stone. The ceilings often drip with water due to the humidity. The moist environment is supposedly healthy for respiration, helping (and possibly curing) people with asthma.

Visitors then walk through a maze of narrow passageways and plunge into great halls. Graffiti remains everywhere from World War II when people hid here waiting for the war to end. Above an alcove, graffiti commemorates the day two people were married under a tuff arch in 1943. Another room has graffiti that reads: "Women are the way to true happiness."

Scuttling through more small spaces, eventually you end back in the hollow space with chairs. Signor Quaranta turns off the lights for a few moments so that you can sit in the pitch black and in silence – an odd feeling when Naples bustles with frenetic activity above. This tour is especially welcome during the hot summer months, the temperate climate of the parallel city making it the most comfortable spot in Naples.

Getting There: Stand outside Caffè Gambrinus in Piazza Trieste e Trento at the designated hour. Someone will be there to lead you to the underground. A wonderful Napoli Sotterranea website exists with more information at www.lanapolisotterranea.it.

NAPOLI SOTTERRANEA

Every visit to Naples should include a tour led by Napoli Sotterranea. Located along a side-street in the *Centro Storico*, don't confuse this comprehensive tour given in many languages, including English, with the tour given at Caffè Gambrinus by the same name. Also don't confuse this underground with the similarly advertised tour one block down at the San Lorenzo Maggiore Underground.

The tour begins with a walk to an apartment building. Some years back, archeologists noticed a recycled Roman marble slab used in the construction of the edifice's top corner. They guessed that Roman ruins lay underneath the building and knocked at the door of an apartment on the bottom floor. The owner told them his apartment included an underground cellar as well as a parking garage for *motorini* (scooters). Archeologists climbed down to take a look,

then asked if they could start digging. Sure enough, they hit upon a Roman odeon built during Emperor Nero's reign.

The tour guide brings you inside the apartment decorated with 1950's furniture. He lifts up a bed, reveals a trap door, and leads you down stairs into the cellar/parking garage. Diagonal lattices (*opus reticulata*) against some of the walls show how the Romans built their structures in such a way as to make them earthquake proof.

Leaving the underground through a side door, the tour guide leads you back to the ticket entrance and takes you down a long stairwell. At the very bottom, you come to a vast underground of hollow areas and narrow passageways.

This underground was first used as an aqueduct during Greek and Roman times and dates back to the 4th century B.C. The water system continued to be used until 1825 when officials shut it down because of a cholera outbreak. The aqueduct was re-opened and used as a bomb shelter during World War II.

Napoli Sotterranea has created a kitsch-like museum in several hollow areas, including World War II displays of army tanks, military uniforms, and toys left by children. Over 20,000 people waited out the war here and graffiti can still be seen on the walls, from the words *Help* (*Aiuto*) to pictures of bombs drawn by children.

In another room, a display of fake rocks and an electric pulley show how the ancient Greeks and Romans once used these cavities to cut tuff stones with large axes, hauling the pieces through holes in the ceiling. The materials were then used in the construction of buildings.

Down one corridor, biologists have set up a bed of plants that never need to be watered because the underground atmosphere boasts eighty percent humidity. The guide explains that when you exhale, you can see your breath.

Next, the guide hands out candles and takes visitors through thin passageways. This part is not for the claustrophobic; you follow the guide through hallway circuits until you reach a water cistern. During Roman times, the public used the larger cisterns for drinking water, while wealthy families would buy a cistern for their private use, pulling up water through holes leading into their homes.

The tour ends in a cavity that sits below the San Gregorio Armeno Church *(see also p. 113)*. Here, the Saint Patricia Order of Nuns store their homemade wine. The tour, terribly enough, does not include a taste of the wine and their cellar remains closed to the public.

Getting There: The address is Piazza San Gaetano 68, Naples. You can find out more at www.napolisotterranea.org.

SAN LORENZO MAGGIORE

In the heart of the *Centro Storico*, San Lorenzo Maggiore is a smaller underground, but you can walk inside without a guide to view crumbled archways and vendor shops. It's also the only underground that has preserved the city's ancient foundations.

The ruins date back to the Imperial Age following the earthquakes of 62 and 64 A.D. Archeologists have found oil lamps imported from North Africa, but the lamps show no trace of usage. In this way, experts hypothesize that the lamps were stock items and, therefore, this must have been a bustling marketplace that offered international wares.

Amphorae were found here in abundance, once holding regional wines that sold in exchange for fish (*garum*) sauce that arrived from the Iberian Peninsula, dried meat from North Africa, and oil that was likely imported from Greece. The vase makers often put their trademark

names on the amphorae, such as A. Vibius Scrofula and A. Valerius Fortunatus.

The names themselves spark unanswerable questions: Who were these people? How did they live? What happened to them?

The amphorae as well as other ceramics are on display in the museum upstairs. Within the underground, you wander along barren dirt paths and up metal stairs, where hollow vendor spaces give only a glimpse into the look and feel of this once bustling market, but one brick oven is so well preserved that it seems that at any moment wooden logs might flicker again with fire.

The **San Lorenzo Maggiore Church** standing right next door to the underground is worth a peek too. First built in the 6th century A.D., a new basilica was constructed over the paleo-Christian site during the 12th century. The writer Boccaccio also fell in love with Fiammetta here.

Getting There: The address is Via Tribunali 316, Naples.

PURGATORY

According to Dante, the Mountain of Purgatory was the only land that existed in the southern hemisphere. It came into existence because of the displaced rock that resulted when Satan's fall created hell. Today, purgatory can be found along a narrow street in the *Centro Storico* at the **Santa Maria Church of the Souls of Purgatory.** The baroque façade has a show of skulls and femurs adorned daily with fresh flowers and candles. Neapolitan noble families commissioned the construction of this church in the early 1600's so that they could bury their loved ones in crypts under the city.

Stairs in the back of the church descend to an underground cathedral, now only hollow tuff stone with niches on either side.

Mozzarella di Bufala

Ostriches, elephants, buffalo and all manner of exotic animals were shipped from Africa to be served at the triclinium couches during lavish Roman banquets. The buffalo stayed, giving rise to what is famously known as a Campania original: mozzarella di bufala.

Probably the most ubiquitous sight in all of Campania, the mozzarella di bufala ball is made from real buffalo milk. The best place to purchase these large balls of cheese is at the many **Caseifici** throughout the region that often provide tours of their factories and show you how the balls are made.

Once you buy a ball or two, never refrigerate. Keep mozzarella balls at room temperature and then, in keeping with the tradition of simplicity in cooking, take them out of their water and serve one ball on a plate plain. Eat with knife and fork as an antipasto or as a snack. You can also combine slices with vine tomatoes and fresh basil leaves for a delicious *insalata caprese*.

For more about mozzarella, see www.mozzarelladop.it.

Across the underground cathedral, a doorway leads to a hallway where rectangular holes display unburied skulls and bones. From here, the visitor enters a cavern that has two long beds of dirt on either side. Looking closer, these are unmarked graves. Niches in the walls display a plethora of skulls and bones, burgeoning onto the sides of the walkways and littered with small pictures of the deceased.

Up at the front of this cavernous room, an altar swells with flowers, rosaries, and other memorabilia left by devotees. To the right of the altar, sickly-sweet smelling flowers and handwritten cards sit underneath the remains of Lucia, the virgin-bride. Legend has it – and many different versions of the legend exist – that Lucia was the only daughter of Domenico d'Amore, the prince of

Ruffano. In 1789, at the age of seventeen, she died of consumption shortly before she was to wed the Marquis Giacomo Santomango. The tragedy caused a tumult of heartfelt emotion by the populous who up until this day still leave fresh flowers and handwritten cards underneath her skull and bones.

After a visit to this church, you can cross to the street named **Vico Purgatorio Ad Arco** and stroll down what feels like purgatory lane.

Getting There: The address is Via Tribunali 39, Naples. The church is open Monday through Saturday from 10 a.m. to 1 p.m., but the underground tour takes place only on Saturdays. You should get there at 10 a.m. for a tour, although they might make you wait until more people show up. In truth, the time of the tour varies according to what's happening at that moment. Best to call this number to make an appointment: 081 551 9547.

SANTA MARIA DELLA PIETRASANTA

With a passionate heart for history and a little knowledge of the Italian language, this is how easy it can be to find underground gems of the city. I write here of my personal experience:

Santa Maria Maggiore Della Pietrasanta Church was named after a holy stone (*pietrasanta*) and built by Cosimo Fanzago over the ruins of an early Christian basilica. When I entered this church, I spotted a young spelunker going inside and asked if I could speak with the custodian about the history of the Church. Instead, she briskly told me to follow and suddenly I was walking down steep steps into the underground belly of the edifice.

There, stones lay scattered everywhere and researchers bustled through an airy space. Excited, I forgot about the Church history entirely and asked about the history of this space. An enthusiastic researcher introduced himself as Raffaele Iovine and immediately gave me a tour.

He explained that the church is the most ancient in Naples, commissioned in 566 A.D. by Bishop Pomponio. It was constructed over a Roman villa, which in turn was constructed over the Greek

foundations of Neapolis. Raffaele took me over to an enclosed area where he showed me the slanted Roman bricks and the Greek walls underneath. Most amazing of all, this space had a massive Greco-Roman aqueduct dating back to 500 B.C. The aqueduct was three kilometers long and began with an four hundred meter deep water tank (cistern) that could be accessed by spelunking down into it.

This underground area has never been officially open to the public. Raffaele, however, did say that anyone interested in Naples' Parallel City can go to **La Macchina Del Tempo** at www.lamacchinadeltempo.info for current information as well as upcoming events and lectures regarding the underground world.

Getting There: Santa Maria Maggiore Della Pietrasanta is on Via Tribunali next to Piazza Miraglia.

THE CATACOMBS OF SAN GENNARO

This old underground is so-named because it once housed the remains of the patron saint of the city, San Gennaro. A tour of the catacombs begins with a walk down many stairs and into a hollow cavern made of tuff stone that dates back to paleo-Christian times. Archeologists think the structure, about the size of a large church, is actually the remains of several

cemeteries and basilicas built on top of one another throughout the ages.

The first area is a fifth century cemetery. Here, poor people paid for their loved ones to rest inside rectangular bunks on the outside walls. The wealthy paid for their families to be buried within alcoves where lavish frescoes decorated their tombs.

The frescoes, although faded, still have a sort of majesty. One depicts a young princess girl who died before her parents, the faces of both parents shown beside her in grief. A crown over the girl's head signifies her ascent into heaven. In an adjacent alcove, a fresco depicts San Gennaro and St. Peter at the gates of paradise.

Walking further into the belly of the catacombs, the guide stops at what used to be a large basilica, called *maggiore*. Thereafter, the guide passes a hollow half-dome that displays a cross and Greek lettering that says: "Christ has won." This probably was the baptismal font of the basilica.

Yet another basilica, called the Bishop's Church, banks toward the left of the catacomb. This area is so named because frescoes – now gone – used to depict a series of Bishops. Here also, a cavernous hole two stories below once held the tomb of San Gennaro. In the 800's, his body was taken to Benevento and then was returned to Il Duomo in downtown Naples where you can still visit his crypt.

Beyond the Bishop's Church, yet another basilica dates back to the second century. Here, ceiling frescoes have Greek and late Roman motifs of cats and other symbols alongside Christian symbols, such as three women holding rocks to symbolize the foundation of the Church. Most impressive of all is a massive ceiling fresco of a Christ in Byzantine style.

Throughout the ages these catacombs were used as a place of study, then as a hospital by the Benedictines during the time of the

cholera epidemic of the 16th century, and finally as a bomb shelter during World War II.

Getting There: Along the slope leading up to Capodimonte, you know you have arrived when you see **Madre del Buon Consiglio**, the Church that is often in panoramic pictures of Naples. The Catacombs are located directly behind it. If you buy a ticket to see the San Gennaro Catacombs, you can use the ticket to visit the San Gaudioso Catacombs as well.

THE MACABRE DOMINICANS

Puozza scula (literally: "May you drain away") is a Neapolitan expression that wishes death upon one's enemies. The saying derives from the macabre burial practices of the seventeenth century Dominicans who painted brightly colored frescoes beside the crypts of wealthy patrons and used their skulls for decoration.

The **Church of Santa Maria della Sanità** doesn't seem to be much on the map of tourist attractions. Taking a walk down Via

Capodimonte, the top of the basilica peeks out from a traffic-frenzied bridge. An elevator along the sidewalk takes you down to the road below, but from there, you walk less than a block and into a church filled with modern architecture and art. The front altar, for example, has translucent sculpted angels that look as if they are ready to fly away.

Beyond the altar, an immense gate leads to the spooky remnants of an old basilica. A barely noticeable passage with no door leads to the catacombs. San Gaudioso's niche comes into view first, then the blue tiles from the original basilica erected in the 5th century.

San Gaudioso was a bishop from Abitina, a village near Carthage. He fled North Africa during the Christian persecutions and arrived in Naples on a leaky boat. Among other things, he preserved the relics of several saints, notably Saint Restituta *(see p. 111)*.

Adjacent to San Gaudioso's niche, a stunning fresco of Saint Catherine of Siena still remains on a wall in the Nostriano niche, so

called because it's believed to be the burial place of Bishop Nostriano who welcomed San Gaudioso and his other African exiles.

The basilica eventually flooded and mud covered it entirely for many hundreds of years. In the 1600's Dominican monks dug up the church and turned it into a burial place. To respect their patrons, they created frescoes of the deceased, embedding their skulls into the walls as well as their bones and spines. Today, the faded images along the walls still show the deceased as they might have looked during their lifetime, wearing skirts and capes. There are also explanatory notes indicating the social status of the person.

Beyond the wealthy crypts, an array of dirt-floor rooms contain carved niches against the walls. In one room, a rectangular hole at the top of the ceiling indicates that the bodies were brought down by pulley. The bones were then broken so the corpse could be put into a tight fetal position, which was believed to help bring the dead back to the Father. The body was put inside the niche and, often, three holes were punctured into the stomach, particularly if a family wanted this space for more than one of their loved ones. The stomach acids and other liquids in the

body ran down and into the shelled out bottom of the niche, helping it decompose more quickly. Hence, they would "drain away."

At the far end of the catacombs, the Dominicans created a cemetery in what had once been an ancient Roman cistern. Interestingly, throughout the church and also within the catacombs and the cistern, contemporary art pieces are on display, fusing together the ancient, Byzantine, Renaissance, and modern.

Getting There: The address is Basilica di S. Maria della Sanità, Piazza della Sanità 124, Naples.

LE FONTANELLE CEMETERY

In the seedy Sanità district, the *O Campusanto de Funtanelle* for many years acted as a bridge to the afterlife where the living tenderly cared for the skulls of the departed. The cavernous space retains an atmosphere shot through with Gothic imagery as fetishistic bric-a-brac is draped upon thousands of bones.

The Sanità district once lay outside the Greco-Roman city and provided a burial place for pagans before Christian interments took over. The vast cavity, which was first a tuff rock quarry, came into use as a burial ground for the excluded – the urban poor, victims of plague (at least 300,000 died in 1656), earthquake, insurrection, executions, and cholera (1836-7).

When the Bourbons razed many churches, the remains of Neapolitans came up to Le Fontanelle. In the late 18th century, despite family members thinking their loved ones had secured a church interment, they might have been bundled into a sack at the dead of night and offloaded here. It's estimated that 40,000 rest in plain sight, but at least four more meters of human remains hide under the floor level.

At some time in the late 17th century a rushing torrent of rain washed much of the contents of the cemetery out into the streets, creating a scene of apocalyptic horror. Then followed the first attempt to put some order into the charnel  house, stacking together the skulls and bones. Father Gaetano Barbati continued this effort until, in 1872, the cult of devotion to the *Anime Pezzentelle*, or Poor Souls, became popular. The ritual included the selection of a *capuzzella* (skull), which was polished carefully and placed on an embroidered handkerchief with a rosary encircling it. Later, a lace trimmed cushion was substituted, small oil lamps lit, and flowers added.

The supplicant waited for the soul to be revealed to him or her in a dream. It was thought the soul needed some kind of refreshment: *'A refrische 'e ll'anime d'o priatorio'*. If the skull seemed to sweat, that meant some success. The grace or favor sought might be the finding of a son missing in war, winning lottery numbers, or a much-longed for pregnancy. If this was not forthcoming, Neapolitans made no bones about putting the pampered skull back in the general mass of remains and beginning the process anew.

Many stories grew up about particular skulls, devotees imposing names and personalities onto their favorite skulls and, if things worked out well, giving them special stone or wooden boxes in which to repose; even a biscuit tin would do. In vain Archbishop Corrado Ursi labored to eradicate this veneration in 1969; even in the late 1970's cars waited outside the locked gates of Le Fontanelle for the

bones of Don Francesco, a Spanish cabalist long departed from this world, to reveal upcoming Lotto numbers.

Step into any of the three huge trapezoidal cavities and the atmosphere will begin to work on you, whether in front of the headless but winged statue of San Vincenzo Ferreri (1330-1419) whose cloth robe moves with the breeze, or before the three crosses set in heaped skulls laced with cobwebs. For many years the cemetery was closed to the public, but now visitors can enter thanks to an overnight occupation by locals that got the municipal authorities' attention.

Getting There: Not an easy drive by car, consider taking the train to Piazza Cavour station (Metropolitana) and then getting on C51 bus in front of Tommaso Campanella School. A twenty minute ride takes you to the Fontanelle stop. Alternatively, walk from Materdei station.

The address is Piazza Fontanelle alla Sanità 154, Naples. Open 10 a.m. to 5 p.m. except Wednesdays, the entrance is free. Call at 081 544 1305 or email: info@catacombedinapoli.it.

THE BOURBON TUNNEL

Near Piazza del Plebiscito and a little way up Via Gennaro Serra, a tiny *vicoletto* provides another route into the heart of the underground. You begin in a former veterinary clinic before descending tuff stone steps down into the Bourbon tunnel.

The year 1848 was tough for any European monarch; riots and revolution were the order of the day in many cities. This made King Ferdinand more than thoughtful as he sat in his new palace in

Naples. What he needed most of all was a possible escape route. So in 1853 he commissioned architect Enrico Alvino to construct a tunnel from the royal palace to a spot near the barracks at Piazza Vittorio. Officially this was to be a double tunnel, the King's and Queen's tunnels running parallel, full of stores and with an elegant interior. But in reality, the workers not only had to dig through the tuff rock to create a new passageway, but they also had to cross the existing water system that Cesare Carmignano had devised in the 17th century. This part, at least, was accomplished by bridging cisterns and carving out new spaces where once only the *pozzari* had ventured with their lanterns. Work stopped after two years and soon Ferdinand and his building projects would be overtaken by political changes that swept across Europe.

As with many other underground spaces, the tunnel was used as an air-raid shelter during the Second World War; cisterns were filled with earth to raise them to usable levels, low voltage electricity supplies were installed along with toilets and showers. One can only imagine how difficult it was to endure months of bombing in these dank spaces. Down here, as you pass along the corridors and through echoing cisterns, you can see heart-rending messages on the walls – *Noi vivi* or "We are alive" – and view the remains of beds and children's toys.

Toward the end of the tour comes a real surprise, the ghostly chassis and frames of cars, vans, and bicycles along the passageways. The tunnel was used as storage for vehicles confiscated from Neapolitans who engaged in contraband trade, chiefly that of tobacco. Just before emerging, blinking into the light of day at Via Morelli (grateful there are no stairs to climb back up) you see the broken fragments of an enormous statue that once stood in Piazza Santa Maria degli Angeli – a monument to Aurelio Padovani, the fascist leader of Campania in the 1920s.

Padovani died, along with eight other people, when he stepped out onto a balcony in Via Generale Orsini to greet enthusiastic crowds on his name day and the railing gave way. Conspiracy theories abound as to whether Mussolini, jealous of Padovani's popularity and power in the south, had orchestrated his demise. *Il Duce* commissioned his statue, whether in a fit of regret or cynicism, and the monument remained in the little square throughout the war.

How the pieces came to be found under layers of trash and rubble in the Bourbon tunnel is yet another mystery.

It took five years for the teams of speleologists and various volunteers to clear out the accumulated lumber and refuse, but now the tunnel offers a great glimpse into the history of Naples at three key points in its history.

Getting There: The address is Vico del Grottone 4, Naples. Walk up Via Gennaro Serra from Piazza del Plebiscito. The vico and entrance are on the left. Expect to see laundry hanging to dry overhead. The website is www.tunnelborbonico.info.

THE WINE SHOP

Every Thursday morning at 5 a.m. trucks come from Terzigno (a vineyard near Pompei) to drop off twenty-five 54-liter jugs of wine at the family-run **Il Vignaiolo**.

Angelo has owned the shop for forty years. He and his son, Antonio, together sell elegant wines and provide a quaint reprieve for regulars who come and sip a cup of wine poured from spouts along the wall. Many people also bring empty plastic water bottles, which they fill for a mere 1.50 Euro.

The wine shop also has its own underground – one of the many privately owned cavities in Naples. The cellar of Il Vignaiolo during ancient times was a street of Naples. Today, a small lift transports beverages to the cellar, which consists of three large rooms. At the very back, an old Greek well is used for storing empty boxes and crates.

A visit can feel like home, with warm welcomes also from Stephanie Dardanello (the American wife of Antonio) and Carolina (the mother who often cooks for everyone in the shop's back kitchen).

Since it's a wine shop, I ask not about their underground, but my most burning wine question: Why are so many red wines in southern Italy fizzy? Often bottles of red wine in this region taste slightly carbonated. Antonio says it's a kind of grape cultivated here. These fizzy red wines are best drunk cold during the summer along with a light dinner.

Getting There: Il Vignaiolo is at Via Misericordiella 4-5, Naples. Go to Piazza Cavour (one block away from the National Archeological Museum – *see p. 60*) and you'll find this small street close by.

AND BEYOND: SAN BARTOLOMEO

World War II weighs heavily on the minds of Neapolitans even today. Whether they remember hiding in the Naples underground caverns or relate stories of their parents and grandparents eating only potato peels due to extreme shortages, vestiges of this stark moment in Italian history remain. In the small town of Campagna, inhabitants played a rebellious, yet compassionate role in Italian history.

Elizabeth Bettina, author of *It Happened in Italy*, is a native New Yorker, who spent many summers of her teenage years with her grandmother in Campagna, not far from Salerno. She had heard references to a few Jews hidden in the surrounding mountains and she began to piece together the part this town played in the story of Jews interned in Italy during WWII.

During the war, the old Convento di San Bartolomeo was overseen by Bishop Giuseppe Maria Palatucci. His nephew, Giovanni Palatucci was working in northern Italy as an Italian police officer for the Mussolini government. His job was to process foreign residents in Italy. Taking advantage of his position in the government, he worked to enable people to leave Italy with false documents, or, if he couldn't, arranged to send them to his uncle in Campagna. Many Jews survived thanks to the Convento di San Bartolomeo, located up a slope too steep for motorized vehicles and backing into a cliff. The ruggedness of the area made the site advantageous for hiding.

Subsequently, Campo di San Bartolomeo acted as a detainment camp for displaced persons, where Jews and other internees were allowed to organize a library, school, theater, synagogue, and their own newsletter. Time might have been spent playing cards or reading. A team also played local soccer.

Families that had been separated were frequently reunited here. In some areas where camps did not exist, apartments were provided and Italian rations granted.

Campo di San Bartolomeo was an *internato libero* (internment that was free). Because of the convent's confined space, internees were allowed to leave, but had to stay in town, signing in at the police office daily. Carabinieri permission was needed if one wanted to leave for the day.

After September 8, 1943 everything changed for the Jews in the camp. Italy stopped fighting on the side of the Germans and joined the Allies. The Germans remained in Italy and began to hunt for the Jews that the Italians would not deport. Entering Campagna that September, officers intended to move the Jews to extermination camps in Germany. They informed those in charge that they intended to come the next day for the Jews. The internees, however, exited a window that night and fled into the local mountains. They disappeared only to the Germans; the Italians continued to care for those in hiding. The Campo di San Bartolomeo remained in operation until September of 1944.

After the war, former internees contributed to the restoration of the convent. The *Itinerario della Memoria e della Pace* (or "Route of Memory and Peace"), in honor of the goodness of Giovanni

The Jews of the Ancient World

Approximately 200 Jews reside in Naples today, but that wasn't always the case. Before the Spanish Inquisition, the Jewish community accounted for thirty percent of the total population. What's more, the Jewish community existed in the Campania region perhaps as far back as when the Greek colonies established themselves here.

Historians give the date of 70 B.C. as a time when Jews came in larger numbers to Italy as slaves after the fall of Jerusalem,[19] but inscriptions found during archeological excavations in the Campania region show that their communities were likely large and varied.

The first written evidence of the eruption of Mt. Vesuvius in 79 A.D. comes from an anonymous Jewish author who told about the catastrophe one year later in a passage of the *Libri Sibillini* (or the *Sibylline Books*). His verse predates Martial's (in 88 A.D.) and Pliny the Younger's (in 106 A.D.).[20]

The port town of Pozzuoli had a Jewish community that contributed to commercial activity as well as the manufacturing of purple fabric and glass.[21] Inscriptions have also surfaced in the towns of Nola, Bacoli, and notably Capua, where an Alfius Iuda is mentioned as having been part of the Council of Elders and a rabbi.[22]

---

19 Carlo Giordano and Isidoro Kahn, *The Jews in Pompeii, Herculaneum, Stabiae and in the Cities of Campania Felix*, trans. Wilhelmina F. Jashemski, revised edition Laurentino Garcia y Garcia (Roma: Bardi Editore s.r.l., 2001) 11.

20 Ibid., 15-6.

21 Ibid., 20.

22 Ibid., 28.

Our best information about the Jewish community comes from the impressively preserved archeological finds in Pompeii. Inscriptions have been found naming Youdaikou a producer and merchant of wine who was wealthy enough to own his own slaves. Coss Libum was a manager of one of the most important hotels in the city.[23] Iesus wrote graffiti along a wall comparing a gladiator to a little fish.[24] Most interesting is the etched word *cherem*, which scholars say is the first Pompeian evidence of a bilingual Hebrew-Greek (in Latin letters) inscription and also may point to the place where Jews assembled on special occasions.

Scholars theorize that it was here that the Jews specifically began to take an interest in Christianity and spread its message among the pagans.[25]

Book Recommendations: *The Jews in Pompeii, Herculaneum, Stabiae and in the Cities of Campania Felix* by Carlo Giordano and Isidoro Kahn. You can find this book at the Pompeii and Herculaneum bookstores, among others.

Primo Levi's *Survival in Auschwitz* and *Reawakening* describe the author's capture by Italians during WWII, his deportation to the Auschwitz concentration camp, and his return home.

---

23 Ibid., 42-3.

24 Ibid., 45.

25 Ibid., 113-4.

Palatucci, was recently dedicated at the restored convent. "There was no difference between us and the Italians," the survivor Walter Wolff said in *It Happened in Italy*.

After being arrested in September of 1944, the Germans sent Giovanni Palatucci to Dachau where he died on February 10th, two months before liberation. He has been called the Italian Schindler.

Getting There: Follow the autostrada A3 east, go about thirty-five kilometers past Salerno and take the Campagna exit. Follow local signs to the town. After entering Campagna, follow the signs to the parking area. Walk back to the main piazza, and across the street from the war memorial where a sign says *itinerario*. You will follow the main street uphill, stopping at other informational signs along the way. The route will end at the Chiesa di San Bartolomeo, where the visitor will find the final sign at the entrance to the convent and museum.

Before you visit, call Carmine Granito at 339 280 9483. He will open the museum for you. He loves to help visitors and groups understand the museum, but a knowledge of Italian will help, as he speaks little English. Most information in the museum is in English, however.

THE ODIOUS WOMEN TOUR

An Odious Woman: A female whose beliefs, words, or actions were unusual, or even considered objectionable, during her time.

(Francesco de Rosa also known as "Pacecco de Rosa"; *Venus, a satyr and two cupids* 1645-1650. Displayed at the National Museum of Capodimonte)

Although the stereotype of Neapolitan women may be that they remain dedicated to private life, whenever you take a sharp left or drive down a narrow street, the public lives of Neapolitan women jump out at every corner. Quite a number of lecherous women have already been mentioned, including Agrippina and Poppaea. The goddesses, including Diana, Sosandra, and Venus had their temples in the Archeological Park of Baia. At Pompeii, one of the wealthiest patricians was the woman Eumachia. Female prostitutes also figured prominently in the city. With so many women playing a role in the myth and history of Naples, this chapter brings the city sights out from ancient times and into the modern day through a chronological description of females who shaped the history of this region.

A 3-DAY TOUR

Day #1: Downtown Naples

Start at Piazza del Plebiscito and walk up the steps behind the Piazza. You'll pass the **Industrial Arts Museum** (now a school). Take a left on Via Egiziaca a Pizzofalcone and then start making your way up to **Pizzofalcone** where the siren Parthenope was born. Lady Hamilton and her husband Sir William also had a villa around here.

Return to **Piazza del Plebiscito** and continue to the **Teatro San Carlo**. The gambling mezzo-soprano Isabella Colbran performed on this stage. You can also search for the bust of her lover, Domenico Barbaja. In the distance you'll see the **Castel Nuovo** (also known as Maschio Angioino) where Queen Joanna I was raised by her grandfather Robert the Wise.

Next, head down Via Toledo where you pass **Piazzetta di Matilde Serao**. Pick up *Il Mattino* in honor of the journalist who founded the Neapolitan newspaper. Many other palazzi are along this street, including that of Gioachino Rossini, Isabella Colbran's husband. The **Galleria di Palazzo Zevallos Stigliano** houses Caravaggio's painting *The Martyrdom of Saint Ursula*. Artemisia Gentileschi studied under this baroque painter for a time and spent her last years in Naples.

From Via Toledo head to Piazza del Gesu Nuovo and then take a right onto Via Santa Chiara. Enter the Spanish tiled **Santa Chiara cloister** where the Clarissa Nuns still live; search for the remains of Queen Joanna I whose body was dumped somewhere inside.

Walk along the bustling Via S. Biagio Dei Librai and take a left on Via Duomo. One block up and to your right, you'll see the **Castel Capuano** in the distance where Queen Joanna II had her court.

Take Via Duomo until you reach the Naples Cathedral or **Il Duomo**. A side chapel inside pays tribute to Saint Restituta, the

African saint whose remains came to Naples with San Gaudioso. This basilica was originally dedicated to her. In the side chapel you can still visit part of the original paleo-Christian basilica.

From Via Duomo, walk several blocks to **Piazza Garibaldi** where Eusapia Palladino used to give her seances at a hotel (no longer standing). Walking from here toward Piazza Carlo III, tucked inside a side street you'll find an **English cemetery** at Piazza Santa Maria della Fede. Eusapia lived and died in an apartment somewhere along the adjacent street of Via Benedetto Cairoli.

Return to Piazza Garibaldi and walk a few blocks to Piazza Mercato, once known as **Execution Square**. The Parthenopean rebel Eleonora Fonseca Pimentel was executed in this space.

Take a bus to Piazza Cavour and then another bus to the **Museo di Capodimonte** where you can search for the works of Artemisia Gentileschi.

Head back by bus to Piazza del Plebiscito and passing the royal palace on your left, stroll down to the seafront. The street is called **Via Partenope** after the siren who lured Odysseus onto the shores. The **Castel dell'Ovo** is where Joanna I was held captive for a time. Sophia Loren dined at the restaurant **Ristorante La Bersagliera** in the Borgo Marinari and they have pictures of her inside.

Stroll along the bay to the district of Mergellina, where you'll hit Via Posillipo and the **Palazzo Donn'Anna** with its ghostly legends of Anna Carafa and Queen Joanna II. The opulent villas along this street also have many beaches for swimming and sunbathing during the summer.

Day #2: The Phlegraean Fields

Visit the trapezoidal **Antro della Sibilla** where the Cumaean Sibyl uttered her oracles.

Make an appointment with Carlo Santillo to see the **Grotta della Sibilla**, located at Lago Averno where the Cimmerian Sibyl gave her oracles.

The **Tomb of Agrippina** in Bacoli has an eerie old theater said to hold the remains of Roman Emperor Nero's mother. There's an Underwater Diving School up the street, restaurants along the water, a lido, and a promenade for walking.

Pozzuoli is a port town with an amphitheater, several archeological ruins, and a wonderful nightlife. It is also the birthplace of the forever elegant actress, Sophia Loren.

Day #3: Caserta – Torre Annunziata – Salerno

The Bourbons created their Versailles-like court in Caserta, a city about twenty-five kilometers from Naples. Queen Maria Carolina lived in the **Reggia di Caserta** and you can see some of her apartments as well as her portrait in the Art Gallery.

Next, head out to Torre Annunziata where you can visit **Oplontis**, the villa of Roman Emperor Nero's wife, Poppaea.

End the day at the **Medical School in Salerno**, about an hour's drive from Oplontis. The physician Trotula worked at this medical school, once considered the best in Europe.

THE SIREN'S HIDDEN TOMB: PARTHENOPE

According to myth, Naples traces its origins back to a siren named Parthenope born on the hilltop of **Pizzofalcone**. The sirens were portrayed in Greek vases as birds with human faces. The Roman writer, Ovid, codified this idea when he wrote that the sirens were companions to Persephone. When she was

abducted by Hades, the sirens couldn't find her and begged to have wings. Demeter granted their wish, giving them sticks for legs, wings, and yet letting them retain their female faces and human voices.[26] Interestingly, the Italian word *sirena* today does not mean siren or bird, but "mermaid" – a creature of the sea.

Beyond the legends and linguistics – could Parthenope have been a real person? Strabo (63/64 B.C. – 24 A.D.), the traveling Greek historian and geographer, mentioned that the tomb of Parthenope existed near Neapolis and a torch race was held every year in her honor.[27]

After Greek colonizers founded Cuma, they ventured down to the Bay of Naples where they settled in a city, which they named "Parthenope." Soon, they founded an additional city attached to Parthenope, which they called Neapolis or the New City. Could Parthenope have been buried somewhere among the Greek foundations of the city?

Today, a sliver of the ancient Greek foundations can be visited in **Piazza Bellini**. Perhaps Parthenope lies close by or perhaps she lies along the street Neapolitans named after her – the **Via Partenope**. Another possible location is the **Castel dell'Ovo** and so her ghost would know the location of Virgil's Egg. While the castle we see today was built by the Normans, the Greeks from Cuma first settled this small island.

From a purely mythological standpoint, Homer's character Odysseus sailed through much of the boot of Italy, and perhaps sailed north, where he passed Parthenope along the island of **Nisida**.

Many myths can be visited all along the city or, perhaps, simply gazing out at the Bay of Naples suffices as Parthenope still lives, swimming somewhere within the hidden underwater villas.

---

26 Ovid, *Metamorphoses*, trans. Rolfe Humphries (Bloomington: Indiana University Press, 1983) 556-63.

27 Strabo, *Geography*, trans. H.L. Jones (Cambridge: Harvard University Press, 1991) 5.4.7 & 6.1.1.

Places To See: You can take an entire day to search for Parthenope in the city of Naples. First, walk behind Piazza del Plebiscito up Via Gennaro Serra and take a left on Via Egiziaca a Pizzofalcone. Walk up a steep hill and you'll see the **Pizzofalcone** rock. There's also a fine view of Naples.

Return to Piazza del Plebiscito and make your way down to the sea to walk along **Via Partenope**. Here you'll also see the **Castel dell'Ovo** *(see p. 146)*.

Next, make your way to the historical center of Naples, passing Piazza Dante and going up Via Port'Alba (with its clutch of booksellers) until you reach **Piazza Bellini** and the ancient Greek foundations.

Finally, if you have a car, drive to Via Coroglio and take a stroll at the island of **Nisida** *(see p. 205)*.

Website Recommendation: For more about sirens see this website: www.theoi.com/Pontios/Seirenes.html.

THE CRAZED FORTUNETELLERS: THE SIBYLS

The sibyl of Cuma foretold wars and wrote her oracles on oak leaves which would often blow away, but which she would not help her listeners re-assemble.[28] Sibyls were known for their trancelike states and shuddering voices; Michelangelo thought that the sibyls were so important that he seated five on the ceiling of the Sistine Chapel. The Cumaean Sibyl, in particular, is depicted as a dark complexioned woman with wrinkles and muscular build. She reads a large manuscript, perhaps the Sibylline books.

---

28 H.W. Parke, *Sibyls and Sibylline Prophecy in Classical Antiquity*, ed. B.C. McGing (London: Routledge, 1988) 82.

The fourteenth century humanist, Giovanni Boccaccio, devoted a chapter to the sibyl in his *Famous Women*, in which he called her a maiden named Almathea or Deiphebe. Boccaccio claimed that she preserved her virginity and had a sanctuary near Lago Averno where she made many predictions.[29]

Boccaccio took his legends from the Roman writer, Varro (116 B.C. – 27 B.C.), who collected a compendium of extant knowledge about the sibyls. Varro wrote that the Cumaean Sibyl went to Rome with nine Sibylline books, which she wanted to sell to the Etruscan Emperor of Rome, Tarquinius Priscus. When the Emperor refused her price, she burned three of them in his presence. She came back the next day to burn another three until he paid the full price for the remaining three books. He acquiesced because the books contained the entire destiny of Rome.[30]

The Roman writer Ovid also mentioned the Cumaean Sibyl in his *Metamorphoses*. Here, the sibyl spoke in her own voice, explaining that she was not a goddess, but a mortal woman who asked Apollo that she remain a virgin and gain eternal life. Apollo granted her eternal life, but forgot to add eternal youth. As a consequence, she lived for seven hundred years, all the while shriveling until only her voice was left.[31]

Pausanias, the Greek traveler and geographer of the 2nd century A.D. reinforced Ovid's myth saying that the temple guides at Cuma showed him a stone water-jug (*hydria*) of small size in which, they said, lay the bones of the sibyl. This was considered proof that before her death, the sibyl had shrunk to diminutive size. Petronius also told a folktale that she hung in a bottle (or ampoule) in Cuma wishing to die.[32]

---

29 Giovanni Boccaccio, *Famous Women*, trans. Virginia Brown (Cambridge: Harvard University Press, 2003) 50-2.

30 Parke, *op. cit.*, 76-7.

31 Ovid, *op. cit.*, 106-156.

32 Parke, *op. cit.*, 81.

Digestivi

It's posited that the sibyls uttered their oracles while in a trancelike state, possibly induced by noxious gases seeping up from the earth. Today, Neapolitans have their own libations that can create oracle induced mutterings – the *digestivi*.

While *aperitivi* are common in most of Italy, Naples doesn't celebrate the beverage much beyond serving *prosecco* (an Italian dry sparkling wine) before special meals. Instead, in the south, the *digestivo* reigns supreme.

Usually enjoyed after a large meal in order to aid digestion, the most renowned is **Grappa**, which comes from different locations throughout Italy and has many flavors, but can also be served as a clear grain alcohol first chilled in the freezer. Other *digestivi* include:

Sambuca: a sweet licorice taste and often mixed with espresso.
Maraschino: a sweet cherry flavor liqueur, also used in cakes.
Anice: a sweet licorice taste like Sambuca, only stronger in alcohol content.
Il Finocchietto: a strong liqueur made of fennel and often good for cooking.

The highest respect to the sibyl was given by Ovid's predecessor, the Roman poet Virgil. In his fourth book of the *Eclogues* he mentioned her as having foretold the coming of Christ.

Virgil also described the sibyl in *The Aeneid* when his character landed at Cuma. He wrote:

> ...her face was transfigured, her color changed, her hair fell in disorder about her head and she stood there with heaving breast and her wild heart bursting in ecstasy. She seemed to grow in stature and speak as no mortal had ever spoken...[33]

---

33 Virgil, *op. cit.*, 47-51.

Averno: a bitter dark drink with a hint of spearmint that boasts many herbs.

Ramazzotti: another dark, mildly bitter liqueur, made with even more healthful herbs.

Amaro Montenegro: a third bitter digestive made of forty herbs.

Le Noci: a walnut alcohol.

Le Dodici Erbe: a twelve-herb grain alcohol.

Liquore di Fragole: a strawberry liqueur with tiny strawberry bits inside.

Limoncello: made of lemon rinds and grain alcohol, this is drunk ice-cold.

Limoncello is the most popular and the town of Sorrento on the Amalfi Coast boasts having the tastiest recipes that are worth the purchase.

For those who want to make it at home, it's fairly simple. The Italian language cookbook *Cucina Napoletana* by Roberta Avallone has the best recipe and the book can be found at the popular Italian chain bookstore **Feltrinelli**, which you can find at Piazza dei Martiri 23, Naples, or online at www.lafeltrinelli.it.

In 1932, Amedeo Maiuri (1886-1963), the Neapolitan archeologist who was installed as chief archeologist for Pompeii, said he re-discovered the entrance to the sibyl's cave that corresponded to Virgil's account. This led to an on-going mystery.

An **Antro della Sibilla** exists at **Cuma** while a **Grotta della Sibilla** exists at **Lago Averno**. Which is the real sibyl's cave?

In the book *Sibyls and Sibylline Prophecy in Classical Antiquity*, H.W. Parke explores this very question. Virgil's sibyl lived at Cuma, but scholars theorize that perhaps there was another, far older Cimmerian sibyl who gave her oracles at Lago Averno. Parke says that the Roman writer, Varro, identified ten sibyls in the ancient world. Two were located in Campania – the Cimmerian and the Cumaean. Varro took his evidence of a Cimmerian sibyl from Gnaeus Naevius who stipulated that the Cimmerians inhabited the area around Lago Averno before the Cumaeans.

Varro would have wanted to make this myth true for the sake of Roman civilization. Why? Although Cuma was recognized as the oldest Greek colony on the Italian mainland, the settlement did not antedate the Trojan War. For Naevius, legend had it that Aeneas fled from Troy after the Trojan War and reached Italy where he consulted the sibyl who prophesied the future to mortals and lived in the town of the Cimmerians. So if Aeneas came to this lake, then a colony must have existed already around 1000 B.C. The sibyl would have been Cimmerian, not Cumaean, and she would have lived during Homer's Greek and Trojan war.

Of course, by the time Varro wrote about the sibyl, she no longer existed, so what comes down to us today is a blend of myth, fiction, and history.

Places To See: Located in the Phlegraean Fields, visit **Cuma** *(see p. 13)* and the **Grotta della Sibilla** *(see p. 17).*

Book Recommendations: A fascinating read, although academic, *Sibyls and Sibylline Prophecy in Classical Antiquity* by H.W. Parke posits these interesting theses in Chapter Four about Cumae.

Another fun read about the Sistine Chapel and Michelangelo's insouciance vis-a-vis the Pope in making the ceiling is *Michelangelo and the Sistine Chapel* by Andrew Graham-Dixon. There is a chapter about the sibyls here also.

THE AFRICAN BONES: SAINT RESTITUTA

Il Duomo is one of the primary destinations for any Naples visitor. The patron saint of the city, San Gennaro, is buried here and his blood is kept in an ampoule in a side niche *(see p. 193)*. But, if you are in search of an odious woman, Il Duomo also pays tribute to Saint Restituta.

Not much is known about her life, except that she was born in North Africa near Carthage and was killed during Emperor Diocletian's Christian persecutions. Although some believe that San Gaudioso brought her remains to Naples, the colorful legends surrounding Restituta put her in the odious category.

In 304, during the reign of Emperor Diocletian, a large number of Christians continued to gather in the city of Abitina to celebrate the Eucharist. Fifty of them, including Restituta, were caught, arrested, and dragged in chains to Carthage. There, they were sentenced to death due to her rebellion against paganism.

Legend has it that Saint Restituta was tortured and then placed in a blazing boat, but her body was left unharmed by the fire. Her boat landed on the shores of **Ischia** where a Christian woman named Lucina walked along the beach and found the incorrupt body of Restituta, who was now dead. Still today the Festival of Restituta is celebrated on the island of Ischia every May 16th to 18th and a church in her name also exists there.[34]

At the Duomo an opulent nave is dedicated to the saint. Tucked away beyond it, the Duomo itself was built above the remnants of a paleo-Christian basilica from the 500's A.D. This older basilica was dedicated to Saint Restituta. Today, you pay an extra fee to get into this one-room vestige where a bulbous dome sparkles with badly

---

34 The information for this sub-chapter can be found at the Italian language website *Santi Beati*: http://www.santiebeati.it/dettaglio/53650.

damaged Byzantine tiles and a fresco of Saint Restituta remains intact against the wall.

A stereotype of women in Naples seems to be that they are expected to be mothers who raise children, remain mostly inside the home, and stay obedient to their husbands. But the large number of

female images within the Catholic Churches throughout the city point to another aspect of women's roles in Neapolitan history. In fact, Naples has over fifty official patron saints, at least twelve of whom are women. Saint Restituta presents a marvelous example of an African woman who stood up for her beliefs and made a strong political statement for her time. Consequently, she was brutally killed, only to be admired centuries later for her courage.

Places To See: Il Duomo is in the heart of downtown Naples at Via Duomo 147. If you go by metro, get off at the Piazza Cavour stop, walk in the opposite direction from the National Archeological Museum, and then take a right onto Via Duomo. Il Duomo is a few blocks away.

You also can take a ferry from either Pozzuoli, the downtown Naples port of Molo Beverello or the Calata Porta di Massa port to the island of **Ischia**. *(See p. 206.)*

SAINT PATRICIA'S WEEKLY MIRACLE

Every Tuesday morning at the **San Gregorio Armeno Church**, Saint Patricia's blood liquifies after the 9:30 a.m. service. She is the patroness saint of Naples and her remains as well as a tooth and a wax imitation of her body lie inside a coffin at a side altar. In addition, during the Tuesday mass, the vial of her blood is hung on the left side of the front altar and is covered with a cloth. After the Eucharist, the priest lifts Saint Patricia's blood from the hook, brings it to the middle of the altar, and worshipers stand in a line to kiss the receptacle. Inside it, one opaque vial has a discernible syrupy dark liquid.

Not much is known about Saint Patricia, her deeds transferred only orally throughout the centuries. According to the little cards given out at the church, she was born rich and noble in Constantinople during the seventh century. She was also a descendant of the Roman Emperor, Constantine the Great. Wanting to lead a life of celibacy, she fled to Rome to avoid an arranged marriage. When her father died, Saint Patricia returned to Constantinople and gave all her inherited wealth to the poor. Thereafter, she embarked on a ship back to Rome, but a furious storm drove the vessel to the Bay of Naples, where she took shelter at the **Castel dell'Ovo**. With her friends, she decided to establish a prayer community in Naples and spent her life helping the needy of the city until her death in 665.

Further legend has it that her body was venerated for several centuries until, between 1198 and 1214, a knight wanted a memento from Saint Patricia and plucked out her tooth. An outpouring of blood came from the empty cavity, thereafter flowing at different periods of time. Calling it a miracle, nuns preserved some of this blood in two bulbous vials.

At the **San Gregorio Armeno Church** today, the "Sisters of Saint Patricia" help with the mass, take care of the cloister, and continue to venerate Saint Patricia's remains. A large number of these nuns, interestingly, come from the Philippines.

On a more tongue in cheek note, the patron saint of Naples, San Gennaro, has his vial of blood at the Duomo, which liquifies every September 19th as well as the Saturday before the first Sunday in May *(see p. 193)*. The blood of Saint Patricia, on the other hand, liquifies on her saint's day of August 25th and each Tuesday after the morning mass, so Saint Patricia performs her miracle at least fifty-three times a year. All this definitively proves, once again, without a shadow of a doubt – that women work harder than men.

Getting There: San Gregorio Armeno Church is located at Via San Gregorio Armeno 44, also colloquially known to the city's expat community as **Christmas Alley**. Make sure to go around the corner and visit the cloister, which has a beautiful **courtyard**. You can also browse the large selection of *presepe (see p. 197)* in the shops along this street.

THE LOST REMAINS OF QUEEN JOANNA

With a reputation as a nymphomaniac and a brothel owner, Queen Joanna I (1328-1382) was orphaned at the age of five and married at the age of seven. She lived most of her life at the **Castel Nuovo**. Very likely one of her best memories was when her grandfather, King Robert the Wise, in 1341 publicly tested Petrarch's knowledge for three days straight, after which he granted him the title of Poet Laureate.

Joanna was crowned queen at the age of sixteen. Two years later, unknown bandits murdered her cousin-husband, Andrew, at the royal court's summer castle in **Aversa**. Joanna was six months pregnant. Andrew's brother – Louis, King of Hungary – took advantage of Joanna's vulnerability and invaded Naples. Without a comparable army, the Queen finally fled to Provence, France, but fearing her son wouldn't make the trip, she left him with some of her staff at the **Castel dell'Ovo**.

Louis of Hungary then entered the city, but Neapolitans revolted. They built fortifications out of cobblestone streets and threw rocks at his army, beating them back. The protests remained so fierce that Louis one night disappeared on a boat back to Hungary. He took with him Joanna's toddler son, who died during the trip.

Rumors flew that while in France she opened a brothel in Avignon used by the nobility of Europe. But once Louis had gone, Joanna returned to Naples and married the son of the Empress of Constantinople, Louis of Taranto. The Pope who married them observed the wishes of Robert the Wise and granted power only to Joanna. This infuriated her new husband and their relationship quickly devolved into political rivalry. Privately, it was said that Louis verbally abused her and even beat her. Nevertheless, she became pregnant with his child and gave birth to a girl, Catherine – who died shortly thereafter. A wave of Black Death in Naples then took the life of her nasty husband.

With many suitors constantly courting her, Joanna felt her most prudent course was to re-marry quickly. With permission from the Pope, she got herself betrothed to James III of Majorca. Seemingly a grand warrior, he had spent twelve years in prison and soon the Queen realized he was also unsound of mind. In a letter to the Pope, Joanna recounted how in front of all her counselors James III had beaten her and called her a whore. He maintained that she slept with other younger men, and indeed, this rumor seemed to stick and heighten. Several chroniclers claimed she was a nymphomaniac. Nancy Goldstone, her modern-day biographer, says slurs were easy to launch against a woman, but the charges were highly unlikely given that Joanna had a strong Catholic practice and faith.

In spite of her matrimonial problems with James, the Queen became pregnant at the age of thirty-nine and was excited about an heir, but she lost the baby through miscarriage. Three years later, James III also died.

At the age of forty-two Joanna had to find another husband. She settled on the lesser-known Otto von Brunswick, a German man a few years her senior and an excellent warrior who defended her realm without seeking the rights of ruling as king. The couple may have been happy for a time, but political intrigue brought them both down.

When Urban VI – a Neapolitan – became Pope he enraged cardinals in Rome with his cruel and irrational behavior. The moment the Pope lowered the number of meals for cardinals to one per day, half of them launched a "great schism." They elected their own Pope, Clement VII (of French origin), and claimed Urban VI had been unlawfully elected.

Historically, the Vatican and the Kingdom of Naples were closely tied together, so Joanna had to make a choice between the two Popes. Rude and abrasive, Urban VI had already written letters to the Queen saying that a woman shouldn't rule and that she should lock herself in a nunnery. He also refused to commute her annual tribute, which Joanna said she couldn't pay because she had sent military reinforcements to the Pope the year before. All this meant that Joanna decided to support Clement.

In reaction, Urban excommunicated her. Worse yet, when the people of Naples found out their Queen had acknowledged a French Pope, they rebelled. Mass protests took place outside her **Castel Nuovo** and Joanna became locked inside with dwindling provisions. The Hungarians took advantage of the situation and invaded. Although her husband launched a battle, he was captured and imprisoned. Forced to surrender, the Hungarians took Joanna to the **Castel Muro** and held her in isolation. There, four men came upon her either in her chapel or in her bedroom and strangled her. Joanna's remains were then dumped in the wall somewhere of the **Santa Chiara Cloister**.

Queen Joanna's excommunication remains in effect today. If you visit the Santa Chiara Cloister and ask about Joanna's remains, most likely you will be given blank looks, but a few aficionados will come to your aide, showing you stairs that lead to a locked door. Some say Joanna lies somewhere behind them.

Places To See: You can take a full day visiting places associated with Queen Joanna I. Begin at **Castel Nuovo** *(see p. 144)* where Joanna grew up and lived much of her life. **Castel dell'Ovo** *(see p. 146)* is where she was held in captivity.

Santa Chiara Cloister and the impressive church at Via Benedetto Croce 1 is where her remains lie and many of her relatives have tombs here, including her grandfather Robert the Wise. Queen Joanna also commissioned building work on the **Certosa di San Martino** *(see p. 198)*. The summer castle in **Aversa** where her first husband was murdered is now a police station. The **Castel Muro**, further away from Naples, can't be found on any map and is closed to the public.

Book Recommendation: To transport yourself into the medieval world of Joanna I, the finest book written is: *The Lady Queen* by Nancy Goldstone.

TROTULA: THE MEDIEVAL PHYSICIAN

To cure a wandering uterus – an ailment which usually afflicts virgins, widows, and women otherwise celibate – insert putrid-smelling herbs such as pitch or burnt hair in the nostrils (if coaxing the uterus downwards) or insert sweet-smelling herbs into the vagina overnight (if coaxing the uterus upwards).[35]

The celebrated female physician, Trotula, gave this advice in her eleventh or twelfth century work *On The Diseases Of Women (De passionibus mulierum).*

Although we cannot verify her actual existence, Trotula may have been the first female professor of medicine who taught at the **Schola Medica Salernitana**, an academy renowned from the 9th through the 13th centuries as providing the best medical training throughout Europe. The school had accumulated extensive amounts of medical knowledge from Arabic sources and held the illustrious manuscripts of Hippocrates and Galen. Doctors often translated the texts into Latin themselves. Physicians and

---

35 Monica H. Green, ed. & trans., *The Trotula: An English Translation of the Medieval Compendium of Women's Medicine* (Philadelphia: University of Pennsylvania Press, 2002) 22-3.

professors then contributed more, producing a large body of literature about their craft.

Particularly fascinating was the large number of female physicians and professors in Salerno. (Their existence, interestingly, coincided with the reign of Joanna I, Queen of Naples.) In all, more than five dozen references to Salernitan women can be found in the medical texts of the 12th and early 13th centuries.

We come to know Trotula only through written manuscripts associated with her name. She seems particularly expert in the fields of gastrointestinal disorders and ophthalmology. Her most well-known *On Treatments for Women* give some wonderful remedies for common ailments:

For Removing Wrinkles: For wrinkled old women, take stinking iris, that is gladden, and extract its juice, and with this juice anoint the face in the evening. And in the morning the skin will be raised and it will erupt, which rupture we treat with the above-mentioned ointment in which root of lily is employed. And first pulling off the skin, which after the rupture has been washed, it will appear very delicate.[36]

A Good Constrictive: For the vagina so that they may appear as if they were virgins. (*Trotula mentions six. Here I give two – my italics*) ... take powder of natron [soda ash] or blackberry and put it in; it constricts [the vagina] marvelously. What is better is if the following is done one night before she is married: let her place leeches in the vagina (but take care that they do not go in too far) so that blood comes out and is converted into a little clot. And thus the man will be deceived by the effusion of blood.[37]

---

36 Ibid., 100-1.

37 Ibid., 103-4.

For Worm of the Ears:
Take an apple and hollow it
out and place it on the ear,
and if there is any worm, it
will come out.[38]

Today, you can visit the
Giardino della Minerva that
claims to be the location
where part of the medical
school once stood. Located
in Salerno's old city center,
the gardens have four terraces that overlook the sea. On each
terrace, plaques mark the various herbs and the floor has many
water canals. Fountains, hanging vines, and trees make this a tranquil
spot. The museum inside consists of one room that displays a
manuscript and old medical implements. However, nothing about
Trotula is mentioned here; the story of her loves, her parents, her
troubles, and her celebrations are left entirely up to our imagination.

Places To See: The **Giardino della Minerva** is located in Salerno's
city center at Via Ferrante Sanseverino 1. It began as a "garden of
simples" or medicinal herbs in the early 1300's. Here you can buy
herbal teas and hear lectures. To find out more, check their website
at www.giardinodellaminerva.it.

Salerno can make a wonderful day-trip. As you walk to the
gardens, you'll likely pass the **Salerno Duomo**, which is worth a
look. Also, don't miss taking a stroll along the seaside **promenade**
and when you return to your car, follow the signs to the **Castello di
Arechi** to finish your day walking around this medieval castle.

Book Recommendation: *The Trotula* has been edited and
translated by Monica Green. The manuscript provides an array of

---

38 Ibid., 108.

medical prescriptions that might ring true for us today (on whitening of the teeth) and prescriptions specific to the time (such as wandering uteruses). Green also provides an introduction with the most comprehensive information on what can be known about Trotula.

THE QUEEN BEE, THE PRINCESS, AND THE CURSED CASTLE

Known for her sexual exploits, Queen Joanna II (1373-1435) was called "The Queen Bee" as well as the vampire or crocodile who ate her lovers after killing them. Another legend says she dumped her lovers in a secret trap door of the **Castel Nuovo** where they were eaten by crocodiles brought from Africa.[39]

She lived at the **Castel Capuano** and allegedly took her many lovers to a castle in **Posillipo**. The castle was known as *La Sirena* and after Joanna's death a curse fell upon the building.

Two hundred years after Joanna II's death, Princess Anna Carafa inherited the villa and ordered the well-known architect Cosimo Fanzago to renovate it. Many stories were told about Anna's lavish parties here. In particular, Matilde Serao in her book about the legends of Naples tells that Anna Carafa competed with her niece Mercede de la Torre for the love of another man. One night, the two women had a fight, after which Mercede was never seen again. It is said that Mercede's ghost haunts the **Palazzo Donn'Anna**. You can't enter the building, but you can see the crumbling structure from Via Posillipo.

Cosimo Fanzago never completed renovations of the palace. Instead, Anna's husband, a Spanish viceroy, had to return to Spain.

---

39 Check the English or Italian version of Wikipedia for Joanna II of Naples. There is no English language biography yet written about this queen.

Anna remained behind, taking up residence in a Portici villa and dying a lonely woman.[40]

Places To See: Castel Capuano *(see p. 148)* where Joanna II lived, **Castel Nuovo** *(see p. 144)* where Joanna II is said to have thrown her lovers to the crocodiles, and **San Giovanni a Carbonara Church** at Via San Giovanni a Carbonara 5, Naples *(see p. 266)* that contains the tomb of Joanna II's lover, the Grand Seneschal Ser Gianni Caracciolo.

Finally, visit the **Palazzo Donn'Anna** on Via Posillipo *(see p. 219)* to see where Joanna II brought her lovers and where later Anna Carafa lived. Across the street, visit the **Caffè Donn'Anna** to taste the spirit of these odious women.

ARTEMISIA GENTILESCHI

Raped at nineteen by her art tutor in Rome and running up high debts with her husband in Florence, Artemisia Gentileschi moved to Naples as a single middle aged woman in about the year 1630. She hated the city "because of the fighting, and because of the hard life and the high cost of living." And yet Gentileschi would spend most

---

40 You can't find much about these two women in books. This is where the internet becomes fun; legends, folklore, and myth can abound with impunity on-line. Anna Carafa's history is here: www.fva.is/harpa/comenius/it_donnacarafa.html.

of the next twenty-six years of her life in Naples. At that time, Naples was the largest city in southern Europe (three times the size of Rome) and the second largest city in Europe after Paris. Having established an excellent reputation for herself in northern Italy, Gentileschi found more abundant art commissions in the South, at a time when it was unusual and difficult for a female artist to obtain success at all.[41]

Today, Gentileschi's works can be found at **Capodimonte**, specifically, on the second floor in room 87. When they are not on tour, you can see *Judith Slaying Holofernes, The Annunciation,* and *Lucretia.*

Capodimonte is also worth mentioning because it's one of the finest museums in Italy. Designed as a royal palace for King Charles of Bourbon in 1738, it sits on a hilltop overlooking the Bay of Naples and Mt. Vesuvius. In 1742, the Baroque Italian architect, Ferdinando Sanfelice designed the forested area to cater to King Charles' love of hunting. Today, the gardens cover 130 hectares and feature over 400 varieties of trees. Whether you want to stroll along the hilltop, find Caravaggio's and Gentileschi's works, or enjoy the modern art section that includes Andy Warhol originals, Capodimonte is a wonderful destination in Naples.

Getting There: The address of the **National Museum of Capodimonte** is Via Miano 2. There's also a large pleasant park for walking. The **astronomy observatory** is nearby (at Salita Moiariello 16 – by group appointments only) as well as the **Torre del**

---

41 Mary D. Garrard, *Artemisia Gentileschi: The Image of the Female Hero in Italian Baroque Art* (Princeton: Princeton University Press, 1989) 88-9.

Palascino *(see p. 215)*. Note that Gentileschi was a contemporary of Caravaggio *(see p. 208)*, who also spent time in Naples.

Book Recommendations: The substantial book *Artemisia Gentileschi* by Mary D. Garrard includes many plates of the artist's works. *Artemisia Gentileschi: Our Contemporary* by Luciano Berti, Graziella Magherini, and Monica Toraldo di Francia can be found at the Capodimonte Museum bookstore.

Artemisia also lived in **Florence**, about a four hour drive from Naples. A tour of female artists is now possible in that city thanks to the meticulous research of Jane Fortune who wrote *Invisible Women: Forgotten Artists of Florence*.

THE QUEEN WHO SWEAT LIKE A PIG

Maria Carolina, Queen of Naples, was born in Vienna. In 1768 she married Bourbon King Ferdinand IV and cried all the way down to Naples because she insisted that Neapolitan Kings were unlucky. She was sixteen years old. The first time she laid eyes on Ferdinand, she thought him very ugly. King Ferdinand, in turn, said that Maria Carolina slept like she'd been killed and sweated like a pig. Together they lived at

Caserta Palace and produced seven children.

Ferdinand spoke in Neapolitan slang, loved nothing better than hunting, and often sold his fresh caught fish on the streets among the *lazzaroni*. Since he was a practical joker and absolutely positively impervious to higher learning, Maria Carolina took over the reigns of day-to-day ruling with ease. She built up the navy, established a silk factory in **San Leucio**, brought the Farnese collection to Naples, patronized artists such as Angelica Kaufmann, and supported the Freemasons for a time.

Then, in 1793 her sister, Marie Antoinette, was executed. Horrified, Maria Carolina turned Naples into a police state in the hope of avoiding a revolution in the kingdom. The army was kept perpetually mobilized, which had the effect of increasing taxation. She set up a spy network as well as a secret police force and sub-divided Naples into twelve police wards controlled by government appointed commissioners, replacing the popular elected system. Becoming paranoid, she employed food-testers and switched the royal family apartments daily. The Queen, however, couldn't stem the tide of revolution. By 1812 Ferdinand abdicated and the very next year Maria Carolina was exiled to Austria where she died in 1814.

Places To See: In downtown Naples, visit the **Palazzo Reale** (in Piazza del Plebiscito) where you can see the **Teatrino di Corte** built in 1768 for Maria Carolina's wedding to Ferdinand IV as well as Maria Carolina's **Revolving Lectern** in the royal apartments.

Today, the **Reggia di Caserta** or Royal Palace of Caserta (at Via Douhet 22, Caserta) still pays tribute to Maria Carolina whose portrait hangs in the **Art Gallery**. She occupied four rooms in the 18th century apartments, which can also be visited today. Ask for a map at the ticket office and you can roam her majestic world.

The **park** surrounding this mansion is particularly opulent, designed by the famous Luigi Vanvitelli. You may also explore the tranquil **English Garden** designed by John Andrew Graefer at the suggestion of Sir William Hamilton, Special Envoy of His Britannic Majesty to the Two Kingdoms.

After visiting here, **Caserta Vecchia** isn't far with its medieval town center full of lovely restaurants and the **Cathedral of San Michele** at Piazza del Vescovado 1, Caserta. Capua is also close by *(see p. 200).*

Book Recommendation: For a biography of this fascinating Queen, see *A sister of Marie Antoinette; the life-story of Maria Carolina, Queen of Naples* by Catherine Mary Bearne.

ATTITUDES: EMMA HAMILTON

A close confidante of Queen Maria Carolina, English-born Lady Emma Hamilton started out as a housemaid who tried her hand at acting and ended up having several rich lovers. Tricked by one of those lovers into being the companion of his uncle, Sir William Hamilton, the British Envoy to Naples, the couple ended up marrying in 1791. Together they entertained guests from all over Europe.

Emma developed a form of entertainment called *Attitudes* in which people had to guess the names of famous characters (such as Medea and Cleopatra) that she portrayed. For her performances, she wore Neapolitan peasant dress; she also created new styles of dance and fashion which were quickly emulated. Considered very beautiful, many portraits were painted of her, including one by George Romney.

Through her husband, Emma became a close friend of Queen Maria Carolina and she even advised the Queen during the Parthenopean Revolution. Emma began an affair with Horatio Nelson, the famous English naval hero, when he came to live in Naples and the affair was tolerated by Sir William.

Several impressive homes around Naples can still be seen where Sir William and Lady Hamilton lived. The **Palazzo Sessa** is where they collected paintings, ancient Greek vases, and samples of minerals. Much of the collection of ancient ceramics formed the nucleus of the British Museum's collection.

The **Villa Angelica** is where Sir William conducted his extensive research in vulcanology and lived during the spring and fall. Then, the **Villa Emma** was the summer home of the couple where they enjoyed sea bathing and a view of Mt. Vesuvius.

Shortly after the Parthenopean Revolution in 1799, Nelson was recalled to England. Sir William and Lady Emma left with him, never to return to Naples. Her husband died in 1803 while her lover Nelson died at the Battle of Trafalgar in 1805, leaving instructions for the care of his mistress and his young daughter Horatia – instructions that were not honored.

Emma became obese and a lavish spender. She went deeply into debt and wondered where all her fame had gone. She spent a year in debtor's prison and fled to France where she eventually died a lonely alcoholic in abject poverty.

Places To See: Palazzo Sessa situated on Pizzofalcone at Vico Santa Maria Cappella Vecchia 31, Naples. **Villa Angelica** is in Portici where you can visit a selection of Vesuvian Villas *(see also p. 217)* as well as the Reggia di Portici, now a university. Go to **Villa Campolieto** at Corso Resina 283, Ercolano and ask about Lady Hamilton's villa there. **Villa Emma** in Posillipo *(see also p. 219)* is located at Via Russo, No. 27.

Website Recommendation: For more about the Neapolitan houses of Sir William Hamilton, see **The Friends of Herculaneum Society** at www.herculaneum.ox.ac.uk.

THE REVOLUTIONARY: ELEONORA FONSECA PIMENTEL

Executed by hanging on August 20, 1799 – her crime was writing pamphlets that denounced the Bourbon Queen Maria Carolina for lesbianism – Eleonora Fonseca Pimentel calmly stepped up to the gallows and quoted Virgil: "Perhaps one day this will be worth remembering."[42]

Eleonora was born in Rome. Her father was Portuguese and moved the family to Naples when Eleonora was nine years old. There, she learned Greek and Latin and by the age of sixteen she published a nuptial hymn written for the marriage of King Ferdinand and Queen Maria Carolina, celebrating the accomplishments of the Bourbon dynasty. Her success catapulted her into the intellectual circles of Naples, where she wrote sonnets, cantatas, and oratorios.

She married the Marquis Fonseca, but the union was a disaster. The Marquis had no compassion for her upon the death of their infant son and he beat her so badly that she miscarried two other children. According to court documents, he also forced her to sleep in the same bed with him and his mistress.[43] They separated and thereafter Eleonora thrust herself into the ideals of the French Revolution, becoming a Jacobin.

---

42 Jordan Lancaster, *In The Shadow of Vesuvius: A Cultural History of Naples* (London: I.B. Tauris, 2005) 178.

43 Ibid., 174.

The Jacobins fought against royalist forces in the city in 1799 and won. They proclaimed the Parthenopean Republic at the **Charterhouse of Saint Martin (Certosa di San Martino)** and created a government modeled along French lines, citing liberty and equality for all. The republic, however, survived a mere five months.

Eleonora fought for Jacobin ideals through her writings. She translated books and articles into the Neapolitan dialect, hoping to incite the staunchly pro-monarchist *lazzaroni* to overthrow the King. To that end, she also wrote for

more than thirty issues of the newspaper *Monitore Napoletano,* the mouthpiece of the Parthenopean Republic. But the Republic had many problems and the Bourbon monarchy soon wrested back control of the city. Eleonora was one of many Jacobins who were executed at that time.

Getting There: You'll see the **plaque** dedicated to the Parthenopean Republic along the wall while walking down the street from Castel Sant'Elmo (address: Largo San Martino 1, Naples – *see also p. 147*) to the Certosa di San Martino. A second **plaque** dedicated specifically to Eleonora can be found across the street from the Santa Chiara Cloister (address: Via Benedetto Croce 1). Finally, **Execution Square** (today named **Piazza Mercato**) is a few blocks from the port as well as Piazza Garibaldi.

For history buffs who'd like to look up more, the other notables executed in Piazza Mercato, include King Corradino (1268) and the popular revolutionary Masaniello (1647).

THE GAMBLING MEZZOSOPRANO: ISABELLA COLBRAN

Isabella Colbran (1785-1845) radiated majesty on stage. Off-stage, it was said, she had as much dignity as a milliner's assistant. Born in Madrid, she studied under Girolamo Crescenti in Paris and by the age of twenty was known throughout Europe for her velvety mezzo-soprano voice. She took her talent to Naples, a city known as the capital of European music during the 18th and 19th centuries.

The opulent Bourbon dynasty had taken over rule of Naples and they built the **Teatro San Carlo**, which quickly became the place every opera singer wanted to be, including the famous castrato Farinelli.

When Isabella Colbran arrived in Naples, she became the lover of the theater's impresario, Domenico Barbaja. A coffee-shop owner from Milan with a knack for business, Barbaja ran the theater alongside a slew of gaming parlors in northern Italy – the likely cause of Colbran's lifelong gambling addiction.

Barbaja commissioned Gioachino Rossini (*Barber of Seville*) to work in Naples on contract for seven years. Rossini quickly fell in love with Colbran, composing at least ten operas with her in mind. The three-some worked together until 1822 when Rossini and

Colbran left for Bologna, where they married. (Barbaja wasn't invited.)

Materially well off, Isabella Colbran exacted high fees and also inherited a large estate. When Colbran's father died, Rossini was so moved by his wife's grief that he commissioned a mausoleum near Bologna depicting a daughter at the foot of the tomb weeping for her father. Colbran is buried there today alongside Rossini's parents.

But in general, Colbran's marriage was a failure. Rossini was thirty and his career was about to take off, while Colbran was thirty-seven, her waning voice sounding the death knell of her career. While in 1824 she still played the star role for Rossini's *Semiramide* in London, asking the high sum of 1,500 pounds, the critics began to pan her performances with such zeal that three years later, at the age of forty-two, her career was over. While Rossini continued to travel and work throughout Europe, taking on a mistress in Paris, Colbran mostly remained at her deceased father's estate in Castenaso near Bologna.

Her health continued to deteriorate, in large part due to the gonorrhea she contracted from her husband. She also began to sell off whatever she could of her estate to support an ever more acute gambling addiction. She died in 1845, at the age of sixty, purportedly murmuring Rossini's name.

Getting There: Today, the **Teatro San Carlo**, located in the heart of the city, is the highlight of any Naples visit. You can get a tour during the day or buy tickets at the window for evening performances. The address is Via San Carlo 98/F, Naples.

Book Recommendation: No English-language biography exists for Isabella Colbran, but the biography *Rossini: His Life and Works* by Richard Osborne details much of the opera singer's life.

MEDIUM OR TRICKSTER?: EUSAPIA PALLADINO

Illusionist, medium, levitator, and trickster, Eusapia Palladino (1854-1918) lived during an epoch that blazed with the determination to prove the supernatural through science. To that end, all manner of scientists and writers, including Pierre and Marie Curie as well as Arthur Conan Doyle, sought out Eusapia — and paid her exorbitant fees — for the sake of finding an answer to the impassioned question of the time: Was she a fraud?

Palladino was born in a mountain village near Bari. Her mother died during childbirth. Her father then sent her to be raised at a neighboring farm until the age of twelve, when he was murdered by brigands. With no living relatives, a family from her village that had moved to Naples took Palladino in.

The family at that time was engaged in holding regular séances, something very common with the rise of Spiritualism (the belief that the spirits of the dead could be contacted through mediums).

When Eusapia was invited to join these séances, she proved able to levitate objects: tables rose, chairs danced, glasses clanked, and bells rang. Thereafter, the family invited all their friends to witness Eusapia's tricks.

But these gifts, as told by Palladino, also tormented her. Palladino explained that she saw ghosts staring at her. Also, her clothes and bed-covers would be stripped from her in the middle of the night.

Fiercely independent, Palladino left the family to work as a laundress. She then married twice, the first time to a conjuror whose name is unknown. Her second marriage was to a Neapolitan merchant whom Palladino helped in his shop while conducting séances in the evenings.

In 1888 Palladino first made headlines when a Professor Ercole Chiaia of Naples wrote an open letter to eminent scientist and spirit-doubter, Cesare Lombroso. Describing Palladino, he said she was "… an invalid woman who belongs to the humblest class of society. She is nearly thirty years old *(actually by 1888 she would have been thirty-four – my italics)*, and very ignorant; her appearance is neither fascinating nor endowed with the power which modern criminologist call irresistible; but when she wishes, be it day or by night, she can divert a curious group for an hour or so with the most surprising phenomena."[44]

Not exactly a clipping to bring to a class reunion, but from that letter forward, Palladino was pushed into the limelight, with respected intellectuals asking her to display her skills. Cesare Lombroso asked her to perform a battery of séances in Milan during which time he made careful scientific observations. Palladino was then invited to cities across Europe. She traveled to Warsaw, Vienna, Munich, Cambridge, and St. Petersburg, among other places. She even displayed her skills in front of Pierre and Marie Curie in Paris. Pierre Curie reported that he saw: "…tables raised from all four legs, movement of objects from a distance, hands that pinch or caress you, and luminous apparitions."[45]

But many intellectuals also caught Palladino cheating. Whenever she resorted to tricks, her clients complained bitterly about her high fees. Palladino, in her own defense, noted that her impatient intellectual clientele put too much pressure on her to perform: that's what caused her to cheat.

---

44 "Eusapia Palladino: Information from Answers.com," *Answers.com: Wiki Q&A Combined with Free Online Dictionary, Thesaurus, and Encyclopedias*; www.answers.com/topic/eusapia-palladino. This link provides the most comprehensive and well-documented English-language summary of all the information known on Palladino.

45 "Eusapia Palladino: Information from Answers.com", *op. cit.*

Did she think of herself as a fraud? And how did she view this high-society interest in her skills? Hereward Carrington's biography of Eusapia tells a story that perhaps reveals more:

> Eusapia says she possessed diamond earrings and bracelets set with emeralds, massive chains and rings with precious stones. Her rich acquaintances Sardou, Aksakoff, Richet, Ochorowicz, Semiraski, Flammarion, knowing her Neapolitan taste for gold ornaments, had loaded her with many gifts. For better security she put these treasures into a sort of strong box in her shop.

> "One night," she said, "I had a horrible dream: I saw a man, of whom I saw not only the face, but all the details of his clothes, with an old hat, a handkerchief round his neck, check trousers; he came into the shop and forced open the box, whilst two companions watched at the door."

> The impression was so strong that she awoke her husband and told him that the shop was being robbed. He paid no attention; but she got up about two o'clock, went into the shop and assured herself that there were no thieves there. But to set her mind at rest she took her precious jewels and carried them to her room, where she shut them up in a piece of furniture after counting them one by one.

> What was her alarm next day when she encountered, near the door of the house, an individual identical in appearance with the person she had dreamed of! Worried by this thought, she went to consult a police functionary whom she knew, but he excused himself, saying: "I cannot, dear Madam, undertake to act as policeman of dreams, but if you wish to make your mind easy take your jewels to the bank."[46]

After several decades of intense interest in her abilities, in 1909 Palladino traveled to America where she was invited to show off her talents at Harvard. There, an eminent psychologist observed her séances and found her to be a fraud. For whatever reason, his publication sounded the death knell of her international popularity. While she may have continued her séances from 1910 onward, we know nothing of what happened to her except that she died in 1918 of unknown causes in an apartment house on **Via Benedetto Cairoli**.

---

46 Hereward Carrinton, *Eusapia Palladino and Her Phenomena* (New York: B.W. Dodge & Company, 1909) 25-6.

Places To See: Folklore has it that Palladino held her séances at a hotel in **Piazza Garibaldi**, but the hotel is no longer standing. Palladino died a few blocks away on **Via Benedetto Cairoli**, the apartment number unknown. A **Magic Café** exists along this road, but if you go inside and ask if they've ever heard about the medium, the barista and customers only shrug.

Another local curiosity, two blocks away is an **English Cemetery** at Piazza Santa Maria della Fede. The adjacent church  was built in 1645 and one hundred years later Carlo III's wife, Maria Amalia of Saxony turned it into a shelter for vagrant women. Later it became a hospital for prostitutes. The cemetery started out as a garden for the church, but in 1826 Sir Henry Lushington bought the land for a non-Catholic cemetery. Herein lie expat protestants who once resided in Naples, including the mathematician and pioneer of modern astrophysics, Mary Somerville.[47]

Book Recommendations: Interest in Eusapia Palladino is long extinguished, even within this city of miracles, but two older books about her are: *Eusapia Palladino and Her Phenomena* by Hereward Carrington and *The History of Spiritualism* by Arthur Conan Doyle.

---

47 Antonio Emanuele Piedimonte, *Partenope E Le Altre: Guida illustrata ai misteri di Napoli e della Campania* (Napoli: La Buona Stampa, 1998) 57.

THE ODIOUS JOURNALIST: MATILDE SERAO

The writer Matilde Serao (1856-1927) wrote twenty-nine novels during her lifetime and is best known for having founded the daily Neapolitan newspaper *Il Mattino*. The newspaper still is the most widely read daily of southern Italy.

At the age of twenty-six, Matilde left Naples to "conquer Rome." There, she wrote everything from literary criticism to gossip. Her rather dumpy figure also managed to attract the attention of writer Eduardo Scarfoglio and the two were married in 1885. Their union was not only romantic, but also professional as they established a newspaper together called *Corriere di Roma*. The newspaper, however, wasn't successful and landed the couple in serious debt.

Fortunately, the owner of the Neapolitan *Corriere del Mattino* promised to pay their debts if they came to Naples and wrote for his publication. Matilde and her husband agreed. They worked for the *Corriere* for many years, until their private life went public.

Eduardo began an affair with a singer and actress and two years later, his mistress became pregnant. When Eduardo refused to leave Matilde, his lover became so incensed that in 1894 she placed their daughter at Eduardo's door step and fired a pistol. While the scandal was at first suppressed, eventually the *Corriere di Napoli* broke the story. A week later, Eduardo's lover died in the hospital and Matilde began to take care of the little girl, Paulina. Although Eduardo and Matilde continued to live together, eventually Matilde couldn't take his philandering and they separated.

Her popularity as a novelist occurred much before this scandal when she wrote *Il Ventre di Napoli* (1884), a realistic portrayal of life in Naples, which criticized the government for its handling of the cholera epidemic and detailed the appalling living conditions of the poor.

Ardently against feminism and against giving women the right to vote, Serao's early fiction, including *Cuore infermo* (1881) and *Fantasia* (1883) explored her dissatisfaction with heterosexual relationships and seemed to say that fulfilling relationships could better be found between women.

Matilde Serao died in 1927 of a heart attack seated at her writing desk.[48]

Places To See: You can pick up *Il Mattino* throughout the city and also visit **Piazzetta Matilde Serao**, located just off Via Toledo near the *Augusteo* funicular.

THE GLAMOROUS CONCUBINE: SOPHIA LOREN

Born on September 20, 1934 in Rome, Sophia Loren was what in those days people called "an illegitimate child." When her father refused to marry Loren's aspiring actress mother, Sophia moved to the port town of Pozzuoli to live with her grandmother. That was during WWII when bomb after bomb rained down from the sky and Sophia was once struck by shrapnel in the chin. After the war, Sophia's grandmother opened a bar where Loren waited tables until,

---

48 Although very well-known in Italy, a biography of Matilde Serao doesn't exist in English. The information for this sub-chapter comes from the Italian-language Wikipedia website at "Matilde Serao – Wikipedia," *Wikipedia. L'Enciclopedia Libera.*

at the age of fourteen, she entered a beauty contest in Naples. The judges selected her as a finalist and from there, she left to Rome to begin a film career.

Soon she met Italian film producer and director, Carlo Ponti, who fell deeply in love with her. He helped launch her career, which was to span over a half-century. The trouble was, Carlo was married and in the Italy of the 1950's divorce was illegal. So Ponti obtained a divorce in Mexico and then married Loren. But when they returned to Italy, the Catholic Church denounced their marriage. The Italian government issued a warrant out for both of them, accusing Ponti of bigamy and Loren of concubinage. Their legal problems in Italy mounted until in 1965-6 Ponti, his first wife, and Loren became French citizens and settled both the divorce and marriage for good. Ponti and Loren thereafter had two children – Carlo Jr. (1968) and Edoardo (1973).

Sophia remained faithful to short and stubby Carlo until the end of his life (in 2007) even as attractive men stumbled all over her. Cary Grant fell so deeply in love with her that he proposed marriage several times during the late 1950's. In spite of Loren's refusals, Grant split with his significant other in order to continue his attempts to win Sophia's heart. Then, during and after filming *The Millionairess* (1960) where Loren co-starred with Peter Sellers, the British actor split with his first wife due to his love for Loren, which she insisted she reciprocated only platonically.

Sophia is best known for winning an Academy Award for Best Actress for her film, *Two Women*. But she never forgot her hometown, filming three movies set in Naples: *Neapolitan Carousel* (1954), *L'oro di Napoli* (1954), and *It Started In Naples* (1960). The latter film co-starred Clark Gable and aptly portrayed the strong cultural differences between Italians and Americans.

Sophia Loren continues to have an affinity for Naples, being an ardent fan of SSC Napoli. In 2007 she promised that if the soccer club won enough games to be promoted to Serie A, she would do a striptease. That year, SSC Napoli achieved this goal, but today, fans still wait and ask: Will Sophia strut her stuff?

Places To See: The port town of **Pozzuoli** where Sophia grew up during WWII *(see p. 10).* The **soccer stadium** is where Sophia's favorite team plays games *(see p. 222).* **Ristorante La Bersagliera** (at Borgo Marinari 10/11, Naples) is a restaurant near the Castel dell'Ovo. The restaurant was frequented by Sophia Loren (as well as Salvador Dalí) and has photos of her on the wall. You can find them on-line at www.labersagliera.it.

You can take a ferry or hydrofoil to the island of **Capri** *(see p. 71),* buy a ticket for the short funicular, and visit the piazza where the cafés and restaurants make you feel like you're inside the Sophia Loren movie, *It Started In Naples,* whose scenes mostly took place on this island.

For a a fantastic dining experience on the Amalfi Coast, go to **Donna Sofia Ristorante** (at Via Talagnano 5, Sorrento). To get there, you drive along sheer cliffs overlooking the sea until you reach Sorrento. You then turn onto a road so small that the walls have thin aqueduct-like lines scooped out from either side to let the belly of cars get through. Be careful though: this narrow road is considered to be a two-way street, so you need to honk your horn often to let those driving in the opposite direction know you're headed their way. You turn onto a dead-end road with overhanging lemon trees. A parking lot is off to one side. The restaurant looks like a secluded private home. Inside, a fantastic restaurant has incredible ambiance and a menu to match. You can find them on-line at www.ristorantedonnasofia.com.

FACES OF NAPLES: THE GLOVE MAKER

On the top floor of an 18th century palazzo, Mauro S. runs an internationally renowned glove business. Fifty years ago, small glove shops filled the Sanità district in downtown Naples, but the Camorra as well as large manufacturers from China and the Philippines drove most of them out of business. Mauro, on the other hand, took over his family business that has existed for over one hundred years. Proud of his company's long heritage, a photo of his grandparents hangs on a wall of his office.

Today, Mauro distributes his gloves internationally, including to France, Germany, and the United States. Many of his gloves have appeared in magazines and the President of Italy even visited his company, writing him a thank you letter.

What's the secret to Mauro's success? Every one of his gloves are handmade by expert craftsmen. His employees still use the non-electric Singer sewing machines from the early 1900's, they cut the leather by hand, and use natural light to distinguish color shades.

Mauro buys his leather from several Middle Eastern countries through intermediaries. From there, the leather goes to a company outside Naples that separates the skin from the wool in large vats filled with water and calcium. The skin goes into a tanning machine, which heats the material for several hours along with vegetable oil and chrome. The leather is then dyed various colors. Mauro takes this prepared leather to make his gloves.

Fifteen people work at the top floor of his palazzo. First, the leather is stretched, being careful to make sure the stretch of the leather will be vertical rather than horizontal. The material is then carefully cut and pounded so that the impression for the fingers becomes clear.

At this point, Mauro has about fifty different elderly women throughout the city who receive the cut leather and sew the gloves together. Many of these women once worked for the glove shops and now continue their craft from home. They return the gloves to Mauro, who gives it to his employees inside the palazzo. They use scraps of leather from the cutting room to fill in the gaps between the fingers. One of these women has worked in Mauro's company since she was eighteen – she is now eighty years old.

The gloves then go on to be lined with cashmere, silk, or other materials. Mauro explains that the only difference between the way he makes gloves and the way his grandfather made them is that his grandfather used one stitch to marry the lining and the leather together, but Mauro uses glue. The lining and leather are then sewn together at the cuff – usually carried out once again to the elderly ladies in the city. The gloves often come and go from this palazzo twenty-four times before they are ready.

At the very end of the process, every glove is put on a hot broiler that looks like a metal hand. Then it's placed between two slabs of marble for several hours in order to make it flat. Mauro checks every glove individually before it's ready to be sent to stores.

Getting There: Mauro gives tours by appointment. You can visit him at Via Stella 12, Napoli, call him at 081 299 041, or email him at omegant@tin.it.

THE CASTLE TOUR

Four medieval castles give Naples a princess and dragon flair: Castel Capuano, Castel dell'Ovo, Castel Nuovo, and Castel Sant'Elmo. For those who live in Campania, I recommend visiting these castles over a series of several weekends, but a day-long tour of all four works just as easily.

A ONE DAY TOUR

Children in particular will love this day-trip to downtown Naples. Start at **Castel Nuovo**, which overlooks the port. Search for the trapdoor where Queen Joanna II dropped her lovers to be eaten by crocodiles.

From there, walk to Piazza Trieste e Trento, pass the Royal Palace on your left and follow Via Console Cesario to the seafront. Walk alongside the Bay of Naples and you will come to **Castel dell'Ovo**, where you can search for Virgil's Egg. Walking further down Via Partenope, the **Villa Comunale** along the Riviera di Chiaia is a park in the middle of the city that has gelato, donkey rides, motorized kids' bikes (on the weekends), Europe's oldest aquarium, as well as playground equipment.

Use the map you obtained from the tourist office and walk to Via Toledo. Here, you can take one of the famous four **funicular** railways to the Vomero district. The Central Funicular opened in 1928 and is one of the longest funicular lines in the world.

Walk to the **Castel Sant'Elmo**, which touts a breathtaking 360 degree view of Naples. Next door to the castle, the **Certosa di San Martino**, a Cistercian charterhouse, has an exceptionally good museum with an exhibition of *presepe* – Neapolitan nativity scenes – as well as carriages, medieval ships, and a lovely garden. Make sure you sing down the wells – the echoes are wonderful.

Return to the historic center of Naples and gaze at the distant **Castel Capuano** on your way to or from **Christmas Alley**, a fun shopping street for kids.

CASTEL NUOVO

Castel Nuovo (also known as the Maschio Angioino) towers over the port in downtown Naples. Charles I of Anjou ordered its construction, which began in 1279. He called it the "New Castle" to distinguish the palace from the older Castel Capuano and Castel dell'Ovo. Throughout the centuries, the castle underwent many renovations. Today it has a trapezoidal plan made up of tuff stone walls with five cylindrical towers.

To understand the history of Naples is to know that after the fall of the Roman empire, the region didn't have a national identity, but rather was owned by many foreign monarchs, including the Normans, the Spanish, the Austrian Habsburgs, and the Bourbon French. The two most notable influences on Naples' structure and architecture today continue to be Spanish and Bourbon.

Spanish rule, beginning at the time of the Italian Renaissance, spanned almost three hundred years and Castel Nuovo remains a strong reminder of this period. In 1422 King Alfonso I moved his capital from Barcelona to Naples and renamed this part of his region "The Kingdom of the Two Sicilies." While he retained Spanish customs, traditions, and language, Alfonso also supported the arts, the philosophical movement of humanism, and launched numerous building projects within Naples. The nobility also at this time rediscovered the ancient city center and built palaces within the **Quartieri Spagnolo** (Spanish Quarter or Spaccanapoli) of the city. The narrow streets with high-rise palazzos along Via S. Biagio Dei Librai and south in the *Centro Storico* still look as they did during this time. Alfonso also made renovations to the Castel Nuovo and took up residence here.

Wandering into the castle, you first enter the grand courtyard. Going up the stairs, the **Baron's Hall** touts a dome vaulted ceiling and noble seating. The room is so-called because in 1486 the barons plotted against King Ferdinand I of Aragon, but were arrested in this space instead, after being invited by the king to celebrate his grand daughter's marriage. The hall is still used for civic meetings.

Ancient ruins have also been found underneath the castle and you can walk through the **Armory Hall** where the floor is made of glass. Beneath your feet, you can view rubble that might have been the swimming pool of a Roman villa.

There's also a bronze door in the upstairs rooms of the **Museo Civico**, which still has the cannon ball embedded in it. This is the original 15th century door of the castle, which was taken as war booty by the French and then later returned.

And finally, search for the **mythical trap door** where Queen Joanna II dropped her lovers to be eaten by "sea monsters," possibly crocodiles.

Getting There: Overlooking the port, the castle is located across the street from where the cruise ships come in at Molo Beverello. The address is Piazza Municipio.

CASTEL DELL'OVO

The Roman poet Virgil, according to medieval legend, was a great sorcerer and while he lived in Naples, he put a magical egg inside the Castel dell'Ovo or Egg Castle. Legend has it that if this egg were ever to break, the city of Naples would experience death and destruction.

But what might have motivated Virgil to lodge an egg inside the castle foundation (or, says another story, inside a cage in its dungeon)?

Today's foundations of the castle date back to the Normans in the 12th century. Thereafter, the castle had numerous occupants throughout the centuries including the Austrians, the French, and the Spanish and it underwent many renovations. Set on the islet of Megaride, this site is said to have been first inhabited by the Greeks in the 6th century B.C. Then, during the 1st century B.C. a Roman villa was erected here.

Did Virgil ever roam this islet? He lived in Naples, so perhaps the poet's spirit does indeed still linger along the causeway where amorous (or libidinous) teenagers usually hang out on Friday and Saturday nights. The castle is open everyday and you can climb to the top courtyard for free. There are often art exhibitions in a variety of cavernous halls and if you explore hard enough, you'll find, perhaps not an egg, but the windows that look down into the **Roman foundations** of the building.

Getting There: The address is Borgo Marinari. If you are on Via Partenope, the castle is in easy sight.

CASTEL SANT'ELMO

Castel Sant'Elmo is best known for its incredible views of the city. The visitor can make a full circle along the open fortifications, passing guard outlook posts and cannons, climbing stairs, and racing down long semi-dark passageways.

Made of volcanic tuff stone, the castle has existed since 1275 when relatives of King Charles I of Anjou lived inside and the fortress went by the name of Belforte. King Robert the Wise renovated the castle in the early 1300's. This is when the building began to be known as the *castrum Sancti Erasmi*, probably because there was a chapel dedicated to Saint Erasmus on the site.

After King Robert the Wise died, the castle was reconstructed over the course of two centuries until it had an unusual hexagonal shape in the 1500's. From 1604 to 1952, the castle was used as a prison. It then became military property until 1979. Six years later, it was turned into a museum. Today a variety of modern art exhibitions can be seen in its echoing spaces and there are permanent sculpture installations by Mimmo Paladino (1948-).

Getting There: The address is Via Tito Angelini 1, Naples. Take any of the three funiculars that run up to the Vomero district. (Get a map from any tourist office and you can locate the four funicular lines throughout the city – *see p. 249.*)

CASTEL CAPUANO

Castel Capuano was built in the 12th century by William I, the first monarch of the Kingdom of Naples. Many kings and queens lived here, including Queen Joanna II. The Parthenopean revolutionaries were also incarcerated here for a time.

Today, the building serves as municipal offices and is generally closed to the public. If you walk down Via Tribunali, you'll see its façade and, bending the rules, you can walk into the courtyard. During the May of Monuments *(see p. 249)* when the archeological parks and museums are free, the castle is open for tours.

Getting There: The address is Piazza Enrico De Nicola and Via Concezio Muzy.

THE BOURBON TOUR

The opulent Bourbon dynasty ruled Naples from 1734 to 1861, not only bringing political stability and the civic ideals of the Enlightenment, but turning what had become a dilapidated city after two centuries of Spanish rule into a modernized metropolis.

In 1734, King Charles III of Spain from the house of Bourbon took over rule from the Austrians and was crowned King Charles VII of Naples. His first stop was to pay homage to the remains of **San Gennaro**, the patron saint of the city, whose blood is said to have liquefied immediately.

The Bourbons, thereafter, initiated Enlightenment ideals. **Herculaneum** and **Pompeii** were discovered during King Charles VII's rule and a flurry of archeological digs were commissioned, including the **Grotta di Seiano**. Well-known artists and writers also visited the city during this era, including Goethe, who was quoted as saying: "See Naples and die."

The most stunning mark King Charles VII left on the city was his building projects, which still impress visitors. The **Teatro San Carlo** turned Naples into an epicenter of musical genius. Farinelli, Rossini, Colbran, and Barbaja worked here. Each theater box featured a mirror along the wall that allowed patrons to watch the show while also staring at the reflection of the King sitting in his royal box. King Charles VII also built the **Royal Palace of Capodimonte**, which houses some of the finest artwork in the city.

During the Bourbon era, Luigi Vanvitelli, who worked in the baroque style was one of the most celebrated architects in Naples. Before he left Rome, he worked on the construction of the Trevi Fountain and stabilized the dome of St. Peter's Basilica. King Charles VII called Vanvitelli to Naples, where the architect spent most of his life constructing the **Royal Palace of Caserta**. The palace marked the pinnacle of architect Luigi Vanvitelli's career and emulated Versailles, especially with its opulent gardens. Vanvitelli also designed the **Palazzo Reale** in Piazza del Plebiscito.

King Charles VII had visions of grandeur, but he also wanted to wipe out poverty throughout the Kingdom. To that end, he commissioned Ferdinando Fuga in 1751 to build a structure that became known as the **Albergo dei Poveri (House of the Poor)**. Work continued until 1829. Unfortunately, the mammoth building was used only for a short time and now, in the last few decades, has been under continuous renovation.

This was also a time when both mysticism and science gained prominence, as seen through the artwork commissioned by alchemist, scientist, and nobleman Raimondo Di Sangro in the **Cappella Sansevero**. Giuseppe Sanmartino sculpted the *Veiled Christ* in this chapel, considered one of the modern day "wonders of the world."

In 1759, King Charles abdicated abruptly and left eight-year-old Ferdinand in charge. King Ferdinand IV of Naples had one of the longest reigns in European history. He was loved for his Neapolitan

dialect and known for setting up a small stand each evening in the market to give away his hunted game or catch of the day. He also established the lottery and a silk factory (or, some maintain, his wife did). Ultimately, the project failed, but **San Leucio** (near the Caserta Royal Palace at Via del Setificio 7) still exists and continues to produce exquisite silk hangings for royal palaces. A community of silk weavers was established, described in 1798 as the *Real Colonia dei Setaioli* (the "Silk Weavers' Royal Colony"). It should have become "Ferdinandopoli," but the project collapsed upon the French invasion.

King Ferdinand also had Luigi's son, Carlo Vanvitelli, design **Casina Vanvitelliana**, a hunting lodge in the Phlegraean Fields. Originally built as a resting place after his hunting and fishing, it was accessible by boat only, but now has a bridge going over the water.

The Parthenopean Republic in 1799 brought the Bourbon reign to an abrupt halt, but the Republic failed within a year and Napoleon's French troops entered the city. A brother-in-law of Napoleon's, Joseph Murat, took over. During his fifteen years of rule – before Napoleon's defeat and Murat's own execution by firing squad – he commissioned the **Piazza del Plebiscito** adjacent to the Royal Palace (Palazzo Reale) in downtown Naples.

Although work on the **Palazzo Reale** was first begun in 1600, the palace was only finished in 1843 after King Ferdinand re-took power. Inside, you can see an enfilade of Royal Apartments as well as the **Teatrino di Corte** built in 1768 for Maria Carolina on the occasion of her marriage to Ferdinand.

King Ferdinand returned to the throne in 1815 and he ruled until his death in 1859. Two years later, the Kingdom of Naples came to an end and the city unified with the rest of Italy.

Book Recommendation: The best English language history of Naples is *In The Shadows of Vesuvius: A Cultural History of Naples* by Jordan Lancaster.

Additional Note: This tour is for the armchair traveler and for those who like to put together much of what they've seen while wandering through the other tours in this book and now turn much of their sights into an additional Bourbon theme. I don't recommend, however, a Bourbon tour *per se* only because the endless opulence of palaces and museums would, well, become excessive.

If you insist that "opulence hopping" is your *forte*, allow yourself seven days to complete the tour: one day for each palace, two days for the archeological sites, and another day in downtown Naples.

The Lazzaroni and Pasta

The "street people" or *lazzaroni* in Naples gained a reputation for being both beggars and riotous, staunch monarchists, resorting to mob violence whenever their Kings or Queens faced attacks from outsiders. By the 1700's and 1800's, they also proved to be the best innovative food vendors and cooks in Europe. Fruit vendors came from the countryside as did the *cepollari* with onions and garlic hanging over their shoulders. *Pisciavinnoli* or fishmongers sold their fresh catch from the sea and *pizzaivoli* invented pizza.

The *maccaronari* or Neapolitan pasta makers also ladled out cooked macaroni from enormous boiling cauldrons that they fired up on the street. By the 1800's pasta became so popular that the first pictures not depicting Mt. Vesuvius were of the *maccaronari*. They are credited with having discovered the food, which has no preservatives and can keep in cupboards for long periods.

Today, pasta is the mainstay of the Italian diet. Most families have pasta for at least one of their meals every day. The varieties are endless, but Naples, in particular, is known for having the largest variety, around six-hundred.

According to Antonio Chiodi Latini and Mario Busso in their cookbook *Pasta: Passione e Fantasia*, pasta entered the Court Kitchen thanks to the Chamberlain of King Ferdinand IV around the mid-1700's who had the idea of using a fork with four short points instead of the hands. The word "spaghetti" was coined in Naples too, the word coming from "spaghi," meaning small strings.

In their book, Latini and Busso give a description of many varieties of fresh and dry pasta, distinguished by their water content. They also say that the South often makes pasta without eggs.[49]

---

49 Antonio Chiodi Latini and Mario Busso, *Pasta: Passione e Fantasia* (Terzo: Gribaudo, 2004) 7.

AND BEYOND: THE PAPER MAKERS OF AMALFI

Paper making first began in the Orient around the 700's A.D. Five hundred years later, the sea empires of Amalfi, Genoa, Pisa, and Venice all traded extensively with the Middle East and the Orient. This network of trade gave rise to the need for documenting transactions. In the 13th century, Amalfi was the oldest Sea Republic – with bases all the way down to what is now Sicily – and became famous for its paper production.

The need for paper increased particularly in 1220 when King Frederick II, Holy Roman Emperor, came up with an epoch-making decision by imposing the use of paper for all public acts. The mills for producing the paper were located in the **Valle dei Mulini** (Valley of the Mills) and people came from throughout the Mediterranean to buy and record documents on Amalfi paper. The quality was so particular and the production so reliable that even the Vatican was said to have contracted with Amalfi to produce all its official paper. Mozart also received a supply of Amalfi paper in exchange for a concert in the home of a wealthy Neapolitan nobleman.

THE HIKE

A hiking trail begins in the small town of **Pontone** along the **Via delle Ferriere**. Walking beyond a stream, you can see ruins of the Iron Works that once produced the metal parts needed by the paper mills. From there, a trail diverts upstream to a cascade. This is the waterway that many mills used to manufacture their paper.

Returning to Via delle Ferriere, the path forks. Another trail goes down to the **Valle dei Mulini**. This route takes you past eleven mills that operated in the valley during the 18th century.

The hills all around are the Lattari Mountains. They produce the water that flows into the Canneto River. In many places along the trail, you can see where man channeled the water into canals to help run the paper making machinery. The valley, ironically, helped the decline of the paper mills in

later years because these roads, railways, and communication systems weren't easily accessible, making the shipping in and out of raw materials difficult.

THE FIRST PAPER MAKING TECHNIQUES

A document from the year 1700 states that this valley had eleven paper mills with a total of 83 pile troughs made of rock. Here, rags were crushed into fibers using large levers with hammers. Some of the mills were huge buildings that had rooms with open windows and large racks to dry the paper, while others were smaller.

In the beginning, old rags from Amalfi and other areas were used to produce the fibers for making paper. Rags were hard to come by. Ironically, when the Black Death killed millions of people in Europe, tons of clothing and rags became available – at just about the time the printing press was invented. Suddenly, more books were printed, people became better educated, and these better educated people scratched their heads, trying to figure out a substance that might provide even more paper making material. In the 1700's a Frenchman studied the paper wasp and discovered that wood could be broken apart and made into paper – a process that is emulated today in paper manufacture.

THE PAPER MUSEUM

At the end of the trail is the **Paper Museum**. The Italians started the first steps toward the process of "industrializing" paper making by mechanizing many jobs once done by hand. In later years, however, the Industrial Revolution struck this region hard. Many

paper mills couldn't modernize to keep up with competitors and they went out of business. In spite of the difficulties, some Amalfi paper makers continued to produce paper using their traditional methods; father passed the trade on to their sons and generations continued making paper in traditional ways.

Because of their geographic location, the mills were always subject to flooding during the rainy season. This flood water, if used in the mill, carried with it rubble that damaged equipment. In November 1954 a massive flood destroyed sixteen paper mills, leaving only three standing.

Because of the size of this valley, these mills have never been, and will never be, large or even middle-sized operations. They will always retain an artisan character. The museum displays some of the artisan techniques used throughout the centuries.

THE PAPER MAKING SHOP

Continuing downhill from the museum, just on the right, you'll find **Arte e Carta di Rita Cavaliere** at Via Casamare. The structure, housing the paper shop, has a mill stone near the entrance. Built in the 13th century, it retains its original stone basin for paper pulp and contains many paper making artifacts.

The Cavaliere family has been making paper from the 16th century onward, an art passed from one generation to the next. Visitors are invited to make a single sheet from wet pulp of one hundred percent pure cotton and peruse the shop with its fine quality paper. Available for sale are single sheets for watercolor or limited edition prints, textured paper embedded with dried flowers and plants, small booklets, blanks for business cards and historical images of Amalfi. The shop is only about ten meters from the museum as you head downhill toward the town center.

Restaurant Recommendation: After your hike, consider having a meal at **Trattoria del Teatro** at Via E. Marini 19, Amalfi. A former theater, you wander up stairs and through an alley before spotting it.

THE ESPRESSO TOUR

There's not a Starbucks for miles around. When you ask for coffee and want something that comes in a cup larger than the length of your thumb, Neapolitans either look confused or smirk. For them, coffee is caffè and caffè everywhere else in the world is called espresso.

Neapolitans drink three kinds of caffè all day long: *lungo* (long, like a double shot), *ristretto* (short, no more than a tablespoon), and *macchiato* ("stained" with a dollop of milk foam on top). What makes a cup of caffè good or bad is the frothy foam or *crema* on the shot. The espresso machine and the barista together perfect this art.

In the morning, Neapolitans also drink cappuccino, which is a shot of espresso with milk and foam that comes in a regular tea cup. Italians, however, don't tend to drink cappuccino past eleven o'clock in the morning. They also don't eat much breakfast, ordering a quick *cornetto* (croissant) instead. Sometimes you can see men drink caffè with a little "top off" or splash of liqueur, such as sambuca, making it *caffè corretto.*

Proper etiquette in these parts dictates that you stir sugar into the caffè before downing the shot in three or four sips. The caffè always comes with a cup of water, either *lisca/naturale* (flat) or *frizzante* (carbonated), which should be sipped both before and after drinking the *tazzino* in order to clean the palette. Most often, caffè is drunk *al banco* or at the counter as a brief sip-and-go.

While Italians don't copy Starbucks, nowadays baristas often do add an extra touch to their caffè. In fact, some of the best caffè renditions come from – you'll never guess it – the cafè-bars at the shopping malls. But just about anywhere in the city, you can get specialty coffee drinks with their own exotic names like *Tiramisu* ("Pick Me Up") or *Il Nonno* ("The Grandpa"). They announce their twists on billboards and each bar considers their speciality drinks proprietary.

In this chapter, I give the history of coffee in Campania, providing a tour of places to visit along the way and beverages to taste at those locations. At the end, I provide a list of my favorite espresso twists – modern artistic delights made by baristas throughout the city that sweeten any moment of the day.

A ONE DAY TOUR

Start the tour in Salerno, parking your car by the promenade and visiting any one of the cafés here to eat either a *cornetto*, *bomba*, *brioche*, or *sfogliatelle*. Next, walk through the old town until you reach the **Giardino della Minerva**, where the Salerno Medical School is said to have been. I maintain that the first written record of coffee on the continent of Europe starts here.

Drive about 1½ hours to downtown Naples and park your car in the port parking lots across the street from Castel Nuovo. Walk to the **Teatro San Carlo** where impresario Domenico Barbaja invented the Barbajata (today *caffè con panna* or espresso with whipping cream) and, possibly even, the cappuccino. Next, walk through **Galleria Umberto I** where Bar Brasiliano serves the popular *Caffè Nocciola* (or Nut Coffee) and spill into **Via Toledo**. Nearby you'll find a plaque that designates the palazzo where Domenico Barbaja lived along with the opera composer Gioachino Rossini.

Walk down **Via Toledo** and then cut over to the **University of Naples** where Mario Schipano received his letters from Pietro della Valle. Next, make your way to **Piazza Bellini**, passing several of the cafés mentioned in this chapter, and end at **Intra Moenia**, where you can try the *Caffè al Baccio* or browse their selection of books.

Return down Via Toledo until you reach Piazza Trieste e Trento and head inside **Caffè Gambrinus** for a coffee delight. My suggestion: the Caffè Gambrinus drink topped with whipping cream.

Head down Via Chiaia and eventually you'll pass the **Sanazzaro Theater** where actor Eduardo de Filippo held some of his shows. He also made the Neapolitan Flip-Over Coffee pot famous.

Take a turn right onto Via Filangieri, walking past some of the poshest stores within the city, until you reach the modern art museum **PAN or Palazzo delle Arti Napoli**. One block away, go to **Caffè Moccia** on Via San Pasquale and buy some of their wonderful pastries.

COFFEE AND HEALTH

Coffee drinking originated in Ethiopia many centuries ago when the beverage was probably used for medicinal purposes. Thereafter, the beverage traveled to the Middle East, where the city of Mocha in Yemen became a coffee trading capital. Coffee historians traditionally give the date of 1615 as the year when Venetian merchants brought the beverage to Italy, thus introducing the dark brew to Europe. However, I maintain that the Campania region knew about coffee far before this date. Medieval physicians from the Schola Medica Salernitana between the 10th through 13th centuries collected a compendium of dietary recommendations called *The Code of Health of the School of Salernum*, in which coffee was mentioned twice. Two Latin hexameters say:

Order of Supping

Begin with meats, with coffee then conclude;
Eschew such drinks as toper hands have brewed,
Which burn our flesh, yet palate all delude.
Be bread the last of anything you eat,
And after meals shun fires that give much heat.
But supper over, then give time beguile
With rest, or gently strolling for a mile.[50]

– and –

Coffee to some gives sleep, to some unrest;
Headache relieves, and stomach when oppressed;
Will monthly flow and urine too procure.
Take it slow-roasted, each grain picked and pure.[51]

The manuscript included chapters on cheese, nettles, wine as well as bloodletting and cures for fistulas. Because the work is a compendium of mostly dietary recommendations, the *Code of Health* demonstrates that at least some people within the region might have used coffee as an everyday beverage. If true, the dark brew in Campania pre-dated the introduction of coffee to the whole of Europe in 1615.

Today, people in Campania still have a strongly held cultural belief that coffee is good for your health and perhaps this dates back to the Salerno manuscripts. Turns out, they might not be very far off in this belief either. Citing several sources, including the Pan-European Coffee Science Information Center (www.cosic.org), an organization established in the United Kingdom in 1990 and whose

---

50 John Ordronaux, trans., *Regimen Sanitatis Salernitanum (Code of Health of the School of Salernum)* (Philadelphia: J.B. Lippincott & Co., 1871) 157.

51 Ibid., 159.

operations are located in Worcestershire, medical researchers have found the following beneficial effects of drinking coffee:

- A study of 72,284 Italians showed that there was an inverse association between intake of coffee and the prevalence of asthma. Risk of asthma fell by 28% when three or more cups of coffee were drunk everyday. Therefore, caffeine is an effective broncho-dilator.
- Coffee possesses greater in vitro anti-oxidant activity than other beverages due to photogenic acid and the meanoidius (color pigment) created during the roasting process. Hence it may reduce the risk of cardiovascular disease.
- Moderate consumption of coffee may lower the risk of Type 2 diabetes.
- A control study in Italy showed an inverse association between coffee consumption and ultrasound documented gallstones.
- Coffee may also protect against liver cirrhosis.
- Studies say that there is a 31% less chance of developing Parkinson's disease if one drinks coffee.
- Portuguese and Canadian studies have shown coffee intake may reduce the risk of Alzheimer's disease.
- Coffee may be an ergogenic aid that improves the capacity to do work and exercise, prolonging the time of exhaustion and enhancing performance.
- Coffee improves alertness, which in particular helps car drivers, thereby reducing the number of accidents.

In spite of these health benefits, Italians actually drink less coffee on average than other EU countries.[52] The small-portioned espresso shot may be the reason and because water touches the coffee grinds for less time in an espresso machine, the caffeine content in an espresso shot is a mere 100 mg in comparison to a 7-

---

52 –, "Kimbo: Consumption," *http://www.kimbo.it/eng/caffe-consumi.asp*.

ounce cup of brewed coffee that has 115-175 mg of caffeine. So if Italians hold the key to "best coffee intake practices," temperate portions also play a role in the dark brew's health benefits.

Curiously, after the written record of coffee in the *Code of Health*, evidence of coffee use in Campania vanished for centuries. Coffee scholars maintain that if coffee was used in the Campania region, then it remained only for home use or quickly disappeared due to its high cost.

Places To See: The **Schola Medica Salernitana**, today called the **Giardino della Minerva**, can still be visited. Inside, they have a café-bar, which also sells an array of herbal teas. *(See also p. 118.)*

Book Recommendation: For more about international coffee history, my favorite book is: *Uncommon Grounds: The History of Coffee and How It Transformed Our World* by Mark Pendergrast.

THE GALLANT COOK

It wasn't until the 17th century when **Pietro della Valle**, born in Rome, settled in Naples. He was feeling suicidal after a love affair went bad but his friend, the physician and professor at the University of Naples, Mario Schipano, encouraged him to travel instead of ending it all.

In 1614, Della Valle set off on a pilgrimage to the Holy Land and spent the next twelve years traveling throughout the East. He continued to write Schipano countless letters and within them Della Valle described how in Constantinople Muslims had an ubiquitous tradition of drinking chave. He explained how it was made, roasting and grinding the beans to dust and sweetening the beverage or better yet leaving it bitter to obtain a benefit from its medical properties.[53] Della Valle's letters would have us believe that coffee was unknown during this time in Naples.

Only at the end of the 18th century did coffee re-emerge as an important cultural ritual in Naples when celebrated gastronome Vincenzo Corrado (1736-1836) wrote a treatise specifically dedicated to the brew. A common household name for Neapolitans today, Corrado studied mathematics, astronomy, and philosophy. He then taught French and Spanish for a time while writing culinary books. In 1773 Corrado published *Il Credenziere di Buon Gusto (The Confectioner of Good Taste)* which became a huge success, catapulting Corrado into a stellar reputation as a chef. Within his book, he listed no fewer than eleven ways of preparing coffee.

Here are some of his recipes, as listed in Lejla Mancusi Sorrentino's wonderful little book, *Manuale del perfetto amatore del caffè* (or *Manual for the perfect lover of coffee*) and translated into English by this author:

Liqueur Caffè: Take two liters of boiling water and add six ounces of roasted and ground coffee. Leave together for two hours and then pass the water through a sieve. Mix the water with two pounds of sugar and two liters of liqueur. Filter the beverage through a cloth.[54]

Coffee Cream: Take roasted coffee and sprinkle into milk that is warmed in a vase above coals. When the coffee flavor has extracted into the liquid, pass the milk through a sieve. Cool the liquid and then mix in sugar, egg yolk, and rice-flour. Cook together. Serve cold.[55]

---

53 Lejla Mancusi Sorrentino, *Manuale del perfetto amatore del caffe: Storie racconti e ricette* (Napoli: Intra Moenia, 2003) 122-3.

54 Ibid., 171

55 Ibid., 171.

Milk Sorbet and Coffee: Create a strong concoction of coffee with three carafes of milk. Dissolve twenty-four egg yolks and three pounds of sugar. Combine with the milk and cook until thickened. Pass through a sieve and allow to cool until frozen.[56]

Candy Coffee: Roast coffee and then grind the beans until they turn to dust. Create a paste from the powdered coffee as well as some sugar until both together turn into a kind of gum. Turn the paste into tiny coffee beans and bake in an oven. The beans turn into candy.[57]

Luciano Pignataro

Assuming the mantle of Vincenzo Corrado, currently the most celebrated gastronome of the Campania region is **Luciano Pignataro** who has published several cookbooks, has a wine blog in both Italian and English at www.lucianopignataro.com, and has written a fabulous book called *I Dolci Napoletani (Neapolitan Desserts)*. Within these pages, he acknowledges the importance of coffee for the region by providing several recipes with espresso as an ingredient. Pignataro mentions the following Neapolitan desserts that include coffee:

Torta Caprese
Cold Cream al Caffè Espresso
Gelato al Caffè
Tiramisu di Ricotta di Bufala

---

56 Ibid., 170.

57 Ibid., 171.

Corrado loved the aristocracy and wanted to choreograph lavish meals to match their style. During his lifetime, he held famous banquets that landed him the moniker of Gallant Chef. By 1794 he wrote another book called *Il Cuoco Galante (The Gallant Cook)* where he elaborated on Neapolitan cooking. This book is still available in major bookshops throughout Campania. Vincenzo Corrado's health obviously benefited from coffee; he died at the age of one-hundred.

Corrado's "Coffee Cream" recipe has now turned into three extremely popular espresso twists: the *Granita*, the *Caffè del Nonno* (or Grandpa Coffee) and the *Caffè Shakerato*.

THE GRANITA

Summer in Naples can be hot, hot, hot. During the month of August everything shuts down and the entire city of one million people clears out. The usually bumper-to-hood bustle turns into a ghost town as Neapolitans flock to the Amalfi Coast and the beaches. A special espresso beverage called the *granita* goes with these hot summer days.

The *granita* comes in many different flavors and is very popular with children who drink *granitas* made of soft flakes of ice sweetened with different syrup flavors, such as strawberry and lime. For adults, the drink has a kick; it's made with an espresso shot. Served in a glass or in a plastic espresso-shot cup to take away, a *granita* is made by putting hot espresso in the freezer for a few hours until slushy, but not frozen. The beverage has a grainy texture, so it's usually drunk slowly in small sips.

The Arx Caffè, located along the road between Castel Sant'Elmo and the Certosa di San Martino serves the best *Caffè Granita*. During a castle tour or a visit to the *presepe* at the Certosa di San Martino, stop at this café-bar and after ordering, sit upstairs and admire a stellar view of Naples.

Arx Caffè
Via Tito Angelini 57, Naples

THE SHAKERATO

Another variation on Vincenzo Corrado's cold coffee cream recipe can be found at Caffè Del Centro Antico in the historic center of Naples. They freeze espresso into ice flakes. Then they add several

teaspoons of sugar and put the concoction into a blender, mixing the ingredients on high for a good ten minutes. As the sugar and espresso ice whip up, air fluffs the drink and turns it into a thick white color. The barista swirls small lines of caramel, chocolate or nut syrup inside the glass cup and then pours the liquid inside. The beverage tastes like a thick drinkable dessert. The sweetened grains of iced espresso also have a sandy texture.

Caffè Del Centro Antico
Via Croce Benedetto 15, Naples

THE GRANDPA

At the Neapolitan chain Il Caffè di Napoli, they create an espresso drink in almost an identical way to the shakerato, but they call it something else: the Grandpa or *Caffè del Nonno*. One of their cafés is on Corso Umberto I, a street that runs from the train station at Piazza Garibaldi down to Piazza Municipio.

Il Caffè di Napoli
Corso Umberto I 345, Naples

THE CAFFETTIERI AMBULANTI

By the early 1800's, coffee had become a public ritual in Naples when coffee street vendors or *caffettieri ambulanti* yelled to customers in the early morning hours: *"Vulite nà tazzulella è caffè?"*

They wore aprons and set up tables along the street replete with small burners, cups, saucers, sugar and a bottle of rum. Served with a little water to clean the palette, the coffee peddlers would serve to workers, maids, apprentices and then slip into offices, serving coffee to employees, managers, and nobles.[58] Thanks to them, caffè became a social leveler – the gourmet drink for the everyman.

Caffettieri ambulanti have been replaced by the café-bar where customers enter for a quick sip at the counter. Thankfully, the rum still exists. Cafés usually tout a wide selection of liqueurs along their back walls from Baileys and Jack Daniels to assorted Italian grappas.

At ten o'clock in the morning, it's common to see a few men drinking *caffè corretto* before heading off to work. The portions of liqueur are so small that the caffè has a bite, but not much more. The most common "correction" is adding about a tablespoon of

---

58 Sorrento Radio provides a picture and description at
http://www.sorrentoradio.com/prova/mestieri/caffettiere.htm.

the licorice-tasting liqueur called sambuca into a frothy shot of espresso. The barista still recommends you stir in a packet of sugar, making the beverage have a kind of bite-sweet-aaaah.

THE BARBAJATA

Caffè Florian in Venice was considered one of the first coffee houses on the European continent and was established in 1720, but generally, the Italian lands didn't take to café culture even after coffee houses blazed their trails of popularity in Austria, France, England, and the United States. It was only with the great Neapolitan impresario, Domenico Barbaja, (1778-1841), that a coffee house culture made a mark upon Naples.

Barbaja started out as a simple waiter in Milan, but went on to build an empire of cafés in northern Italy that were often fronts for his gambling parlors. His money brought him to Naples where in 1809 he became the director of the prestigious Teatro San Carlo. He brought opera singer Isabella Colbran to the theater as well as Giachino Rossini.

Folklore has it that Barbaja made his first big windfall of money through the creation of a signature beverage called the *Barbajata*. Today, however, nobody has ever heard of the *Barbajata* anywhere in the Campania region. Some claim Barbaja actually invented cappuccino, but that seems far-fetched. More likely the beverage still survives in a modern day form called *Caffè con Panna* or Coffee with

Whipping Cream. Simple and elegant, the drink is made from one shot of espresso doused on top with whipped cream.

Places To See: Tribute to Barbaja can be found at the **Teatro San Carlo** (*see also p. 130*) where his bust stands inside an intermission hall. Domenico Barbaja lived in the palazzo at **Via Toledo 202** close to the theater; you can still see the plaque dedicated to him on this street.

CAPPUCCINO IN NAPLES

Although claims that Domenico Barbaja invented the cappuccino seem far-fetched, we do know that the name stems from the Order of Capuchin Friars who in 1520 broke away from the mainstream Catholic Church, considering the Franciscan lifestyle of their day too opulent. Under Matteo da Bascio they created their own sect in the Marché region. The order spread and by 1538 a group of nuns, known as the Sisters of Suffering, founded a cloister in Naples.

These bearded friars wore brown robes with a white hood called a *cappuccio*. When the beverage was invented, a man like Domenico Barbaja – who loved expletives, gambling, and the high life – might not have wanted to name a drink that sounded so, well, austere. Whatever the truth behind the folklore, Neapolitans do have their cappuccino. They drink the beverage only until eleven o'clock and cappuccino is served in a porcelain teacup with milk that is frothed silky, not foamy. Neapolitan food is always kept simple, so for goodness sakes don't expect any heart, leaf, or elephant decorations pressed into the foam!

Italians also don't eat big breakfasts. Instead, they choose from an assortment of pastries to eat at the counter along with their cappuccino. The most common are:

Cornetto: a sweet croissant either plain or filled with confectioner's custard (*crema*) or chocolate.

La Graffa or La Bomba: La bomba is also a colloquial expression meaning something fantastic. This is a large donut covered on both sides with granulated sugar.

Brioche: often warmed, this is a sweet bread that is round and has a small cap on the top.

And finally, the Neapolitan original pastry, rarely made at home due to the complexity of the recipe – the *sfogliatelle* made from layers of thin dough. The inside is filled with ricotta cheese perfumed with vanilla beans and candied orange rinds. Puff *sfogliatelle* are baked until the many layers of dough turn a golden crispy brown (also called *ricca*). A smooth, shortcrust version (called *liscia*) is almost as popular.

CAPPUCCINO FROTHANTE

For those who want a sweet cappuccino delight at all hours of the day, the café-bar across the street from the San Lorenzo Maggiore Underground makes this cappuccino twist:

Swirl caramel or chocolate syrup into two beer glasses. Sprinkle powdered sugar on the sides here and there. Add a shot of espresso. Add milk and silky milk foam to the top. Sprinkle cacao on the top.

Caffettiere di San Lorenzo
Via Tribunali, Naples

CAPPUCCINO GALAK E LINDO

Across the street from the Albergo dei Poveri, Caffè Vanvitelli touts an abundance of espresso twists, including the *Cappuccino Galak e Lindo*. They won't say what's inside – the drink is proprietary – but suffice to say that it includes milk foam, white chocolate syrup, and an espresso shot.

Caffè Vanvitelli
Piazza Carlo III 49, Naples

THE CAFÉ-CHANTANT

After Domenico Barbaja's death in 1841, the illustrious reputation of theater culture in Naples continued, as did the coffee tradition. In 1860, Il Gran Caffè opened one block from the Teatro San Carlo. A *café-chantant* (or singing café) in the style of Parisian coffee houses, it hosted painters, writers, and famous actors of the day. The name changed in 1870 to Caffè Gambrinus and then hosted, among others, Oscar Wilde and Benito Mussolini.

As a singing café, Gambrinus and the rest of the city saw the rise of the Neapolitan *canzone*. Wandering street musicians went from restaurant to restaurant serenading for tips. Mostly males singing solo and in dialect, they played on either a mandolin or guitar. By 1918 coffee tradition in Naples had taken such a hold on the city that Giuseppe Capaldo wrote *A Tazze 'E Caffè* with music added by Vittorio Fassone.

À Tazze 'E Caffè

by Giuseppe Capaldo and Vittorio Fassone

I'd like to know why, when you see me
You always look so disappointed
But even when you put that bitter expression on your face
You still look so beautiful to my eyes
Yes, you look wonderful to my eyes
I'm not sure you realize that

But to me, Brigette
You are like a cup of coffee.
Sweet as sugar underneath,
And bitter on the surface.
So I'll stir and stir so much,
And stir and stir some more.
Till the sugar from the bottom of the cup, finally rises to the top for me.

Time goes on and you get colder and colder
Rather than being "a good cup of coffee"
The fact is that even if you get as cold as ice
You would still be some delicious iced coffee
Even better than a simple lemon slush

But to me, Brigette...

You are the mother of a teaser,
And I, darling, am the son of a fortuneteller
If you have to turn the lover's card,
I'll tell your fortune, free of charge,
What a nice couple we would make.

But to me, Brigette...

CAFFÈ GAMBRINUS: THE DRINK

The baristas at Caffè Gambrinus are brusque, but they know their coffee. The highlight of their beverage menu is, of course, the Caffè Gambrinus.

The drink consists of a shot of espresso, a teaspoon of cacao powder, milk foam, whipping cream, and chocolate sprinkles on top.

**Caffè Gambrinus
Via Chiaia 1-2, Naples**

THE NEAPOLITAN FLIP-OVER COFFEE POT

In the early 1900's northern Italians invented the espresso machine and a new kind of coffee culture was born. However, the espresso machine, at first, didn't take hold in the south and coffee house culture still didn't gain corner-to-corner popularity. Instead, coffee remained for use at home as part of a healthy diet. Today, offering a cup of coffee to guests is essential to Neapolitan culture. For any warm gathering, Neapolitans have their own coffee pot known as the *macchinetta Napoletana*.

A French tinsmith invented the *macchinetta Napoletana* in 1819.[59] Not much is known about its history beyond that, including when it was introduced to Italy. But in 1946 Eduardo De Filippo, who

---

59 William H. Ukers, *All About Coffee* (New York: The Tea and Coffee Trade Journal Company, 1922) *Chapter 34. The Evolution of Coffee Apparatus*; http://www.web-books.com/Classics/ON/B0/B701/39MB701.html.

published thirty-nine plays and acted beside Sophia Loren in the 1954 classic *L'oro di Napoli* turned the coffee pot into a Neapolitan original through his comedy *Questi Fantasmi* or "Three Ghosts."[60]

In the movie, De Filippo sits at the balcony, presumably already having boiled the water and flipped the *macchinetta Napoletana* over. He then waits while the water drips down through the filter and into the second pot. Pretending to talk to a professor neighbor, he explains that a paper cone put over the spout is essential; this keeps the aromas from escaping.[61]

In the 1970's, Alessi asked the Neapolitan architect, Riccardo Dalisi, to create a new version of the Neapolitan Flip-Over Coffee Pot. After roaming for many years through junk dealers and tin-smith shops, Dalisi's design ended up winning the Golden Compass, the most prestigious Italian industrial design award.

Today, the *macchinetta Napoletana* isn't used in households as much as the moka pot (a similar stove top coffee maker, but simpler). Mostly, it's sold by souvenir shops as a distinctly Neapolitan trinket. Still, for those who want to make authentic Neapolitan coffee in their home, a tin pot can be found throughout Campania and costs a mere 10 Euro, *più o meno*.

Here are the instructions on how to use the *macchinetta Napoletana:* First, take the top pot and fill it with water. Next, add fine grinds to the filter and place it inside the water. (You can add more or less grinds depending on the strength of coffee you like.)

---

60 Eduardo De Filippo, *Theater Neapolitan Style: Five One-Act Plays,* trans. Mimi Gisolfi D'Aponte (Massachussetts: Rosemont Publishing & Printing Corp, 2004) 12.

61 Scene from *Questi Fantasmi Scena del Caffè* found at http://www.youtube.com/watch?v=YllQLj0h6mo.

Add the second pot to the top. Place the pot on the stove and let boil. Here's the first catch: once the *macchinetta Napoletana* is on the stove, you can never see the water boiling. Instead, you must decide this intuitively.

When the water is ready, take the coffee pot off the stove and flip it over. This is both art and skill. If not done properly, the boiling water can end up all over the floor.

When the *macchinetta Napoletana* is flipped, the pot with the spout will then be on the bottom. The water from the top pot slowly drips through the filter. Again, you will have to know intuitively when all the water has drained to the bottom and if you use De Filippo's advice, you'll put a little cone on the spout to keep the aromas from releasing into the air. When the coffee is finished, heaping spoonfuls of sugar are stirred into the cups.

THE ROASTERS

When people made coffee at home, they also roasted their own beans, but in the 1960's the tin can was invented. A watershed moment in coffee history, the tin can allowed beans to stay fresh for longer periods and then coffee could be transported over wider distances. Coffee roasting businesses sprouted up everywhere and today more than 600 coffee roasters compete on the Italian market.

In Naples, people view large companies with skepticism (their products considered shoddy), so the small Neapolitan coffee roaster reigns supreme. Café owners use three main criteria in choosing their roasters: 1) they tend to buy local; 2) roasters should be family owned and run; and 3) the company should have a long history — if they've been in existence several decades, they are coveted.

Café owners usually have placards both inside and outside their establishments telling customers which roaster they use. The roasting company then supplies the cups, saucers, and bean grinders that display their logo.

Neapolitan roasters pride themselves on having a taste unique to the South. Southern Italian coffee has a reputation for being darker, stronger, richer, and tends to taste like semi-sweet chocolate. More specifically, Neapolitan roasters say that while they use up to seventy percent of the sweet arabica beans (more often found in the South), they also add a mix of the bitter tasting Robusta beans that come from Africa. Their beans aren't oily (like the French), they aren't acidic, and they are roasted both evenly and longer. Finally, Neapolitan roasters deliberately leave out the medium notes in their coffee.

Roasters generally own companies located in the suburbs so that trucks can more easily access the highway. Their roasting machines also work behind security manned gates. Because competition is so fierce, the secrets of their blends are guarded jealously and visits by the public are generally not allowed.

At least fifteen roasters exist within the region. Café do Brasil is the most well-known, holding third place in the whole of Italy for coffee roasting market share. Other roasters include: Tico, Castorino, Toraldo, Kenon, Izzo, Caffen, Passalacqua, Borbone, Moreno, and Greco.

Most of these roasters sell only to café owners, so you'll have to make a visit to Naples in order to enjoy their flavors. But mmmm. It's well worth the trip!

TAKE-OUT CAFFÈ

In Naples, businessmen don't sit down at a café with their laptops, college students don't linger doing homework, and mothers don't bring their children for a playdate to a café. The emphasis isn't on lingering, but rather on taste.

At any café-bar, a customer can ask to take coffee on the go, in which case the barista makes the caffè in a plastic cup the size of a *tazzino*, putting the plastic cup right under the espresso machine, then providing a packet of sugar and a clear plastic stirrer.

A bustling sight on the Naples landscape is always the coffee waiter who carries a tray of plastic coffee cups filled with hot espresso and carefully covered on the top with aluminum foil.

Businesses call to order these drinks for delivery. Bus drivers may have a caffè served to them at a stop. At any given time throughout the day, a store clerk, a museum tour guide, or even a barista will stop everything for a moment to take their own *riposo*. In these few moments, everyone knows that they must wait until the coffee moment is finished – then, and only then, the frenetic bustle of the Neapolitan service sector may strike up again.

ESPRESSO TWISTS

The espresso machine itself came into existence a mere one-hundred years ago in Milan, but because coffee history in Naples is more about home use, the beverage drunk at café-bars can be considered more modern – providing the cultural top-layer of the city. Espresso twists in Naples veer toward the aristocratic and wealthy tradition of Vincenzo Corrado and Domenico Barbaja, sometimes so rich that they taste more like drinkable desserts.

Riccardo Dalisi is the modern artist who fuses this modern and Neapolitan traditional culture together in his Alessi version of the

Neapolitan Flip-Over Coffee Pot, but baristas throughout the city have followed suit, producing elegant modern twists that can be enjoyed throughout the day. Here are some of the best espresso twists the city has to offer:

SUGAR CREAM AND THE BRASILIANO

In many café-bars throughout Naples, baristas ask if you'd like to have a spot of *zucchero-crema* (sugar-cream) in your cup. If you say yes, they daub a teaspoon of the fluffy concoction in a *tazzino*, then put the cup under the espresso maker.

At the famous Moccia Caffè (established in 1922) they gave me the recipe:

- 1.5 kilograms of granulated sugar;
- 20 shots of espresso;
- Blend together in a mixer until you have a frothy tan cream.

Sugar-cream adds a sweet-syrupy taste to the espresso. It also means that you have to stir a long time before taking that ever-satisfying coffee gulp.

Moccia is located on a narrow street several blocks from the seafront and one block away from the modern art museum, PAN or *Palazzo delle Arti Napoli (see also p. 229)*, which offers temporary exhibitions of artists from around the world.

Caffè, too, has an international flair in Naples. A reigning favorite coffee beverage throughout the city is the *Caffè Brasiliano*. Caffè Moccia gave me their recipe for this too:

A small glass cup is filled with an espresso shot. A half teaspoon of cacao is sprinkled on the shot as well as *zucchero-crema*. Next milk foam, made with whole milk and foamed only until silky, is poured to the rim of the cup. At last, some cacao is sprinkled on the foam.

Moccia
Via San Pasquale a Chiaia 21/22, Naples

THE KISS

Intra Moenia sits right next to the excavated Greek foundations of Naples. The café-bookstore has its own publishing house and is frequented by artists and students. A reigning favorite on the menu is *Caffè al baccio* or "Coffee with a Kiss."

The barista coats a brandy glass with syrupy nutella. She then adds a healthy shot of espresso and a dollop of milk foam. Cocoa flakes sprinkle the top. It's expected that you'll stir the hot beverage for a long time before taking it down in four or five gulps.

Caffè al baccio also comes with an auditory twist. Intra Moenia is one block away from the music conservatory, so often a soprano practices her scales from an open second story window while you drink to her tunes.

Intra Moenia
Piazza Bellini 70, Naples

THE PICK ME UP

At Caffetteria dell'Arte Antica, located in the *Centro Storico* of Naples, the café has turned the delectable dessert Tiramisu (which means "pick me up") into a beverage.

The barista coats a martini glass with thick lines of Tiramisu syrup squirted from a bottle. He then adds some chopped nuts. He pours a healthy shot of espresso into the glass and sprays a large helping of whipping cream up to the rim. Cacao and more nuts sprinkle the top.

A rich beverage, it's still liquid enough to drink as a sip-and-go at the counter. Everything you ever wanted in a drink and a dessert.

Caffetteria dell'Arte Antica
Via Tribunali 30, Naples

THE PIGNATELLI

Gran Caffè Pignatelli is located down the block from the neo-classical Villa Pignatelli *(see also p. 215)*. The café has its own twist in honor of the villa, but the beverage isn't on the menu, so you must ask for it specifically.

The barista thickly coats a champagne glass, including the rim, with granulated sugar. Next he sprinkles a half-teaspoon of cacao inside the glass. Using a cappuccino frother, he blends a double shot of espresso, a teaspoon of cacao, and a splash of amaretto together. He pours the frothy concoction into the glass, then adds milk foam and a sprinkle of cacao on top.

Gran Caffè Pignatelli
Via Francesco Morosini 26, Naples

NUT CAFFÈ AT GALLERIA UMBERTO

Galleria Umberto I was named after Italy's monarch from 1887-1891; today the gallery is enlivened by high-end clothing stores, cafés, and pastry shops. Located in the heart of the city across the street from the Teatro San Carlo, architects worldwide study this glass ceiling with its iron arches as an example of quintessential modern design.

All the glitz and glamor of this airy space also means that you can find an excellent *tazzino* of caffè. At Bar Brasiliano, baristas leave out several elegant pitchers of *zucchero-crema* at the counter. They also offer an array of coffee twists; see the list by the cash register. The most highly recommended is *Caffè Nocciola* or "Nut Coffee."

The base of the caffè is made from *zucchero-crema*, a tablespoon of which the barista daubs at the bottom of the glass cup. He squeezes some nut syrup from a bottle. He then pours a shot of espresso on the top and sprinkles the top with cacao.

You must stir the ingredients together before sipping, but waiting just a few moments reveals how the *zucchero-crema* begins to rise to the top while the espresso sinks. The last sip includes a few bits of nuts. The drink is not overly sweet and nicely nutty.

Bar Brasiliano
Galleria Umberto I 78, Naples

NUT CAFFÈ AT PIAZZA GARIBALDI

Giuseppe Garibaldi is the man considered responsible for uniting all of Italy in 1871. The history, of course, is more complicated, and suffice to say that Neapolitans weren't completely happy with unification. Southern Italy had had its own illustrious Kingdom with magnificent monarchs residing in Naples. The rich and famous, for centuries, had always stopped in this city, but after unification, Rome became the capital and Naples was eclipsed.

Today, Piazza Garibaldi has a reputation of being seedy and full of crime, but recently its train station has been completely revamped and the square isn't far behind. The train station has turned into a large underground shopping mall with clothing stores and a two-story bookstore on the top floor. The surrounding area is also the most multi-cultural location in the city. One block away, Africans lay out all sorts of wares along the streets. Close by, the Chinese community has restaurants as well as their own shops, including hair dressers and clothing stores. There's also excellent espresso twists to be had.

The café-bar Antica Pasticceria Napoletana gives an array of coffee beverages from *Kinder Caffè* to more exotic orange twists. *Caffè Nocciola* was the drink recommended by the barista.

He coats a small glass with *zucchero-crema* and then drizzles nutty syrup from an automatic glass dispenser. A half teaspoon of cacao and the glass teacup is then put under the espresso machine for a shot of caffè. The result, after copious stirring of the sluggish ingredients, is a syrupy consistency drunk in two or three sips.

Antica Pasticceria Napoletana
Piazza Garibaldi, Naples

THE MOROCCO

When Italians speak about shopping malls (*i Centri Commerciali*), many immediately say they can't stand them. They prefer to walk through an open market where vegetables, seafood, and clothing come at great prices. They also prefer small shops to chain stores.

And yet, every evening and every weekend the shopping malls in the suburbs of Naples teem with people. The parking lots are full, people push through crowds outside stores, and the food courts draw families and teenagers to eat at the food courts or at the chain restaurant Fratelli La Bufala. You can find movie theaters as well as snazzy clothing stores such as Zara. The French-owned grocery stores Auchan and Carrefour are versions of Walmart with electronics, music, books, toys, clothes, beauty products, and gourmet foods.

All this glitz has also given rise to excellent caffè. At the mall in the suburb town of Giugliano, a café-bar called Lino's Coffee (www.linoscoffee.com) has an array of proprietary drinks.

Caffè Morocco is made with a teaspoon of cacao powder, a layer of espresso, a layer of flavored chocolate syrup, a layer of milk foam and then – optionally – a dollop of whipping cream with or without chocolate powder on top. Once you get the drink, you must spend a good amount of time stirring until all the ingredients mix together. Thereafter, three or four gulps are enough.

Galleria Commerciali Italia SPA
Giugliano

FACES OF NAPLES: THE RUBINO COFFEE TRADITION

Coffee aromas saturate the air along the freeway next to Melito, a town ten miles outside of Naples. A little beyond the off-ramp, a security guard monitors the gate to Café do Brasil's roasting factory (also known by one of its brands, Caffè Kimbo). Like most roasters, the factory is located in a suburb where transport vehicles can travel to their destination points with ease, but with more than six hundred coffee roasters throughout Italy, blends are proprietary and fierce competition makes most companies shy about opening their doors.

Café do Brasil, however, is the second largest retail seller of coffee in Italy and the number one international exporter in the south. The company has an external relations department headed by Dottoressa Signora Marizia Rubino, the daughter of Francesco Rubino – one of the three brothers who established the roasting plant.

Café do Brasil traces its roots back to the three Rubino brothers – Francesco, Gerardo, and Elio – who in the 1950's began to roast coffee beans in their father's pastry shop and sold their blends in paper bags. Their successful roasting techniques contributed to the reputation of the south's dark bittersweet blends. Soon, they created the company name, Café do Brasil, which gave an exotic aura to their roasts.

Coffee roasting, grinding, and boiling remained predominantly an art passed down by parents in the home until, in the 1960's, a grand split occurred with the invention of the tin can. Roasted coffee could now be preserved for longer periods and shipped over wider distances, so people began to buy ready roasted beans from a store. Café do Brasil became one of the forerunners of this trend, establishing their Melito factory in 1963.

Café do Brasil blends and roasts the coffee, whereas Interkom, a company located in downtown Naples, goes abroad to acquire the beans and then sells them to various roasters. While the legacy of the *caffettieri ambulanti (see p. 168)* can be seen today, with café-bars on every block offering a mere counter to sip-and-go, more than seventy percent of coffee drinking in Italy still takes place in the home. Café do Brasil meets this specific market need, their brands a near ubiquitous sight at any grocery store.

A warehouse rumbles with wall-to-ceiling machinery inside the Kimbo complex. Hidden from the naked eye, coffee beans whisk through long tubes into silos, scales, and roasting machines. In the middle stands the "brain" of the warehouse – a trailer brimming with hi-tech computers. Here, several operators in white coats control the roasting process. They first use remote controls to tell the  machines to separate the raw beans into a number of different silos. Operators can distinguish from 101 to 117 different qualities of beans and their skill lies in blending them together. Once they have a blend ready, they send the beans to a scale where they are weighed. Operators then wait for one of four roasters to open and tell the computers to drop the beans inside. Café do Brasil roasts 400 kilograms of beans approximately every eight minutes at temperatures ranging from 200-220 degrees Celsius.

Inside the computer trailer, raw beans chink through a metal tube where operators can actually see and touch a sample of raw beans they plan to roast. A few minutes later, the same beans clank in an adjacent tube, giving operators the chance to evaluate the quality of the final product. The roasted beans are then transferred through tubes into other silos for maturing, a process which takes anywhere from a few days to a maximum of seven days.

Once mature, the beans move on to the packaging side of the warehouse where assembly-line equipment automatically pulls and folds large Kimbo labels on a turnstile to create coffee bags. A machine drops coffee grinds inside the packages and then clamps down to vacuum-seal them. Next, a conveyor belt sends the packages to a monster mechanical arm that lifts them onto a palette. From there, a bright yellow robot drives up, digs a fork into several palettes, and transports the coffee to trucks waiting outside.

Café do Brasil supports two different brands – Caffè Kimbo and Caffè Kose. Each brand has its own blends that range from the fragrant taste qualities of Aroma Espresso to the milder acidic tones of Caffea Arabica. Their best selling Macinato Fresco has a nutty aroma with a bittersweet taste.

According to the company website, the Macinato Fresco is made up of beans from Brazil, but if you ask what kind of beans Café do Brasil specifically uses, Signora Rubino explains that the company buys beans that come from many different parts of the world. What's more, when beans are roasted they give off more than eight hundred flavors and aromas. The roasting process, therefore, is complex.

But Café do Brasil surely wants to maintain the reputation given to southern Italy of making dark semi-sweet coffee? Signora Rubino answers no. Their company doesn't want to be known for creating one strong flavor, but rather they strive for an equalization of many flavors and aromas, balancing astringency, acidity, and sweetness together.

So what is the roast recipe for any one of their blends? Aaah. Now that's a secret. Only the nose and palette can truly ascertain, but the delight, for a coffee lover, lies in the guessing.[62]

---

62 This article first appeared online at: Barbara Zaragoza, "A Tour of Café do Brasil's Roasting Factory," *INeedCoffee.com* 14 April 2010: http://www.ineedcoffee.com/10/cafe-do-brasil-tour.

HOLIDAY TOURS

If you find yourself in Campania during the various holidays, a tour of seasonal sights can be delightful. While the Christian and pagan traditions blend together on La Befana day, for Easter several churches are worth a visit. I have added a few lesser known holidays and then also the most quintessential Neapolitan celebration: the Feast of San Gennaro. With so many Americans living in the region, Neapolitans are also slowly adopting Halloween, so this chapter provides a tour of the gory. Finally, Christmas is the most celebrated season of the year – a season so important to Neapolitans that it can be celebrated all year long. You can visit Christmas Alley from summer to winter or admire *presepe* (nativity scenes) throughout the city. This chapter doesn't provide a comprehensive list of holidays, but rather a smattering of the most accessible for the expat and visitor.

WITCHES AFTER CHRISTMAS

On the eve of January 6th, La Befana who in some traditions is considered to be a witch and in other traditions is simply an elderly woman, swoops down into the chimneys of little children and fills their stockings with either gifts or coal. She travels on a broom, wears a black shawl, and is covered with soot. Once children have received their presents on the morning of the 6th (and usually also candy coal because no child is solely good all year long), parents shuttle them to school in costume where the festivities continue.

Many believe that La Befana dates back to ancient times when the Romans gave each other gifts for the New Year in celebration of the festival of the goddess Strenia. (The word "strenna" in Italian means "Christmas gift.") The actual word "Befana" derives from the Christian word "Epifana" or "Epiphany."

Folktales say that when the Three Kings set upon their journey, they stopped to ask La Befana directions. She didn't know where the baby Jesus might be, but provided them with shelter and was noted to have been an excellent housekeeper, hence the broom. The Three Kings asked if she wanted to accompany them on their journey, but La Befana declined, explaining that she had too much housework. After they left, she regretted her decision and set out to find the baby Jesus by

herself. She was, however, unsuccessful and continues to search for him to this day.

On the night of the 5th, it is customary to leave out a glass of wine along with some food. Parents tell their children that if they catch a glimpse of La Befana, she will thump them with her broomstick. Consequently, this sub-chapter goes out to everyone as a warning – don't leave your beds on the night of January 5th or you'll catch the tail end of a woman's housekeeping stick!

THE EASTER TOUR

While the Vatican is certainly a popular visitor destination on Easter Sunday, Naples and the surrounding region also contains its own Easter pearls. With over two hundred Catholic churches – and that's just within the city limits – a church tour offers innumerable delights (see p. 265).

Contorni

For those who fast during Lent or for those who are vegetarian, Naples is a haven for alternatives to meat dishes. *Contorni* or vegetable dishes feature on all restaurant menus, including many variations of Eggplant Parmesan, bell peppers, olives, rucola, zucchini, and *lampacioni*.[63] Here are two common *contorni* that can be made at home:

Garlic Artichokes
* ½ kilograms (or 1 lb.) globe artichokes
* extra virgin olive oil
* several cloves of garlic
* parsley
* kosher salt

Cut the stems off the artichokes and place in boiling water for 3-5 minutes. Drain the artichokes and then place in a pan. Douse with olive oil. Slice several cloves of garlic and stuff inside the leaves. Chop parsley coarsely and stuff inside the artichoke leaves also. Sprinkle with kosher salt. Place the artichokes in the oven at very high heat (about 220 degrees Celcius or 450 degrees Fahrenheit) for about 10 minutes or until the tips are golden brown. Let cool for ten minutes. Eat leaf by leaf. The artichokes are soft and melt in your mouth. (Another way to prepare the artichokes is, after boiling and stuffing, place them on a grill.)

Zucchini Flowers
Zucchini flowers are often battered, fried, and served as an antipasto, but after buying a package at the grocery store or market, you can brush them off gently with a paper towel and then throw them into a pan filled with hot oil for a few minutes until they turn crispy. Then, they are ready to eat.

---

63 Dating back to ancient Roman times, *lampacioni* were known as "Bulbi for Love" by Apicius who wrote that honeymooners and young lovers should use them as aphrodisiacs. *Lampacioni* are very similar to little reddish onions. To eat, they must be boiled several times to take out their bitter taste.

Two churches, in particular, give Naples the reputation of being "the city of miracles." At **Il Duomo** (or main cathedral) the blood of the patron saint of the city, San Gennaro, liquefies twice a year. **San Gregorio Armeno Church**, located down Christmas Alley, houses the remains of the patron saintess of the city, Santa Patricia, whose blood liquefies every Tuesday after the nine o'clock mass.

Saint Paul's legacy also marks the city. In the New Testament it says that, as a Roman citizen, Paul requested transfer to Rome to protest his punishment and imprisonment for professing the new Christian faith. He traveled by sea from the Holy Land and was briefly shipwrecked on Malta before arriving in Italy. The voyage is described in the Acts of the Apostles (28: 13-14), which says that after one day, a south wind sprang up and Paul reached **Puteoli**. There they found Christians who invited them to stay a week.

St. Paul is then said to have celebrated mass in a chapel on the site of the 13th century church of **San Pietro ad Aram** (Corso Umberto I 292). The church still exists and is very close to Piazza Garibaldi.

Another Easter wonder is **Split Rock** in Gaeta, located about an hour and a half drive from Naples. The **Chapel of the Crucifix** was erected on a huge mass of rock that hangs between two adjoining rock walls. The "split" between these rock walls is said to have occurred at the precise time that Jesus died on the cross. Subsequently, a doubter came to visit the rock and when touching the side of the split, his hand print became forever emblazoned on the wall.[64]

---

64 Directions to Split Rock can be found at: http://www.italy-weekly-rentals.com/webpages/accessori/TOTHESOUTH/Gaeta.htm. This website also has a fantastic tour of Gaeta in general.

SOLSTICES AND EQUINOXES

Every solstice and equinox, a group of universal-minded Italians hold a Solstice Ceremony at the **Temple of Apollo in Lago Averno** *(see p. 16)*. The ceremony is well attended, open to everyone for free, and has a charming desire to unite all religions and all peoples.

It begins at about sundown outside the Temple. While everyone gathers around, an elderly gentleman gives an introduction about the coming service, urging the group to respect silent moments.

Then people file inside the Temple. The ceremony begins with two circles, one inner and one outer and the first recitation is "The Invocation of the Seven Directions." Throughout the service, songs are sung and individuals read poems. Symbols of the earth, wind, fire, and water are passed around: a plate of Lago Averno water, bread, incense, and a torch is passed from person to person.

An elderly woman gives a speech explaining that we come together with our sayings and songs from different religions in order to appreciate our unity. Once the ceremony is finished, the group makes their way from inside the Temple to the lake where candles are pushed on lily pads into the water. Stones are also thrown into the water as offerings. The ceremony ends with a long "OM..." just as the sun sets across the crater.

Centro Nuova Era sponsors these events and their center is in the Vomero where they offer massages, yoga, and other activities. You can find them at www.centronuovaera.it.

THE FEAST OF SAN GENNARO

San Gennaro's blood liquifies every September 19th as well as every Saturday before the first Sunday in May. The miracle is suppose to usher in a year of good fortune for Neapolitans.

According to legend, San Gennaro was born sometime in the 3rd century to a rich patrician family. At fifteen years of age, he became a priest. During the persecution of Christians by Emperor Diocletian, San Gennaro was sentenced to death for his beliefs and beheaded in Pozzuoli. His bones and blood were then saved by a woman named Eusebia just after his death.

Today, his tomb is located underneath the altar of **Il Duomo**, the city's cathedral located downtown. In a side niche of the church, San Gennaro's dried blood is stored in two hermetically sealed ampoules (vials) and adorned in a silver reliquary.

The blood doesn't always liquify on command, sometimes taking several hours, or liquifying several days before the celebration, or – most ominously – not liquifying at all.

Scientists have wanted to study the phenomena, but are not allowed to open the ampoule as Church leaders fear they will damage or ruin the blood. Hence, scientists have used alternative methods, but have been unable to come up with an adequate explanation for the phenomenon. Many people note that during the years when San Gennaro's blood has not liquified, bad things have happened to the city. Others maintain that when they come to mass and witness the liquefaction, in particular kissing the reliquary, they are healed of all sorts of ailments.

At the September 19th mass, the church is usually packed and the mass begins at 9 a.m. The Cardinal himself holds the mass, thereafter processing to the side altar and taking out the reliquary.

The Cardinal then moves to the front of the church while the congregation applauds and waves white handkerchiefs. He walks with the liquefied blood down the middle aisle for all to see. He continues his procession outside and announces to the city that the liquefaction has occurred, then he returns the blood to the altar. The reliquary is left there for the next eight days to show the people of Naples that San Gennaro has yet again blessed the city.

Thereafter, the streets of Naples are closed off for religious processions. Candies and children's toys are sold on the streets, decorations are everywhere, and a festive ambiance fills the city.

INTERNATIONAL PASTA DAY

Celebrated since 2005, October 25th is International Pasta Day. The International Pasta Organization founded in Rome, designated this day to give the world more awareness of the health benefits of pasta. According to the organization, pasta was officially "discovered" by Marco Polo who brought the product to Italy from China in the 1200's, but variations of pasta date back to the Greeks, Etruscans, and Romans. In Naples, the Greeks are said to have mixed barley-flour and water together and dried it in the sun. They called the final product "macaria." For more about the organization, see www.internationalpasta.org.

THE HALLOWEEN TOUR

Paying tribute to the deceased can be a Halloween treat in Naples. A few sights, in particular, stand out.

WHERE TO SEE THE MACABRE

The **Catacombs of San Gaudioso** have frescoes painted by Dominican monks who wanted to honor their wealthy deceased patrons by using their skeletons and skulls for decoration. *(See p. 87.)*

The **Santa Maria Church of the Souls of Purgatory** has an underground catacomb which bristles with unburied bones. *(See p. 82.)*

The **Sansevero Chapel** has an underground chamber displaying two gruesome anatomical machines – a male and female skeleton with vein and artery structures modeled upon them – built by alchemist and freemason Raimondo di Sangro. *(See p. 209.)*

WHERE TO SEE THE EERIE

The **English Cemetery** is all that remains of Eusapia Palladino's legacy. The graveyard is located off the street where the medium and levitator once lived. *(See p. 132.)*

Execution Square has a spacious, yet hollow feel that matches perfectly with the number of executions that took place here, including that of Eleonora Fonseca Pimentel. *(See p. 128.)*

The **Garden of the Fugitives** is the eeriest attraction in Pompeii. A row of men, women, and children lie eternally frozen, victims of the Mt. Vesuvius eruption. *(See p. 49.)*

WHERE TO SEE THE JUST PLAIN GROSS

Any **Tripperia** will do, but the one on Via Pignasecca is particularly gory, with its tripe hanging outside the restaurant dripping with water and lemon. *(See p. 235.)*

THE *PRESEPE* TOUR

A *presepe* is a depiction of the story of the birth of Jesus in three dimensional form. Saint Francis of Assisi is credited with creating the first nativity scene in 1223 at Greccio, Italy. His intent was to shift the focus of Christmas back to the worship of Christ from the secular materialism he saw during his time. His nativity scene was a living one with humans and animals. Over the centuries such scenes became ever more elaborate, figurines being made of ivory, wax, and other materials.

Most Neapolitans set up *presepe* (also known as crèches, cribs, or nativity scenes) in their homes during Christmas. The *presepe* are often very elaborate and the pieces are collected little-by-little over many years.

The famous *presepe* sold all year round down **Via San Gregorio Armeno**, called **Christmas Alley** by foreign expatriates, are a "must-do" for any visitor to Naples. The street also provides some fantastic shopping for the holidays, although during December hordes of people trample through.

From there, walk to Via Duomo, take a left, then take another left on **Via Anticaglia**. This street is at the heart of Greco-Roman Naples. The walls on either side are part of what was once a bathhouse and a theater that could hold up to 8,000 spectators. Walking by shops and apartments with overhead laundry, you'll find stores that sell maps of ancient Greco-Roman Naples (the paper looks old, but the cartographer clearly took modern artistic license;

nobody knows exactly what the ancient city looked like) and tout
their wares of elaborate handmade *presepe*.

Return back towards Piazza
Dante and once you get there,
walk down Via Monteoliveto until
you come to Piazza Monteoliveto.
Take a right into the piazza and
you'll find the **Sant'Anna dei
Lombardi Church**. Go into the
back caverns of the sacristy to
find Guido Mazzoni's *Lamentation
over the Dead Christ* (1492), with
seven life-size terracotta figures
surrounding Christ. Beyond it,
you'll also find Vasari's refectory
with wood marquetry and a
stunning ceiling fresco. In a room

between these two amazing works,
you'll find a sprawling *presepe* scene.

From here, find the Montesanto
funicular and ride up to the Vomero to
visit the **Certosa di San Martino** that
displays an exquisite number of *presepe*
as part of their museum collection.
While the exhibition is open all year

round, most people come during Christmas. The *presepe* exhibition
here was established in 1879 by architect and playwright Michele
Cuciniello. Over time it was enriched with other collections.
Notably, a figurine on display at the museum was created by the
artist who sculpted the *Veiled Christ*, Giuseppe Sanmartino.

Wandering the *presepe* here, the life-like scenes portray a dream
factory where the everyday frenzy of Naples melts into scene after
scene of idealized rural life. The Certosa also has a rich collection of

carriages and medieval ships. To get there, the address is Largo San Martino 8; the Certosa is located next to the Castel Sant'Elmo.

Next, take the Chiaia funicular from the Vomero to Parco Margherita and walk to the **Santa Maria in Portico Church** (Via Santa Maria in Portico 17). Go to the sacristy where you'll find a life-size *presepe* created in the 17th century.

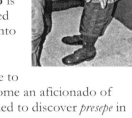

On another day, you can also visit the **Reggia di Caserta** and look for a massive *presepe* behind glass.

Finally, next to the **Duomo in Salerno** is an extraordinary *presepe* of life-sized painted wooden figures by Mario Carotenuto set into various tableaux and including modern personalities from local and national life.

These are my top seven picks of where to find *presepe* around Naples, but if you become an aficionado of these finely crafted pieces, you'll be charmed to discover *presepe* in nooks and crannies throughout the city.

THE NOOKS OF NAPLES

The nooks of Naples came about as a way to describe some of the gems of the city, but I wanted to make sure they were short enough to read "in the time it takes to drink an espresso." Many of the nooks turned into the tours described in the previous chapters, but I selected the following gems because they generally never make it into the guidebooks or because my descriptions add an idiosyncratic twist to the visit.

For a comprehensive list of sights to see in all of Campania, I highly recommend the on-line **Portal of Cultural Heritage and Activities: Region of Campania** at www.culturacampania.rai.it. Written in both Italian and English, you can click the sidebar index entries to find updated addresses, hours of operation, and histories of the many museums, archeological sites, nature parks, churches, and more.

OF GLADIATORS AND MITHRAS: CAPUA

Situated sixteen miles north of Naples within the fertile plains of the Caserta province, Capua dates back to at least the 7th century B.C. when Etruscans and Euboean Greeks settled the area. Today, the ancient city lies mostly underneath the modern town of Santa Maria Capua Vetere, which came into existence at the end of the 18th century.

The ancient city has several claims to fame. In Roman times, Cicero said that the "fleshpots of Capua" defeated Hannibal because his Carthaginians became soft due to the high living in the city. At the time, Capuan residents were considered wealthy, well-groomed, and always perfumed. The city was also called the *terra di lavoro* or "land of work" due to its cornucopia of agriculture, metal-working, pottery, ceramics, and extensive trade in other goods. The ancient writer Livy referred to Capua as the granary of Rome because of its abundant wheat crop.

The amphitheater is easy to find at the center of Capua. It's the second largest in Italy next to the coliseum in Rome. Built in the late 2nd century B.C., the well-preserved ruins used to hold up to 60,000 spectators. The amphitheater is open so visitors can roam the vaulted corridors, the gladiator field, and the underground tunnels where once elaborate stage machinery as well as caged animals were kept. During Roman times, the shows at the amphitheater admitted both men and women for free. Exotic animals and fantastic scenery made the events extremely popular.

A **Gladiator Museum** next to the amphitheater contains two rooms of artifacts as well as a display of fighting gladiators. At one time, Capua boasted the best gladiator schools that trained both slaves and freemen. The gladiators were divided into categories according to the type of armor used and their

combat specialty. The amphitheater put on two kinds of shows: the *munera* where gladiators fought each other to the death and *venationes* where gladiators fought against wild animals, sometimes even being thrown unarmed into the arena. Spartacus, the leader who led the slave revolt in 73 B.C. against Rome, first distinguished himself as a gladiator in the Capua amphitheater. It was also here that he broke away from his training camp and, joined by slaves who broke out of their barracks *en masse*, Spartacus plundered towns up and down the Apennines for two years.

The travel tip for Capua is to make sure to ask at the entrance gate to see the **Sanctuary of Mithras**. (It's the only way to gain access.) The custodian at the entrance window nods and disappears for a moment, then returns with a key, and tells you to follow him by car. You drive through the bustling streets of Capua where signs for the sanctuary appear and then vanish. The custodian stops his car at a dead-end road, in the middle of which a red-brick building with a Latin plaque marked *Mithraevm* is squished between apartment houses. He unlocks double iron doors and brings you down a flight of stairs to a vestibule. A rectangular vaulted room has a ceiling with vestiges of red and green stars on a yellow background. In the front niche a fresco depicts the god Mithras slaying a bull.

The cult of Mithras originated in Persia during the 14th century B.C. His cult traveled across Asia Minor to Greece and then to Rome where by the 1st century A.D. it gained popularity, especially among the common people. Scholars have written extensively about the syncretism between Mithraism and Christianity due to the many Christian churches that were formerly Mithraean and the fact that Christ's birthday coincides with the birthday of Mithras – December 25th.[65]

---

65 But also note that scholars compare the images of the bearded god Serapis with the first images made of Christ. Again, in these parts, the Christian Church absorbed the

Capua holds more ancient wonders if you have the patience to wind through the streets asking for directions at every block. The **Etruscan Furnace** still remains from the Archaic period, the **Carceri Vecchie** is the old jail whose inmates included gladiators, and further afield are the **Temples of Diana Tifata** and the **Temple of Jupiter Tifatina** (merely stones wedged into a mountain).

An absolute must for a visit to Capua is the **Museo Campano di Capua**. Tucked halfway down a narrow street, this small museum houses mosaics, medieval paintings, and funerary epigraphs of the Roman period, but the highlight are two rooms filled with mysterious tuff stone statues of seated mothers, *Le Madri*, holding swaddled infants. These statues date back to the Etruscan period and not much is known about them except what can be gleaned by gazing at their inscrutable faces.

Getting There: Capua is about eleven kilometers from Caserta and about thirty-five kilometers from Naples. If you are coming by car, the nearest exit from the A1 autostrada is marked *Capua*. If you come by train, the station is one-kilometer from the city center.

The **Capua Amphitheater** address is Piazza 1° ottobre, Santa Maria Capua Vetere (CE).

The address for the **Museo Campano di Capua** is Via Roma, Palazzo Antignano, Capua (CE). They also have an informative website at www.capuaonline.it/museocampano where you can take a glimpse of the *Le Madri*.

Book and Movie Recommendations: *A Guide of Ancient Capua* by Stefano De Caro and Valeria Sampaolo, eds. is hard to find, but a gem because it's the only English language book that comprehensively describes the sights in Capua.

---

many gods and goddesses in order to gradually convert the pagan populace, who worshipped as many gods as there were people.

The Spartacus War by Barry Strauss details the rebellion led by the charismatic leader, Spartacus. Stanley Kubrick also made a movie about the gladiator titled *Spartacus*.

The Roman Cult of Mithras: The God and His Mysteries by Manfred Clauss examines the Mithraic god and his followers during the Roman period.

THE BASILICA IN CAPUA

The **Basilica Benedettina di S. Michele Arcangelo**, located in the outskirts of Capua, used to be an impressive Temple of Diana. The church lies at the bottom of a hilly area, known as *Tifata* that during ancient times was densely forested. Rich with oak trees and spring waters, the cult of Diana – goddess of the wood and hunt – flourished here.

We don't know exactly when construction of this temple began. Scholars say that active building work took place at the end of the 4th century B.C. and the beginning of the 3rd century B.C. According to an inscription still visible on the floor, the Romans rebuilt the temple in 74 B.C.

The date that the temple was transformed into a church is unknown. Few manuscripts remain that detail the construction of this church. The Lombards may have built a church consecrated to the Archangel Michael about the 6th century

A.D. By 1065 the Norman, Richard I of Capua built a monastery over the church.

As happened at the Temple of Jupiter in Cuma *(see p. 15)* and at Virgil's tomb where the Church transformed the pagan sanctuary into the Madonna of Piedigrotta Basilica *(see p. 32)*, this basilica also recycled the ancient temple's stones to build a paleo-Christian church. The Corinthian columns from the temple remain intact and the brilliant fresco colors along the walls have been well-preserved.

Getting There: The address is Via Luigi Baia 120, Capua (CE).

ET TU BRUTE?: NISIDA

Three islands sit off the coast of Naples – Capri, Ischia, and Procida. On a clear day, they're visible from the Bay of Naples as well as from Mt. Vesuvius.

Capri is where you can visit the Blue Grotto, the **Villa Jovis**, or enjoy the cafés and restaurants that make you feel you're inside the movie with Sophia Loren and Clark Gable, *It Started In Naples*.

Procida has a stunning panorama of the sea, restaurants by the port, and is also where the movie *Cinema Paradiso* and much of *Il Postino* was filmed.

Ischia is the spa island where you can receive all kinds of massages, herbal treatments, or take a bus ride to the lavish **Gardens of Poseidon**. There, you can linger on their private beach or bathe all day in more than twelve different swimming pools.

But a fourth island struts directly off the Bay of Naples –
Nisida. Harder to find by car (you get there by passing an industrial
area near the **Children's Science Center** or Città della Scienza at
Via Coroglio 104, Naples) Nisida has a causeway monitored by a
security guard who always lets people pass.

Legend has it that sirens perched upon these stones, luring
sailors into crashing their vessels. Roman history says that Brutus
had a villa here where he plotted to kill Julius Caesar in 44 B.C.
During the 18th century, the Bourbons turned the island into a
notorious prison.

Today as you approach the island, you can see Italian yachts
lining the harbor. If you have an American military pass, you may
go down the causeway, hang a left, and flash your ID in order to get
past the gate. Here, a tiny military base has yachts that Americans
can rent for day-long sailing. There is also an American yachting
club that holds competitions during certain times of year. Find them
at www.nnyc.it. Additionally, the island serves as a juvenile detention
facility where many of the youngsters learn a new trade: pizza-
making.

Getting There: Go down Via Coroglio, Naples and you'll find the
island on your right.

You can reach the islands by going to either the Pozzuoli port,
the Molo Beverello port across from Castel Nuovo, the nearby
Calata Porta di Massa port or the Mergellina port on the Riviera di
Chiaia. Check timetables (*orari*) at any tourist office or on-line at the
ferry and jet services, including: www.caremar.it and www.snav.it.

Book Recommendation: Legend has it that Odysseus sailed all
along the coast of Italy trying to find his way home to Ithaca, so it's
charming to read *The Odyssey* by Homer while traveling through
these parts.

ST. THOMAS AQUINAS

St. Thomas Aquinas lived in Naples for many years and if you make an appointment, you can find one of his handwritten works in the Manuscript Department of the **National Library** *(see p. 61)*.

Author of *Summa Theologica*, St. Thomas Aquinas remains the foremost philosopher and theologian of the Catholic Church. A Dominican priest, he studied for a time in Naples and it was here that he read Aristotle's works. After taking up residence in many cities, including Rome, Monte Cassino, Orvieto, and Paris, he returned to Naples in 1272 to found his Theology University, located at what today is the **San Domenico Maggiore Church** in downtown Naples. Rumor has it that the saint's arm still resides somewhere in the clavicles of the church.

If you visit, make sure to look inside the sacristy where forty-two coffins are arranged along the balcony. One contains the remains of King Alfonso I and another of King Ferdinand I of Aragon.

A mystery attaches to this sacristy: the **Treasure Room** was suppose to hold the hearts of King Charles II as well as King Alfonso and King Ferdinand I, but when the French occupied the Kingdom of Naples in the 19th century, the relics disappeared forever.

Getting There: The address is Vico San Domenico Maggiore 18, Naples. Look for the piazza along Via Benedetto Croce/Via S. Biagio Dei Librai.

WHERE TO SEE CARAVAGGIO IN NAPLES

Known for his love of prostitutes, young boys, and brawling, in 1606 Michelangelo Merisi da Caravaggio killed a young man in Rome and fled to Naples. The Colonna family gave him protection and in that year Caravaggio painted *The Seven Acts of Mercy*.

A few months later, he left for Malta where he found wealthy patrons in the Knights of Malta, but he was soon arrested and imprisoned for another brawl that left a knight seriously wounded. Caravaggio escaped to Sicily where he received more well-paid commissions while displaying strange behaviors such as sleeping fully armed in his clothes. After nine months, he returned to Naples to ask the Colonna family to protect him once more while he waited for a pardon from the Pope. He then painted *The Martyrdom of Saint Ursula*, his last picture.

Today, at least three important Caravaggio paintings are on display in Naples. Seeing them can make for a charming day-trip through the city:

The **Galleria di Palazzo Zevallos Stigliano**, Via Toledo 185, Naples. Built by architect Cosimo Fanzago in the 17th century, the Banca Commerciale Italiana bought this Palazzo in 1920. When you first walk inside, you enter a stunning courtyard with a glass roof and opulent balconies. Climb up two flights of marble stairs and a gallery houses Caravaggio's *Martyrdom of Saint Ursula*.

Pio Monte della Misericordia, Via Tribunali 253, Naples. A once important charitable organization in the city, this church houses Caravaggio's *The Seven Acts of Mercy*. (Down the street from here, along Vico Dei Panettieri, the Missionarie della Carita now has replaced the charity and passes out food to the homeless.)

Capodimonte, Via Miano 2, Naples. Once the Bourbon Royal Palace, Capodimonte is one of the finest museums in Italy. The museum collection includes Caravaggio's *The Flagellation of Christ*, painted in 1607 for the di Franco Family and meant to be displayed in the Naples church of San Domenico Maggiore. (The family, incidentally, was connected with the Confraternity of the Pio Monte della Misericordia.)

In 1610, Caravaggio took a boat from Naples to Rome in order to receive the Pope's pardon, which would be granted thanks to his powerful friends. But he never made it, apparently dying of a fever during the journey. Speculation continues about lead poisoning – which might explain Caravaggio's uncontrollable violence. Only in 2010 did researchers exhume certain remains found in a church in Porto Ercole, Tuscany, and, subjecting them to DNA and carbon dating analysis, they concluded that the remains were almost certainly those of Caravaggio.

THE VEILED CHRIST

Only meters away from Christmas Alley, one of the "wonders of the world" lies tucked down a narrow street inside the **Cappella Sansevero**. *The Veiled Christ* was sculpted by Giuseppe Sanmartino during the Rococo period. Little is known about the artist except that he was part of a larger group who bedecked this church with more than thirty works of art.

Also of great interest is the man who reconstructed and commissioned these pieces during the 1700's. An Italian noble and scientist, Raimondo di Sangro invented a long range cannon while serving in the military and created a water-proof cape for his friend King Charles VII.

Raimondo's interest in alchemy led to many rumors that he could create blood out of nothing, that he could replicate the liquefaction of San Gennaro's blood, and that he killed people to use their bodies for experiments. We do know that he was the master of the Neapolitan masonic lodge, for which the Church excommunicated him. Although the Church eventually revoked his excommunication thanks to Raimondo's influence within the city, after his death in 1771 the Church threatened to excommunicate Raimondo's family if they didn't agree to destroy his writings as well as the results of his scientific experiments. Raimondo's family acquiesced and today the man who brought us such wonderful art is himself shrouded in mystery. The astronomer de Lalande described him as not an academic, but an entire academy.

If you walk down the steps to an underground chamber, two anatomical machines – a male and female skeleton with vein and artery structures – display Raimondo's scientific work.

Getting There: The address is Via de Sanctis 19, Naples.

Book Recommendation: The dual Italian-English written book *A Fantastic Journey In the Light of the Everlasting Lantern: the extraordinary inventions of the Prince of Sansevero* written by Mario Buonoconto and translated into English by Albert Coward describes Riamondo's experiments to make artificial blood, alchemic coal, vegetable wax, and anatomical machines.

HEALING YOUR AILMENTS

Catholic devotion and miracles go hand in hand in Naples. The liquefaction of the blood of San Gennaro and Saint Patricia are examples of the abundant miracles taking place in this city. In the church of **Gesu Nuovo** (built in 1584), the walls and ceilings of two side chapels are crowded with silver *ex-votos* representing body parts. These ornaments are most numerous in the side chapel that houses the remains of San Giuseppe Moscati, a physician canonized in 1987. Worshippers place these silver body parts here to either ask San Giuseppe to heal an ailment or to thank him for having already healed their disease. But first, they must purchase the ornament from a religious shop, many of which pepper the two main parallel streets of the historic district of Naples: Via Tribunali and Via San Biagio dei Librai.

At **Statuaria Sacra** the owner has a shoe box behind the cashier's desk with a slew of silver and faux-silver body parts that range in price from 20-60 Euro. They include legs, arms, heads, livers, stomachs, pancreas, throats as well as full figure men, women, and children. Buy one or more for the healing of your or your loved ones' ailments – it's a Neapolitan original tradition.

Getting There: The address is Statuaria Sacra, Via S. Biagio Dei Librai 76, Naples. The Church of Gesu Nuovo is at Piazza del Gesu Nuovo 2, Naples.

THE HIDDEN FACES

The **Cappella Pappacoda** is owned by the Oriental Institute of the University of Naples and gets its name from the tombs of two aristocratic brothers: Bishop and Cardinal Pappacoda. The church was founded in the 15th century and the doorway retains the original late Gothic style. There's also a campanile that is noted for its color contrasts created by the use of different materials.

The real treat here is searching for the hidden faces along the façade. Why was this pair stuck up on high and who were they? You can search for these hidden faces or ask the custodian of the church to point out these solemn figures.

Getting There: The address is Largo San Giovanni Maggiore, Naples.

THE UNIVERSITY OF NAPLES

Along the shopping street of Corso Umberto I lies a mammoth structure that flaunts security guards and lion statues. Turn the corner and an entrance leads to a maze of impressive stairwells and courtyards. It's the University of Naples, which dates back to the 17th century and houses a handful of excellent museums.

The **Museum of Paleontology** is located in the west wing of

the Santi Marcellino e Festo Cloister and preserves more than 50,000 artifacts, the oldest dating back 600 million years. The first finds to be displayed were the Ittioliti deposits of Campania – fossils found by Oronzio Gabriele Costa (the founder of Italian Paleontology).

The **Royal Museum of Mineralogy** is located inside the University itself. There's a Vesuvian collection, a collection of scientific instruments, and two hyaline (glassy) quartz from Madagascar given as a present to King Charles VII.

The **Zoological Museum** has one thousand skin specimens dating back to the 18th century and several extinct animals are on display, including the Norfolk Island Pigeon, the Crescent Nail-Tailed Wallabi, and the Berber Lion. They also have 30,000 specimens of insects and 2,000 specimens of parasitic worms.

The **Museum of Anthropology** houses archeological finds from Troy, including polished stone axes and milling querns from about 3,000 B.C.

The **Biblioteca Università** contains one million volumes. The books themselves are hidden away within the building, accessible only to librarians. However, ask the lady at the top of the stairs if any exhibits are on display. The library often has exhibitions and curators are more than willing to give you a tour.

Getting There: The address is Via Mezzocannone 8, Naples.

THE SPANISH PALAZZO

Depicted in the Italian films *Processo alla Citta* by Luigi Zampa and *Giudizio Universale* by Vittorio de Sica, the Palazzo dello Spagnolo is an apartment complex with awe-inspiring architecture.

In Naples generally, the triumvirate of Bourbon architects include Luigi Vanvitelli, Ferdinando Fuga, and Ferdinando Sanfelice. Sanfelice's signature style was the hawk-winged staircases that he designed around the city center; he also was believed to have created the stairs of this palazzo – but that's untrue.

Marquis Nicola Moscati built this palazzo in 1738 and the edifice became a famous example of Neapolitan Rococo. Although Sanfelice was said to have designed the building, his name never appeared on any notary deeds, leading scholars to surmise that he only gave out advice on its construction.

Afterwards, financial problems marred the palazzo in scandal. Moscati ceded it to the Marquis of Livardi after incurring high debts. In 1813 Livardi had to sell it again to a Spanish nobleman, don Tommaso Atienza, from which the building gets its Spanish moniker.

Atienza commissioned a new architect to do extension work, but he was so unhappy with the result that he went to court. The proceedings cost Atienza an exorbitant amount and he too had to sell the palazzo, apportioning several sections to three different owners; four portions, however, remained empty due to lack of buyers. Let's hope they have better luck today.

Getting There: The address is Via Vergini 19, Naples. Privately owned, you can walk into the courtyard and take a peek at the staircase. It's near the National Archeological Museum (see p. 60) and The Wine Shop (see p. 94).

THE BOTANICAL GARDENS

If you need a reprieve from the bustle of downtown Naples, the Botanical Gardens lie smack in the middle of the city, and yet cover thirty acres of quiet land. Created in 1807, they bring together plants from many differing climates, including an oasis of cacti.

Ring the bell at the front gate and a security guard will buzz you in. It's free.

Getting There: The address is Via Foria 223, Naples.

VILLA PIGNATELLI

Villa Pignatelli was built in 1825 for Lord Ferdinand Acton. Twenty years later Carl Mayer von Rothschild bought the villa, which today has concerts, often hosts an excellent series of temporary exhibitions, has a splendid ballroom filled with sculptures, re-creates rooms to look like the inside of Pompeii villas, and cultivates a quiet garden. Children love the ducks in the pond.

If you walk over to a little administrative building along the left side of the villa, you might go inside and, with a friendly smile and a passion for history, ask if someone can give you a little tour of the **Carriage Museum**. Located in its own building, this exhibition has been closed for the last twenty years or more. It houses Italian, French, and British carriages from the 1800's and 1900's. You can even pull out the back drawers of the carriages to see where they stored wine for longer trips.

Getting There: The address is Riviera di Chiaia 200, Naples.

THE MYSTERY TOWER

Visible from the autostrada near the Naples Financial District, a tower pokes its head out of the hills. It's reddish and from the freeway it looks crumbling – or even like an Arab tower with overtones of neo-Gothic and Renaissance.

A bit more reading about Naples history, however, reveals that while Arabs from North Africa may have traded with Naples, they didn't settle in these parts. In fact, no mosque exists in the modern city today. So what is this strange tower that pokes into view when you are driving along the tangenziale and peeks through the vegetation near the botanical gardens?

Located a few blocks away from Capodimonte, the **Torre del Palascino** was designed to look like the Palazzo della Signoria in Florence. Antonio Cipolla directed construction that builders completed in 1868. Today, private residents live inside the tower, which is surrounded by high gates.

The surgeon Ferdinando Palasciano (1815-1891) once owned the entire complex. When he provided medical care to both sides in Messina during the riots of 1848, the King considered his care of the enemy an act of treason and consequently Palasciano served one year in prison. His case gained international attention and provided the basis for the Geneva Convention of 1864 that gave life to the Red Cross. The good doctor thereafter lived in this abode, which included a large garden of fruit trees.

Today, the Culture Hotel Villa di Capodimonte is located next door, providing wonderful views of the city as well as a view of the tower.

Getting There: The hotel address is Salita Moiariello 66, Naples. If you'd like to stay at their hotel that has a restaurant, a garden, and plush rooms, check their website at villacapodimonte.culturehotel.it.

THE VESUVIAN VILLAS

In a dilapidated area close to the ruins of Herculaneum, the nobility built 122 villas during the 1700's. They wanted to keep up not with the Jones', but with the king himself, Ferdinand IV who built one of his palaces here. After the villas cropped up, the area became known as the *Miglio d'Oro* or the Golden Mile.

The centerpiece here is the **Reggia di Portici**, currently a university. If you roam around and ask, you might find the **Herculanense Museum**, which houses reproductions of items found in Herculaneum. The gates to the **Botanical Garden** may also be open. Students sprawl through the airy courtyards during the weekday and anyone can do the same. On the weekends, however, custodians lock up the palace and the Golden Mile looks more like an abandoned and crumbling ghost town.

A few blocks away from the Reggia, the lavish **Villa Campolieto** welcomes tourists during the weekdays as well. Ask at the tourist office inside what other villa's are open to the public at that moment: Villa Favorita, Villa Prota, or Villa Ruggiero might be some options and each have their own interesting history.

Sir William Hamilton owned a villa here and the famous architects Sanfelice and Vanvitelli designed some of the splendors.

Getting There: The Reggia di Portici is at Via Universita 100, Portici. Villa Campolieto is at Corso Resina 283, Ercolano.

For the Herculanense Museum, check the website: www.museoercolanense.unina.it. The Villa Campolieto also has a nice website at www. villevesuviane.net.

THE ELEVATORS

ANM (Azienda Napoletana Mobilità) is the company that runs the bus service in Naples. It also offers a transportation oddity – three public elevators. Each elevator takes pedestrians between a top level street and a bottom level street. The best thing about them is that the fare is free.

Across the street from Piazza del Plebiscito, the **Acton Elevator** takes you down to the port of Molo Beverello.

The pedestrianized **Via Chiaia** connects Piazza Trieste e Trento (by the Teatro San Carlo) to the upscale stores near the Piazza dei Martiri. Smack in the middle of this walkway is a seventeenth century arch with a bas-relief of horses, the Ponte di Chiaia. The elevator inside takes you up to a less visited part of the city. Here, you can see the **Palazzo Serra di Cassano** (at Via Monte di Dio 14-15) that was once owned by a Prince whose son Gennaro was executed during the 1799 revolution, the façade of the **Museo Artistico Industriale** (at Piazza Demetrio Salazar 6), and visit **Pizzofalcone** hill. The elevator is manned by friendly operators; don't press any of the buttons.

Finally, in the seedy **Sanità district**, a bridge going toward Capodimonte has an elevator that runs down to the **Church of Santa Maria della Sanità** and the **Catacombs of San Gaudioso**.

But watch out! The elevators also have hours of operation. When the green light is on, the elevator is open. When the red light is lit, the elevator is closed and you'll have to find another (longer) way to the street either below or above you.

A WALK THROUGH POSILLIPO

The Greeks called this area Pausilypon (respite from pain or toil) and some say Virgil lived here. The Spanish aristocracy began building seaside villas in the district of Posillipo during the 17th century. In the 1950's property development intensified and many claim that this destroyed the beauty of the district. Others maintain, however, that Posillipo today is the posh area of Naples.

If you walk from the tip of the Chiaia district along the bay, a slope goes upward to Via Posillipo. Here, you can wander past many villas, some converted into elegant restaurants. Search for the **Palazzo Donn'Anna** along this street and find the **Villa Rosebery** at Via Ferdinando Russo 26 where the Italian President resides when he is in Naples.

A stroll up Via Posillipo leads to **Piazza San Luigi**, which has a WWI memorial with an obelisk. A longish hike further along the road takes you to either **Parco Virgiliano** (Via Salita Grotta 20) a landscaped park overlooking the sea, or walk down a winding road to reach the **Santa Maria del Faro** church (Via Marechiaro 96). Here, stairs go down to **Marechiaro**, a fishing village with wonderful seaside restaurants and a labyrinth of stairs that lead into many little outlets to the sea. This walk can be done on a casual Saturday afternoon.

LIDO LIFE

Summer in southern Italy means beaches, but in this sprawling metropolis, it's hard to find a beach that's free and open to the public. Instead, private companies own strips of beach property. Although Lidos can be somewhat expensive and are packed with people on the weekends, they can also feel luxurious.

Lidos line the shore from the seaside town of **Castel Volturno** all the way down to **Lago Patria** and beyond. To name them all would take a decade. Driving along the road, once you select a Lido (you can choose one randomly), an attendant directs you to a

parking lot. The procedure for entering a Lido tends to be the same everywhere. You pay an all-day fee at the front gate and then walk into an espresso bar replete with caffè, sodas, candy, and gelato. You forge ahead to the promenade and give a beach attendant your ticket. He picks up an umbrella and chairs, which you pay extra for at the front gate and you select a sandy plot. He then sets up the beach furniture for you.

Lidos often have playgrounds for kids and delicious cafeteria food with panini, spaghetti, mozzarella balls, and other hot *primi,*

Fast Food

Who says Italians don't have fast food? Although this is the land where McDonald's has repeatedly gone out of business, food courts at *i Centri Commerciali* (or the shopping malls) bustle with customers, cafeterias at the Lidos provide quick bites, and fast food restaurants line the streets outside the soccer stadium. Fried or laden with olive oil, these treats still tend to be healthier because Neapolitans use less sauce, such as ketchup and mayonnaise, and they add vegetables. Here are three fast food delights to make at home:

Panini with Roasted Bell Peppers

Roast several bell peppers under the broiler or grill. Allow to cool and cut into thin slices. Place in a dish and add liberal amounts of olive oil, salt, and pepper. Scoop the roasted peppers into the middle of bread rolls and eat. (Neapolitans eat these without condiments.)

Panini with Eggplant and Mozzarella

Fry eggplant in a pan with healthy heaps of olive oil. Slice mozzarella cheese. Place the eggplant and mozzarella inside the panini and eat.

Hot Dog and French Fry Panino

Slice a panino in the middle. Place a hot dog (cut once lengthwise) and a heaping bunch of french fries inside.

secondi, and *contorni piatti*. It's delicious, though a bit pricey, so families tend to bring their own panini and spaghetti in tupperware.

To avoid the bumper to bumper Lido traffic, arrive close to 10 a.m. and leave at 2 p.m. At those hours, you'll have your choice of parking and beach space. If you head for the beach at noon and leave at 4 p.m., the traffic will be intense and the beach will be very crowded. Also, know that the Mediterranean in most of Campania isn't considered particularly clean. For information (in Italian) about the current state of beaches in the region, you can check this website: www.arpacampania.it.

SOCCER IN NAPLES

It's impossible to talk about life in Naples without mentioning soccer. The fans are rowdy, the **Stadio San Paolo** is old, and you can frequently see flairs and firecrackers launched inside the stadium during games. Soccer is a huge sport here and it seems that all young males devote their afternoons and weekends to honing their skills on the field.

For those of you who don't know much about soccer, here's a small summary: the season runs from August through May. The Naples team plays forty regular season games per year – twenty at home and twenty away, playing each Serie A team twice. The Naples team is excellent, so they are in Serie A or the Italian Premier League. This league is  considered one of the three best in the world alongside the English Premier League and the Spanish La Liga.

Throughout Italy, almost every town has its own team, so there are also Serie B, C, and D. Each year, the top teams in each division move up to the next division the following year. The bottom four teams of a Serie move down a division. This makes the competition within each Serie fierce.

The top teams in Italy tend to come from Northern Italy, in particular AC Milan, the Internationale from Milan, and Juventus from Turin. They are the ones who usually win the Serie A. Naples usually finishes somewhere in the middle of the Serie A.

The top Italian teams – just like other teams in Europe – buy their players from all over the world. AC Milan, for example, recently had the likes of David Beckham from England and Ronaldinho from Brazil. Most of the players on the Naples team are from Italy, but they also have their fair share of foreign players, including Edison Cavani from Uruguay and Ezequiel Lavezzi from Argentina. The great Argentinian Diego Maradona played for Naples from 1984 to 1991 and led the *Azzurri* to its only two Serie A championships.

The sport can get complicated because not only do Italians play teams within their country, but European tournaments also run throughout the year. The most famous tournament is the Champions' League, which pits the top teams in Europe against each other in a year long competition with a finale in May.

Getting There: Take the tangenziale to the Fuorigrotta exit. Once you get off, you'll see the stadium to the East. The address is Via Giambattista Marino, Naples.

To see a live game, it's best to go downtown and purchase the tickets near the stadium rather than buy on-line. Go to Azzurro Service at Via Francesco Galeota 19, Naples, which has a TicketOnline s.r.l. inside. For more information, see the ticket website at www.azzurroservice.net/biglietteria.

Website Recommendation: The Naples soccer team is known as Società Sportiva Calcio Napoli or SSC Napoli. Their English language website is here: www.sscnapoli.it.

GRAFFITI

Some claim it's art, others say it's vandalism. What we do know is that in Pompeii, some of the best information we have about the daily life of the ancient Romans comes from graffiti. So whatever graffiti is – it lasts. And it tells a story about what Neapolitans find important today.

A visit to Pompeii reveals graffiti such as magic spells, declarations of love, and political slogans. One inscription gives the address of a prostitute, Novellia Primigenia, known for her great beauty.

In World War II when Neapolitans escaped the bombings by hiding in the underground, they scratched prolific amounts of graffiti into the tuff stone. Still today visitors to the underground can see what adults feared and cared about during those crisis days through the pictures on the walls.

But graffiti as a modern art form gained popularity during the 1960's and 1970's in New York City when gang members and political activists spray-painted subway cars. They then extended their markings throughout the city. Within a decade, the well-known Jean-Michel Basquiat went from graffiti artist, with a tag of SAMO, to having his works displayed in New York art galleries.

Today, Italian graffiti artists are heavily influenced by the movement in New York City, most often marking up subway cars. At least some Italians take this art form seriously. In 1979, for example, graffiti artist Lee Quinones and Fab 5 Freddy were given a gallery opening in Rome by art dealer Claudio Bruni.

Experimentation continues to this day and Naples is no exception. On Via Bagnoli, a stretch of walls are left untouched by police and city officials, allowing graffiti artists to work unimpeded. They display brightly colored images using spray paint and stencils.

When you arrive along this road, parking is easily available. Not too many people seem to stop in this gritty part of downtown

Naples. Once you get out of the car and walk, you have to keep your eyes to the pavement because doggie poop, broken glass, and trash litters the sidewalk. But when you stop and look up, Neapolitan graffiti stretches for over a kilometer in panels along the concrete walls.

The most prolific artist along this street tags himself as "Iabo." Here are some of the stenciled words:

Tutti sordi per i soldi (Everyone deaf for money.)

Where is Respect?

Reduci di Pace ("Ex-Servicemen." A dead man is depicted next to the words.)

Libbbertà (Liberty, spelled with three b's.)

Amore amaro amare (Love, bitter, to be in love)

Progettare in fondo e il miglior modo per evitare (To plan carefully is the best way to avoid problems)

A little love lost, a little politics, and a somewhat unpleasant smell makes this street an off-the-beaten track destination.

Getting There: The address is Via Bagnoli. From the tangenziale, take the Fuorigrotta exit, pay the toll and bear left through two underpasses. When you reach the stadium (behind you), go straight ahead until the last street and make a right. The graffiti on Via Bagnoli begins about five kilometers down, straight ahead.

Book Recommendation: *Graffiti Writing: Origini, Significati, Tecniche e Protagonisti in Italia* by Alessandro Mininno. This Italian language book with many pictures can be found at the Capodimonte Museum. The author focuses on influences from New York City and the book presents a wealth of photographs, particularly of box-car graffiti from around Italy.

METRO STATION ART

Named after the Neapolitan baroque painter Salvator Rosa, this metro station is a divine place to roam. Designed by architect Alessandro Mendini, during its construction builders found an ancient Roman bridge, which archeologists then excavated.

From the metro station, a long escalator takes people up to a piazza where boys play soccer among robot-like science fiction characters and a copper hand that holds a sundial. The artwork featured here is by Mimmo Paladino and several other modern Italian artists.

Walking one block down from here, the **Piazza Salvator Rosa** has a pulcinella statue in the bushes, golden flames shoot across the face of a building, and a triangular monument in the middle has images of volcanoes on each side.

As the new Line 6 of the Metropolitana is completed, each stop along the way will show off its designer tags; architects and artists of international renown have been commissioned to design or decorate the new stations.

Getting There: You can find the Salvator Rosa Station on Line 1 of the Metropolitana.

RUA CATALANA

The buildings along this narrow street display modern sculptures created by Riccardo Dalisi and artists from his workshop. A professor emeritus of architecture at the University of Naples, during the 1970's Dalisi set up art workshops for children in the most impoverished districts of Naples. Their works went on to be displayed at international exhibitions.

The Italian household goods company, Alessi, also asked him to create a new version of the Neapolitan flip-over coffee pot, for which the architect visited countless tinsmith shops and junk dealers for his research, inspiring him and his artist friends to create junk yard sculptures. To see modern art inspired by Dalisi, go to Rua Catalana and visit the artisan shops of **Allfer** and **Artistic Sud**. They sell modern sculptures made of tin, copper, and bronze. Artwork also peppers the buildings along this street.

Getting There: Allfer is at Rua Catalana 111, Naples and **Artistic Sud** is across the street. In the heart of downtown Naples, this small street lies off the congested Via Agostino Depretis.

MADRE

To experience a little night life, to find a children's center, or to see frescoes inspired by Giotto who lived in Naples for a time, the *Museo d'Arte Contemporanea Donna Regina Napoli* or MADRE is the place to be. Relatively new, the museum opened its doors in 2005 and houses a permanent collection of modern art by some of the greats, including Andy Warhol, Robert Rauschenberg, Claes Oldenburg, Mimmo Paladino, Roy Lichtenstein, Robert Mapplethorpe, and Anish Kapoor.

MADRE hosts lectures, films, and even children's art classes. You can also wander to the far back of the museum and enter the

8th century church **Santa Maria di Donnaregina Vecchia**. Ask there about the Giotto frescoes. This is also a great place to hangout in the evenings since the museum stays open on Saturdays and Sundays until midnight.

Getting There: The address is Via Settembrini 79, Naples (near Piazza Cavour). Their website is: www.museomadre.it.

THE BOOKSHOP

Life just isn't complete without a Saturday morning spent lingering inside a boutique bookshop. Across from the excavated Greek foundations at Piazza Bellini, **Colonnese** offers a wonderful range of antiquarian books, posters, and photographs. They focus mainly on selling Italian language books about Neapolitan history, food, and culture. Some Italian titles I've enjoyed, include: *The Naples Underground: ventures through the mysteries of the parallel city* and *Comme te l'agia dicere?* – the art of gesturing in Naples, replete with pictures.

Colonnese is about a block away from Piazza Dante – the square where book dealers abound, selling both used and new titles. The music school and Intra Moenia are also nearby.

Getting There: The address is Via San Pietro a Majella 32-33, Naples. They also have a website at www.colonnese.it/intro.php.

PAN

Located in the 17th century Palazzo Rocella, the Palazzo Delle Arti Napoli (PAN) has no permanent collection. Instead, exhibitions from around the world rotate through the airy spaces. A fourth-floor archive has catalogues and pictures of art in Naples from the last few decades. The museum also hosts film screenings and lectures. Along the way there, stop at Caffè Moccia on Via San Pasquale a Chiaia.

Getting There: The address is Via dei Mille 60, Naples. You can find more information at www.palazzoartinapoli.net.

THE NAPLES BONSAI CLUB

The **Naples Bonsai Club** offers classes in the Japanese art of cultivating Bonsai. The club itself is a sprawling greenhouse consisting exclusively of Bonsai. Well, okay, not all the plants are Bonsai because students begin their training with indigenous Mediterranean plants that are easier to pluck and prune.

The Bonsai Club is a bit difficult to find, hiding down a steep incline behind a gated parking lot, but with a GPS and a little adventurous spirit, plus the telephone number from the website on hand, you'll enter a take-me-away world of plants and sunshine.

The owner proudly gives visitors a tour, including the Bonsai he himself has cultivated for over eighteen years. They're all Italians and if you stay a while, they'll offer you espresso from a thermos.

They adhere to strict Japanese forms of Bonsai cultivation and over the years, as the pictures on the walls attest, they have invited Japanese teachers to Naples many times. You can find out more at www.napolibonsaiclub.it.

A FEW NOTABLE RESTAURANTS

WHERE THEY INVENTED PIZZA

Antica Pizzeria Port'Alba invented pizza. No really – they did. And don't confuse this restaurant with Brandi's. Brandi's invented the Margherita Pizza, but Antica Pizzeria Port'Alba started out as a street stall in 1720 and became a restaurant in the 1800's. Their signature dish is the Napoletana. Made from fresh mozzarella di bufala, fresh tomatoes, basil leaves, and olive oil, the crust is left thin on purpose.

Located in the center of town, the restaurant offers inside seating or an outside stall where you can buy slices of their pizza and eat it as a snack while you wander along the bookstalls and bookstores that clutter the street from **Piazza Dante** up to **Piazza Bellini**.

Getting There: The address is Via San Biagio dei Librai 115, Naples.

PIZZA MARGHERITA

Brandi Pizzeria is the second oldest pizzeria in Naples, established in 1780. The cards given out at Brandi's recount the margherita story.

In 1889 the legendary pizzaiolo Pietro, a.k.a. Raffaele Esposito, received a visit from an employee of the royal household who invited him to prepare pizza for the Royal Family at Capodimonte. Raffaele accepted the challenge and when he cooked the meal, he topped a pizza with tomato, buffalo mozzarella, and basil to create a pie with the colors of the Italian flag. He presented this special dish to King Umberto I and his Queen Margherita when they visited Naples in 1889. The Margherita Pizza was thus born and remains the most popular pizza here today.

The restaurant has kept the letter written by the Royal Palace on June 11, 1889:

The Royal Household of His Majesty
Dear Mr. Raffaele Esposito (Brandi)

I would like to officially state that the three varieties of pizza prepared by you for Her Majesty the Queen were found to be excellent.

Humblest regards,
Camillo Galli
(Head of Table Service of the Royal Household)

Now that's a letter that might make a die-hard foodie want the monarchy to come back!

Getting There: Salita S. Anna di Palazzo1-2, Naples. If you are standing next to Caffè Gambrinus in Piazza Trieste e Trento, walk up Via Chiaia and you will see the signs. You can find them also at www.brandi.it.

PIZZA A METRO

On summer weekends, Neapolitans flee to the Amalfi beaches or into the mountains. **Monte Faito** is particularly welcome because the air is at least ten degrees cooler than in Naples. You can drive up the winding roads to the mountain peak where you find hiking trails, cozy restaurants, and wooden houses. As you walk through the trees, bells clang from the necks of wandering goats.

It can be reached by aerial tramline from Castellamare di Stabia station on the Circumvesuviana train line while for drivers a good place to park is the **Funivia del Faito**, where you can then take a ride on the tram. The views of Mt. Vesuvius and the sea are stellar from here. The tram ends at the Circumvesuviana train stop in Stabia. From there, take the train four stops to Vico Equense and walk a

few blocks to the famous **Pizza a Metro**, which makes fresh pizzas in a wood fire oven while you watch. The waiter cuts the pizza at your table.

Getting There: From Monte Faito, take the Funivia down to Castellammare di Stabia. Get out of the Funivia station and walk to the adjacent Circumvesuviana. Hop on and go four stops to Vico Equense. When you disembark, **Pizza a Metro** is four left turns and three blocks away from the station. The address is Via Nicotera 15, Vico Equense. Their website is www.pizzametro.it.

Pizza, Pizza, Pizza

Although versions of pizza existed in the ancient world – notably adding toppings to different kinds of pita bread – pizza as we know it first became common among the *lazzaroni* of Naples. By the 17th century, tourists visited the poor section of the city just to sample the new creation. Pizza today is a staple within the region, eaten as a full meal (usually with cold beer and using a fork and knife) or as fast food. Neapolitans make pizza with a thin crust and spread their toppings in only small portions, not heaped on the dough.

The **Napoletana** and the **Margherita** are the most popular (and basically the same pizza by two different names). Other variations include **Sailor's Pizza** (with shelled shrimp, mussels, clams, and octopus), **Four Season's Pizza** (with green olives, artichokes, anchovies, and mozzarella), **Anchovy Pizza** (with slices of garlic and fresh anchovies), and the most innovative **Walnut and Provolone Pizza** (a white pizza made with slices of smoked provolone cheese and finely grated walnuts).

A TASTE OF JAPAN

When you ask a Neapolitan: "Where are you from?" you usually get the same answer: Naples. In general, people are born and live in the Campania region all their lives surrounded by family. Neapolitans also tend to be fiercely proud of their local heritage, from their two thousand year history to their internationally famous cuisine.

Living here, therefore, means being immersed in everything Neapolitan. It also means that the visitor or expat accustomed to international food choices, might feel a bit of a challenge in finding cuisine other than Italian. But never fear, four exquisite Japanese restaurants in downtown Naples mirror the seriousness of the Italian cooking experience and a little slice of the Orient feels apropos considering that Naples was once home to international merchants who came to this port bringing spices, exotic animals, and more.

Today, Neapolitans are intensely conservative about food, eschewing even other regional Italian cuisines, but the popularity of the following restaurants show how highly the Neapolitans prize sushi, sashimi, and tempura:

Kukai at Via Carlo de Cesare 52, Naples;
Ristorante Zen 2 at Vico della Quercia 24, Naples;
Ristorante Tokyo at Via S. Maria delle Neve 26, Naples; and
Nero Sushi at Via Partenope 12, Naples.

THE TRIPPERIA

Most Neapolitans prefer to buy their groceries, shoes, clothing, and electronic equipment at the bevy of open markets around the city. The most famous is located along **Via Pignasecca** where locals haggle for clothes or shoes and seafood vendors display their catch

in huge shallow tins. Any day of the week, visitors can push through the throngs and experience the blessings of retail therapy.

Somewhere along the way, lunch is also in order. What better place to stop than the **Tripperia Trattoria** that advertises fresh tripe in a glass case surrounded by lemons?

Getting There: Get out at the Montesanto Funicular, Circumvesuviana, or Metro Station and turn right. Otherwise, walk down Via Toledo and once you reach Piazza Carità, take a left onto Via Pignasecca. The Tripperia is along this street on the left hand side.

THE ULTIMATE FEAST: MAKING OUT, ITALIAN STYLE

Okay – so learning Italian has turned out to be a little harder than you thought. Although you've driven in Naples, you still think horn-honking is road rage rather than just a salutation and queues at shops still look like a crush of people instead of the organized lines that they are for Neapolitans. But fear not! There is something particularly Italian that you can master – Italian kissing.

It's not entirely easy. The art can take months if not years to perfect. You must observe, observe, observe. And then, naturally, practice.

Admittedly, this author has been fascinated with Italian kissing ever since she landed on the shores of Naples. Now, she's willing to share the tidbits of learning so far, whittling down the intricacies into what any Italian would likely tell you should be presented as a luscious *primo piatto*.

Here are the cultural steps you can attempt to master:

Step 1 – Choose a public venue. While the causeway going to the Castel dell'Ovo is the best choice in Naples, parking lots at shopping malls are also adequate. A little more out of the way might be inside a Fiat on the shore of Lago Averno or consider renting a lounge chair at one of the many Lidos in summertime.

Step 2 – When you begin kissing, don't keep your mouth almost closed. Wide open is better, but not to the point where the lips are stretched. The lips must look loose, natural. The lips must say: so you think you can kiss?

Step 3 – Keep the tongue outside of the mouth. Keep the tongue active. Not too fast. Not too slow. Always adventurous and possibly even surprising. Remember, this is Italy. You *are* amore.

Step 4 – Yes, it's good to keep your partner in mind, but more importantly, think of all those around you. Think of their feelings. Are they entranced? Do they look like they want more? If the answer is yes, then you are serving up the right meal.

With that, I bid you *Tanti Baci*.

FACES OF NAPLES: THE TIN-SCULPTURE ARTIST

Inside a run-down apartment building, tin pot puppets sprout from shelves, copper birds dangle from the ceiling and painted canvases line the walls. A cross between a tinsmith workshop and an academic's experimental laboratory, this is Professor Riccardo Dalisi's art studio, down a narrow cobblestone street in the Naples district of the Vomero.

Dalisi introduces himself with a jovial smile and immediately offers to give a tour of his artwork. "They're doing the tango," he chuckles, holding up two tin pots with pointy noses, hats, and arms soldered together.

Born in 1931, Dalisi grew up in Italy during World War II when often he had nothing more than potato peels to eat. While still a child, he moved with his family to Naples from the small town of Potenza, southeast of the city. His father, a postman who loved working with his hands as a hobby, encouraged his son to do the same, and to study. Dalisi enrolled in the University of Naples department of architecture, earned a degree, and by 1969 he became a tenured professor there.

He found teaching very taxing and, believing that art should be for everyone, he embarked upon an experiment. In 1971 he set up workshops for children in the most impoverished district of Naples, the Rione Traiano. On his first day with the children, he brought along wooden sticks and strings. He told the children to design whatever they liked. They didn't question him, but instead began to work without any inhibitions. From these simple materials, the

children created complex geometrical designs that, Dalisi says, could
have been signed by Paul Klee, Wassily Kandinsky, or Marc Chagall.

In 1979 the household goods company Alessi asked him to
create a new design for the Neapolitan Flip-Over coffee pot.
Because the pot was made of tin, he began visiting countless
tinsmiths and junk dealers in Naples. The pot reminded Dalisi of
the 18th century Neapolitan theater movement's opera buffa, which
depicted common people in everyday situations. Often a pulcinella,
a joker wearing a mask, came into the scene and overturned things.
Dalisi began to sketch tin pots with stick arms and stick legs,
forming characters such as vestal virgins, traffic cops and the
pulcinella-like comedian.

Dalisi handed over his sketches to a tinsmith, Don Vincenzo,
who took the designs and soldered the features onto the pots. Dalisi
never met the old Neapolitan recluse, communicating with him only

through a nephew, but together they
created more than two hundred
prototypes and sent them off to
Alessi.

Alessi felt some frustration with
the architect's endless experiments but
stuck with Dalisi. Its loyalty paid off:
in 1982 he won the premier industrial
design award in Italy – the Golden
Compass – for his new rendition of
the pot. MOMA – the Museum of
Modern Art in New York City –
exhibited Dalisi's tin pots and they
soon became part of the private
collections of museums in Paris,
Montreal, Milan, and Denver, Colorado.

Today Dalisi, a retired professor emeritus, spends most of his
time at his studio surrounded by artists and gallery directors. Since
the 1990s he has devoted himself mostly to sculpture, using simple

materials such as brass and copper. In one doorway, a female statue clasps her hands to her chest, her glassy eye welcoming people into the room. Strutting out in the middle, a Don Quixote holds a shield. Dalisi ambles to a table where a medieval farmer on a horse pulls shearing implements. "Horses used to be an important part of medieval Neapolitan culture," he says.

Dalisi explains that modern art flourishes in Naples today. He not only cooperates with many other contemporary artists, but also uses the city's history for his ideas. He lifts up a metal mask with a horse-like face, bulging golden eyes and mischievous smile, then explains that these masks were inspired by the theater masks of ancient Greece and Rome.

Accessible and friendly, Dalisi shows his studio to anyone who calls and makes an appointment.[66]

Getting There: Studio Dalisi is at Calata San Francesco 59, Naples. Call at 081 681 405 or e-mail at studiodalisi@libero.it.

---

66 This article first appeared in print, cited as: Barbara Zaragoza, "Tin sculpture artist wows modern art community," *Stars and Stripes* 29 April 2010: 30.

TRAVEL TIPS & NEWS HEADLINES

Certain issues will probably remain perennial problems for Naples, such as the fear of another volcanic eruption, the imminent collapse of Pompeii, and the trash problem. In this chapter, the first five headings provide travel tips, including those specific to Naples. The

next five headings delve into the seedier aspects of the city that expats and tourists want or need to know, but guidebooks often do not cover due to their controversial nature. The essays respond to newspaper articles found during the years 2008-2010,

but they are examples of problems that have plagued the city for decades and will likely continue to persist. Be aware, however, that these essays are in no way comprehensive research on the topic and they do not speak for everyone; they are simply reflections that broach the topic and are meant as starting points for you to draw your own conclusions while exploring the city.

The greatest concern about Naples relates to the stereotype of rampant crime and the ubiquity of the Camorra (mafia). These two issues have been addressed in the **Introduction** *(see p. 3)* but the gist will be reiterated here: Naples, for all its imperfections, also happens to be one of the safer cities in Europe in terms of violent crime.

A FEW TRAVEL TIPS FOR NAPLES

Although it can be dry and boring to drone on about travel tips, it seems necessary because Naples is a world unto itself where visitors will likely enjoy their time much more if they know a few basics. Here are some practicalities that add to the myth and romance:

WHY IS THE CITY SO DIRTY?

The complaints about Naples are that the city is gritty and polluted. The truth about Neapolitan *grit* is that the city is more than 2,800 years old. In addition, Neapolitans have preserved so much of their past that the buildings almost by necessity tend to blend into the natural look and feel of the ancient ruins.

If you live in Naples and acclimatize to the environment, when you travel to other cities, such as Barcelona or Berlin, those cities look so clean that they seem both inauthentic and superficially hygienic. Certainly Naples has its share of problems, but it's best to look at Naples as more than a travel or living experience – it's a personality type.

SAFETY

You wouldn't leave your wallet on a park bench in New York City. You wouldn't walk down the street in East LA with your Louis Vuitton purse. Naples is a big chaotic city. Be smart and be safe. You can stay tranquil in the knowledge that violent crime is unusual and so is child kidnapping since children and their mothers are considered sacred. The crime is almost exclusively one of pickpocketing and home burglaries.

DRIVING

Neapolitans see nothing wrong with their driving, but tourists and expats should remember that in these parts traffic signs and signals are only a suggestion. The Neapolitan attitude is that common sense should always override the law, and the law generally defies common sense. So pay less attention to traffic laws and more attention to what the cars, *motorini,* and the people around you are doing.

Drive defensively. Watch the flow of traffic. If lots of cars are not stopping at a particular red light or stop sign – slowly and carefully do the same. Why? Because if you don't follow along with everyone else – yes, perhaps someone will get angry and honk at you – but more likely you'll get rear-ended. Traffic accidents are frequent, so don't be complacent about your safety.

Also, motorcycles have the right of way – even over pedestrians. I repeat: crazy *motorino* drivers, often with a cigarette in their mouth and a cell phone pressed to their ear, dart through every crevice of the city and have the right of way over pedestrians. If you're driving, always look in your right *and* left rear-view mirrors to watch for *motorino* darting on either side of you.

For pedestrians, be aware that Neapolitan drivers are alert and ultra-attentive since they have to be. You can cross even multiple lanes of traffic by locking eyes with an oncoming driver.

IF YOU GET LOST

Neapolitans themselves get lost or confused often. The less than well-marked signs necessitate that locals as well as tourists ask, ask, ask. But don't worry: it's part of the culture to ask directions – you'll even see men doing it often and shamelessly.

HOW TO TAKE PUBLIC TRANSPORTATION

Public transportation is somewhat of a mystery. Mass construction projects can be seen everywhere and Naples is attempting to build a comprehensive metro system with stations in many parts of the city and suburbs, including by the main port of Molo Beverello located across the street from Castel Nuovo. Unfortunately, construction often gets delayed due to lack of funds and the discovery of archeological finds. No matter what, the non-unified nature of public transportation will likely continue.

The Circumvesuviana runs out to Pompeii and the Amalfi Coast, while the Cumana train goes to the Phlegraean Fields. Two metro lines (and possibly more in the future) run through the city and into the suburbs. The funicular rails are owned by the bus service ANM, which also owns only one of the Metro lines. Confused yet?

Fortunately, you only need one ticket – the Uniconapoli – to get onto any one of these modes of transportation. You can always buy a ticket from the ticket office outside the metro, bus, or train stations. Also, newspaper stands sell tickets. The basic rate gives you 90 minutes of travel time on any mode of transport, so the system is unified in this sense. Note that longer trips, such as out to Pompeii or Sorrento, costs more, so state your destination when buying.

When you get on the bus or metro, make sure to put it through the machine that stamps a date and time on it. Sometimes you can hop on public transportation without a ticket and not get caught, but if the conductor comes along, you're out 36 Euro or more, so it's not recommended.

GREETING ITALIANS

Neapolitans can seem brusque or grumpy at times, but if you unlock a little cultural key, they'll turn chocolate-sweet within an instant. Wherever you are and as often as possible, greet people around you (the bus driver, the barista, the waiter, the store clerk) with a *buon giorno* if it's before 2 p.m. and a *buona sera* if it's after 2 p.m. Also use the word *grazie* as often as possible. It seems that Italians are always saying *grazie* even if there's nothing to be thankful for. When you enter anyone else's space, whether their home, store or even the airport bus, the question *'Posso?'* (may I?) is often appropriate. When foreigners use those few words often, their travel experience goes from being pushed around to being very welcomed.

KEEPING HEALTHY ON THE ROAD

For any international travel, a few tips occur that can prevent the most unpleasant travel experience of all: getting sick on the road. Here are a few recommendations for avoiding a stay in a hotel bed with the curtains drawn.

Eat the yogurt. Everywhere you go, try to eat a little of the local yogurt everyday. Yogurt is probiotic, which means that it promotes the growth of healthy bacteria in the digestive system, taking over and beating back any bad bacteria that can cause the flu, stomach illness, or colds during a trip.

Drink Coca-Cola. Tummy aches are common on the road. A little Coca-Cola during the day settles the stomach. Countries cultivate their vegetables and meats differently, so this beverage helps soothe any aches. Ginger Ale also works well, but it's less available throughout the world.

Wear shower shoes. Take along flip-flops and use them as shower shoes. When you're walking a lot, it's essential to avoid athlete's foot.

Keep a few over-the-counter drugs handy. Take along a bottle of children's and adult Motrin. Motrin (also known as Ibuprofen) is better than Tylenol because Tylenol relieves only aches and pains, while Motrin brings down inflammation. Too much

Tylenol can also be hard on your liver. For back aches or high fevers, Motrin will knock those out for an entire day.

Also bring Claritin or another anti-histamine (in case of allergies), Dramamine (in case of motion sickness), anti-diarrhea medicine, and bug spray during the summer months for keeping away mosquitoes.

Carry toilet tissue. It always comes in handy, particularly on trains and in public restrooms.

Wash Your Hands. Wash your hands any chance you get, especially before eating meals. If there are paper towels, use them to open doors to the public restrooms. The largest number of germs exist on door handles. Hand sanitizer gels are useful too.

Wear bags across your shoulders and wallets in your front pocket. No matter where you are, tourists generally are considered targets. People know that you've got more cash in your bag than anyone else in town. Keep your purses criss-crossed along your chest, which makes it harder for people to pull off your shoulder and run with it. Men – carry your wallets in your front pockets.

These tips can easily become habits and make for a much more enjoyable trip.

HOSPITAL EMERGENCIES

Lynn La Benz, a military spouse who lived in Naples for three years, provides the following information for emergencies that may arise while traveling abroad:

I know we all travel with our passports at the outset of our trip because we need them for customs and checking into our hotel. However, many of us then pack them back into the suitcase during our stay. Instead, I decided to make a copy of the passport photo page (showing all passport information) for each of my family members, then I cut them down and stuck them into my handbag.

This turned out to be a good thing. When my son needed stitches, at the emergency room and again at the hospital before his stitches, I was asked for both my and his passport. I didn't have them on me (too heavy) but I did have the copies, which were accepted immediately.

I also found that when you are injured overseas, there is a go-between to help you find your way to the hospital, translate services, and provide authorization for the payment of treatment. It's called **SOS International**. They are London-based and the staff there is friendly, efficient, and helpful. Although we had to pay about 35 USD for the ER triage, the treatment was covered by the fax that SOS International sent to the hospital authorizing payment.

EMERGENCY PREPAREDNESS TRAVEL TIPS

1) Carry either your passport or copies of your passport at all times.

2) Find the plan and health benefits that apply to you at International SOS (www.internationalsos.com).

3) Keep the relevant numbers in your cell phone and write the information on the back of your passport copies.

THE ARTECARD

In this region, Starbucks is nowhere to be found and that can feel a bit problematic for the traveler or expat who is accustomed to being able to "rent a space" at a coffeehouse to sit quietly with a laptop or book for an hour or two. Although the beaches are everywhere, almost every sandy strip is privately owned, so it's difficult to walk freely along the shores at any time of day. Sidewalks are also scarce in these parts, so taking walks or runs isn't common. Riding on a bike without a group of professional bikers will likely have Neapolitans calling you to come to their soup kitchens as most people who ride bikes while wearing jeans are considered homeless. This means that travelers and expats need to re-define how they spend their moments of reprieve.

The Artecard can become essential. The Artecard is for anyone who plans to stay in Naples for more than one day (they offer three and seven day passes also). The year-long card for 40 Euro is nothing short of divine. For Americans, buying one adult Artecard allows your children to get into museums, ruins, palaces, and castles for free.

(Children who do not have EU passports usually must pay the full price of entry.) The card says you get thirty percent discounts here, fifteen percent discounts there, but all these rules are often at the discretion of the person sitting behind the entrance counter. (I suggest you always just take their word for it. Over time your savings will be large no matter what.)

You can purchase the Artecard at any museum, tourist office, or newspaper stand. It comes with a coupon pack as well as a brochure that lists an abundance of sites, some more well-known than others.

With the Artecard, you can use Pompeii as a date-day with your significant other or go hunting for princesses with your children to Castel Sant'Elmo. On days when you'd rather be at a café or take a long walk, the Archeological Park of Baia is a nice substitute. Thanks to the Artecard, leisure time is re-defined and after you've enjoyed the richness of the places offered, the transition back to

Starbucks, well, might not suffice. You can find lots of information about the Artecard at www.campaniartecard.it.

MAY OF MONUMENTS

Every year the **May of Monuments** in Naples or **Maggio dei Monumenti** is a time when most museums and national parks are entirely free to the public with extended hours of operation – including sights like Pompeii. Many museums open up that are usually closed the rest of the year. This is a great time to come out and enjoy the rich sights of Naples.

   Tourist offices around the city provide a directory of guided tours given during this month also. The four tourist offices I recommend are run by the *Azienda Autonoma di Soggiorno Cura e Turismi di Napoli (AAST)* and can be found at these addresses:

> Piazza Trieste e Trento 1, Naples;
> Via San Carlo 9, Naples;
> Piazza Gesu Nuovo, Naples;
> Piazza dei Martiri 58, Naples. (Walk inside the courtyard past the guard and up the stairs on your right.)

A FEW WORDS ABOUT TRASH

Trash in Naples has been an on-going discussion within the national, European, and international press for decades. The trash topic is also of great embarrassment to Neapolitans. Trash, after all, holds connotations of people being dirty and environments being unsanitary, if not toxic. So when outsiders discuss trash in Naples, a cultural sensitivity gets hit upon. And perhaps rightly so. What city or country doesn't have its problems that are an embarrassment to its inhabitants?

Ever since the seventies, the old adage has been: "You come to Rome to see Italy, you come to Naples to smell it." While nothing can ever be pinned down to exact facts, here are some observations:

First, during local and national elections, and for mysterious reasons, trash is not collected. This holds true for Naples and, apparently, for other Italian cities such as Parma, up north, where residents have complained about the same trash phenomenon.

Second, when a trash crisis occurs (unrelated to elections), the city of Caserta thirty-five kilometers north of Naples and the city of Salerno fifty-four kilometers south of Naples continue to have trash collection and the streets are clean. This baffles everyone.

Third, by the humid summer Neapolitans make sure that the bulk of the trash is cleared away – and it happens. Sometimes the European Union threatens to fine Italy for the Neapolitan trash, at which point the Italian army comes into the city and takes everything away in  trucks, depending on the whim of the national government of the day and its attitude towards the local authorities looking after Naples.

Fourth, the city can also face massive shut downs due to strikers who not only affect the businesses they are protesting, but also have a considerable effect on all the other citizens around them. Trash collection frequently stops due to disgruntled sanitation workers who say they aren't getting paid, which is all too often true.

Fifth and most interestingly, New York City also has quite a bit of trash lying around the streets, including during the height of the humid summer. Local folklore in New York maintains that decades ago, certain Neapolitan families immigrated to New York City and they set up a business that happened to be in the sanitation industry. There seems to be a tradition here. Many Neapolitans explain that the trash problem is bound up with the stranglehold that the Camorra has had on the region since all the way back in the 1700's. There is undoubtedly a heavy involvement of the Camorra in the trash collection business and in local politics.

Perhaps – and only perhaps – some aspects of the problem of trash collection are bound up with the culture. In daily conversations both in Naples and in Italy at large, Italians often say that they feel the largest problem in their country is a lack of civic mindedness. The culture prides itself on maintaining strong family bonds, especially in Naples where children often never leave their hometown and remain in close proximity to their family, coming together almost by ritual each Sunday for a large lunch. While you take the good with the bad, these admirable family ties also mean that people outside this circle can often be treated as less important. Other drivers on the road or other people waiting in line are less important because they are strangers. As a consequence – some say – you can see people throwing trash out their car windows (it's not, after all, their own house which usually is kept pristine). Here in fact is a key issue, the vast divide in attitude towards public and private space. Having left your car window and hit the ground, the trash is now in public space and someone else will pick it up, possibly an employee of the state and we never did like the state anyway...

Lest these generalizations about civic consciousness go too far, the people of Naples and Italy are constantly debating the trash problem in the media, instead of ignoring it, and Neapolitans have been known to launch protests during trash crises. Meanwhile, some local politicians have debated whether they could use the Naples underground cavities as repositories of trash. On a more positive note, following the election of a new mayor, Luigi de Magistris, on an anti-mafia ticket, the new administration is attempting to get to grips with the garbage problem with a modest measure of success. New initiatives in recycling have been announced (slowly coming into play) and the streets appear cleaner. What's more, a civic-minded social network based group called *CleaNap* has begun organizing people into cleaning squads to clean the city, piazza by piazza and foreigners are very welcome to join in.

DELUGE IN POMPEII

On December 1, 2010 the *Christian Science Monitor* reported that the walls of the house where the gladiators once trained for combat as well as a wall of the so-called *small brothel* had collapsed due to heavy rain. Italians, UNESCO, the European Union, and reporters generally blame Italian politicians for Pompeii's imminent collapse.[67]

But rest assured, Pompeii remains as it always has – in ruins.

The all-important Forum remains intact. So does the newly renovated Forum Baths and the famous House of the Faun and the Villa of the Mysteries. Walking along the main artery of Via dell'Abbondanza, the street remains in excellent sloped condition and the heavy rains that flow each year down toward the Stabia Gate shows how Pompeii inhabitants would have welcomed any deluge because all the trash during ancient times, from animal feces to human body parts, would have washed out of the city.

Interestingly, the *Christian Science Monitor* dressed up the devastation of the little brothel as a tourist catastrophe, even though it is not on the tourist map, has never been part of any tour, and

---

67 Alessandra Rizzo, "Pompeii collapse affects 2 ancient walls, UNESCO inspecting damage," *Christian Science Monitor* 1 December 2010:
http://www.csmonitor.com/World/Latest-News-Wires/2010/1201/Pompeii-collapse-affects-2-ancient-walls-UNESCO-inspecting-damage.

thus far has never been open to the public. The House of Gladiators is cordoned off and, indeed, rubble appears. This house has also never been open to the public and has never shown up on the map of tourist attractions.

Across the street and a little further down, the House of Venus – with its vibrant fresco of naked Venus – still looks fantastic. During WWII, bombs fell on Pompeii and the House of Venus was obliterated, but archeologists received money in 1952 to reconstruct the villa piece-by-imaginative-piece.

Perhaps some of the newspaper reports are about politics. The EU will always want a reason to embarrass Italian Prime Ministers or Italian politics in general – which can boast of having had at least forty-eight political parties and at least seventeen Prime Ministers in the last two decades.

But also a touch of ignorance or at least unreasonable expectations may be behind these fears of imminent collapse. Archeologists (especially for tourists' sake and often under pressure from benefactors who fund the reconstructions) have always taken artistic license when studying artifacts and rebuilding ruins. They often liberally add modern day plaster or add wooden beams, they restore color to frescoes, and sometimes surmise from a few pebbles what an entire villa may have looked like. Their creations are highly breakable, yet Pompeii's sights sustain the weight of three million visitors per year. Pompeii is, in fact, Disneyland by another name.

And what's wrong with that? Archeologists do painstaking work and have layered methodologies that create a blend of fact and, yes, fiction. Because, in the end, walking through ruins such as Pompeii is not so much about accuracy as it is about erecting shadows of a lost history that smacks down our modern day hubris. After a visit, one is thrust into asking: do we really do things better?

Living among these ruins certainly has a strong impact on the culture of Naples. Neapolitans strongly believe *the old ways are better*, whether it be the old ways of making wine, making vintage gloves, or hearkening back to a coffee roaster's decades-long history in order to sell their product.

So perhaps another frightening suggestion lies behind the fear of Pompeii's collapse. In the end, our world, too, will collapse. So another travel tip may be that when you return home, consider scratching obscene graffiti along your walls and leaving buckets of paint in the middle of your living room. You never know when your community might be ossified in ash. In such a case, you'll want archeologists to find what you've left behind and whatever it is, you can be sure that tomes will be written about the many lovers and quarrels you had inside your humble domicile.

THE UNDERGROUND DISASTER

At about 4 a.m. on September 29, 2009 three chasms opened in the historic Spaccanapoli district of downtown Naples. The largest chasm was about twenty meters deep and opened in the middle of a street considered a major nerve center for traffic. Six buildings had to be evacuated and 297 people had to leave their homes. Tensions arose among the evacuees who feared remaining homeless without any help from government institutions. Another chasm then also opened beneath a church, putting it at risk of collapse and making its entrance practically disappear. The local Neapolitan newspaper, *Il Mattino*, suggested that the chasms were caused by the heavy rains.[68]

In the end, these collapses will remain forever an alarming possibility in a bustling city that does, and perhaps must, live for the present moment.

---

68 –, "Napoli, voragini nei Quartieri Spagnoli 297 sfollati, 188 famiglie a rischio," *Il Mattino* 23 Settembre 2010: http://www.ilmattino.it/articolo.php?id=74230&sez=NAPOLI.

THE LYSISTRATA SISTERS

Let's face it, full-time wives and mothers can often be the most odious of women. Having given up dreams of career, money, and promotions, they spend their days cultivating the practice of serving others without gain. When three or more of these women get together, kings, presidents, decorated military men, and husbands quake. These women demand odious things like crosswalks at schools for their children, strict punishments for drunk drivers, and that grand word – peace.

Neapolitan women have also flexed their muscle in the recent past. Bringing their history as part of Magna Graecia to the forefront, they have used *Lysistrata* by Aristophanes as a guide to protest their men folk. (In the ancient Greek play, women refuse to have intimate relations with their husbands until they agree to stop the war with Sparta.) On December 31, 2008, the BBC reported that hundreds of Neapolitan women went on a sex strike, refusing to have intercourse with their husbands unless they refrained from lighting firecrackers on New Year's Eve.

Every year, boys and men light firecrackers or *bombe* throughout the city during the New Year's festivities. *Bombe* explode with much of the force of conventional armaments and yet, they are thrown off balconies, down narrow streets, and into the middle of traffic. Injuries as a result of firecrackers have occurred all too frequently and have led to lost eyes or paralysis or worse.

Now, the local authorities have backed the women and the women have urged their male-folk to **"make love, not explosions."**[69]

AFRICAN-ITALIAN BECOMES PRIME MINISTER OF ITALY!

Black Neapolitans constitute the largest minority population in the region. Nevertheless, it's near impossible to encounter a black barista, waiter, or shop keeper working anywhere in the city – occupations that usually provide on-the-job training.

Some locals say that black Neapolitans are a new group who landed on these shores during the last twenty years only. In fact, African-Italians have been a part of Italy, and particularly Naples, since ancient times. From the great warriors of Hannibal to the imported slaves for Roman patricians, this port town has had a close relationship to the continent of Africa and its people for more than two thousand years. Africans settled here during the Byzantine era, including San Gaudioso and his followers. He brought the remains of Saint Restituta, an African woman, to Naples and she is still revered, having her own niche in the Naples Duomo itself. Furthermore, the artists who created the *presepe* displayed at the Certosa di San Martino added an abundant number of kings, sheep herders, and musicians who were black.

Today in the Naples area, blacks are relegated to living almost exclusively in the suburb town of Castel Volturno where they have their own churches and shops. One black Neapolitan, wanting to remain anonymous, admitted that blacks aren't able to live outside this suburb town because white Neapolitans refuse to sell or rent to them elsewhere. And blacks aren't necessarily welcome in Castel

---

69 –, "Naples sex strike over fireworks," *BBC News* 31 December 2008: http://news.bbc.co.uk/2/hi/europe/7806367.stm.

Volturno either. On September 18, 2008, for example, six blacks were gunned down in a suspected mafia hit, the Camorra unhappy that people of darker skin color were starting to become successful in their slice of the Campania black market economy.[70]

Then, on January 7, 2010 in the town of Rosarno (about five hours south of Naples), some caucasian Italian males in a car decided to shoot air bullets at two Africans as they walked home from work. The incident set off riots and protests by the African immigrants living in the town. Three days later, policemen decided to solve the problem, not by finding the gunmen, but by evacuating more than 900 black African immigrants from their homes. While watching their departure, many caucasian Italian inhabitants cheered.[71]

On a national level, even while the well-known Jean-Leonard Touadi (of Congolese background), serves his country as the third black-Italian member of Parliament[72], legislation has become increasingly disturbing. The Bossi-Fini immigration law maintains that if a legal immigrant looses his or her job, he or she is considered an illegal immigrant and is subject to immediate expulsion. To remain in the country is to become a shadow worker. The government has also debated whether to segregate schools for the children of immigrants.[73]

The use of the words "African immigrants" rather than "black Neapolitans" within the media is itself interesting. Currently, Italian citizenship laws favor *jus sanguinis* (right of blood). This means that U.S. citizens, Argentinians, Chileans, Canadians, Australians, New

---

70 –, "Man arrested for Italian shooting," *BBC News* 22 September 2008: http://news.bbc.co.uk/2/hi/europe/7630352.stm.

71 Gavin Jones, "Italy in racism debate as migrants quit riot town," *Reuters* 10 January 2010: http://www.reuters.com/article/2010/01/10/idUSLDE60906D.

72 Tom Kington, "Black MP in warning to "racist" Italy," *Guardian.co.uk* 19 October 2008: http://www.guardian.co.uk/world/2008/oct/19/italy-race-touadi-mafia.

73 Sabina Zaccaro, "Election Bings New Hope for Migrants," *Inter Press Service (IPS)* 8 April 2006: http://ipsnews.net/news.asp?idnews=32824.

Zealanders, Brazilians and Venezuelans who have an ancestor (parent, grandparent, or even great-grandparent) born in Italy may apply and receive Italian citizenship automatically by descent. However, those who don't have Italian blood or haven't married an Italian citizen can become naturalized only after ten years of legal residence, provided they do not have a criminal record (including getting caught for working illegally), and they have "sufficient financial resources." In contrast, EU citizens – meaning not from the "third world" – who live in Italy but don't have Italian blood or marital bonds can naturalize after four years and thereafter can refer to themselves as Italians.[74]

Black Neapolitans understand well that they are targets of discrimination. They refuse to be photographed and refuse to participate in any interviews, avoiding conversations about their lives. Why so much fear? Their reluctance leads one to believe that they indeed have something to fear and this is truly a shame within a port town that has been a salad bowl of diversity for thousands of years.

---

74 –, "Italian Nationality Law," *Wikipedia, the Free Encyclopedia:* http://en.wikipedia.org/wiki/Italian_nationality_law.

AND BEYOND:
THE ARBËRESHË

Drive into the mountains of Calabria near the Ionian Sea and signs start to be written in both Italian and Arbëreshë, a pre-Ottoman language still preserved by these small village communities. Linguistic enthusiasts come here to study how a Christian folk escaped the Muslim Turks and retained a tongue replete with five hundred year old archaisms no longer understood by their cousins across the sea.

The Arbëreshë today comprise the largest ethnic minority in Italy, their towns mostly located in southern provinces, such as Calabria and Basilicata. They sailed from Albania to these shores in the 15th to 18th centuries, on one notable occasion at the request of King  Ferdinand I of Aragon. In 1459 Albania's national hero, Skanderbeg, created an army and fought with a combined Neapolitan-Albanian force to crush the French insurrection, effectively saving Naples. The King rewarded Skanderbeg's troops with land in Apulia where they settled in many villages; today they are present in fifty communities.

After the death of Skanderbeg, the Ottomans overran Albania, forcing Christian inhabitants to convert to Islam. Many refused and fled to the Italian lands. Legend has it that Skanderbeg's son spearheaded the immigration. For centuries thereafter, waves of immigration and intercultural interactions continued between Italy and Albania. By the 1990's when a pyramid scheme sent the

Albanian economy toppling, more than 300,000 Albanians fled to Italy, sometimes settling in Arbëreshë villages where they clashed with the descendants of their medieval countrymen in both language and customs.

To visit the Arbëreshë, two towns in particular stand out. **Cività** (or Cifti) has an **Arbëreshë Ethnic Museum** and a **Devil's Bridge** that is part of the **Pollino National Park**. The town itself is cut into the mountain with beautiful views and tortuous cobblestone streets with a piazza, B&B's, wine makers, and restaurants. The Arbëreshë also have their own cuisine, such as Strangujet, a kind of gnocchi with tomato sauce and basil.

At the edge of the town, a **monument to Pal Engjelli** (1417-1470) perches above a valley. A priest and close counsellor to Skanderbeg, he wrote the first known sentence in Albanian.

The Arbëreshë language derives from the southern Albanian Tosk dialect, but still retains all the archaisms of the 15th century. Interestingly, Arbëreshë was only a spoken language until the 1980's – Albanian itself only became a written language in the 20th century – so Pal Engjelli's written words in 1462 are particularly significant. His written

sentence is about baptism, probably the phrase used for Albanian people in the countryside who were unable to take their children to church to be baptized.

Another town nearby, **Frascineto**, has a Church and an **Arbëreshë Library** founded by a Byzantine-Catholic priest, Antonio Bellusci (1934-). Today, the majority of Arbëreshë have a unique religion; they are Christians of the Eastern Rite, but adhere to the authority of the Catholic Pope. Frascineto also has a **Museum of Albanian Costume** and a **Museum of Byzantine Iconography**.

Once remote, these villages are still sleepy. There's much to explore, but you'll find that strolling through the streets and waving at the locals is the best way to experience this slice of a dual-culture world.

TOP PICKS

Rather than provide a comprehensive list of places to stay, eat, pray, and shop, which becomes quickly obsolete and can easily be found on-line by Googling travel websites such as **Trip Advisor** (www.tripadvisor.com), here I only add "Top Picks" that are especially meant as brief insider tips.

PLACES TO STAY

For those who would like to stay in the center of Naples, I suggest you choose hotels located near the Castel dell'Ovo. Exploring the streets at night is not recommended for tourists with the exception of this area, where you can wander along the promenade until late and enjoy the nightlife. However, I recommend only the excellent four star hotels along here:

1) **Royal Continental** at Via Partenope 38/44, Naples (www.royalgroup.it).

2) **Excelsior** at Via Partenope 48, Naples (www.excelsior.it).

3) **Grand Hotel Santa Lucia** at Via Partenope 46, Naples (www.santalucia.it).

4) A nice alternative to downtown Naples is **Hotel Paradiso** at Via Catullo 11, Posillipo (www.hotelparadisonapoli.it).

5) A cheap option is the youth hostel near Virgil's Tomb and close to the Castel dell'Ovo called **AIG Ostello Mergellina** at Salita della Grotta 23, Naples (www.ostellonapoli.com).

6) Choices *outside* the city abound and are highly recommended as an alternative to staying in the city. The most popular and least

expensive is to stay at an **agriturismo**, where the owners usually make their own fresh food and wine on the property. You can find lots of agriturismo choices at www.agriturismo.net/campania.

7) For the Phlegraean Fields, try **La Tripergola** at Via Miliscola 165, Pozzuoli (www.latripergola.it/hotelnapoli.htm).

8) A cheap option is **Camping in Solfatara** (www.solfatara.it).

The islands provide a wonderful getaway, especially for honeymooners:

9) In Capri there's **Hotel La Tosca** at Via D. Birago 5, Capri (www.capri.com/en/c/la-tosca-2). This is near the town center where *It Started In Naples* with Sophia Loren was filmed.

10) In Ischia there's **Hotel Da Raffaele** at Via Roma 29, Ischia (www.daraffaele.it). This island is known for its wonderful spas. Make sure to try out the multi-pool, waterfalls, and beach strip at the Gardens of Poseidon (www.giardiniposeidon.it/uk).

PLACES TO EAT

Because food plays such an important role here, you'll rarely go wrong at any of the restaurants or cafés in this region. The following are my top picks:

1) In the Phlegraean Fields and overlooking the Temple of Apollo, **Agriturismo Terra Mia** offers fresh vegetables and wine made on the property at Via Lago D'Averno 9, Pozzuoli.

2) For fine dining at a high-end restaurant that overlooks wonderful views along the cliffs, try **La Sarrestia** at Via Orazio 116, Posillipo.

Book Recommendation: For a comprehensive English-language recipe book, *Naples At Table* by Arthur Schwartz is worth the purchase.

3) The new city of Pompei has a charming town center with the restaurant **Il Principe** that boasts ancient Roman cuisine, including Tutti-Frutti of Oplontis. The address is Piazza Bartolo Longo 1, Pompei. *(See p. 54.)*

4) **La Bersagliera** at Borgo Marinari 10/11, Naples. *(See p. 139.)*

5) **Donna Sofia Ristorante** at Via Talagnano 5, Sorrento. *(See p. 139.)*

6) Along the Amalfi Coast, **Trattoria del Teatro** at Via E. Marini 19, Amalfi is a former theater. *(See p. 157.)*

7) **Antica Pizzeria Port'Alba** is at Via Port'Alba 18 in downtown Naples. *(See p. 231.)*

8) **Brandi's** is at Salita S Anna di Palazzo 1-2, Naples. *(See p. 231.)*

And my top picks for cafés in the city are:

9) **Intra Moenia** at Piazza Bellini 70, Naples. *(See p. 180.)*

10) **Moccia** at Via San Pasquale a Chiaia 77, Naples. *(See p. 179.)*

PLACES TO PRAY

More than two hundred Catholic Churches exist in downtown Naples alone. Open to everyone, they provide quiet reprieve from the frenetic city traffic and display stunning works of art for free. They also transport visitors back through centuries of medieval, Byzantine, and ancient history. But with so many Churches in the area, which ones are the most important?

Here are my top picks of churches to see in downtown Naples, which can also be followed as a day-long tour:

1) **Santa Maria del Parto** at Via Mergellina 21 is a wonderful little treat because you must take an elevator up to this church built in the 1520s. Jacopo Sannazaro, the Neapolitan humanist and poet during Angevin times, has his tomb behind the altar. There's also a *Mergellina Devil* painting that shows St. Michael vanquishing the devil disguised as a beautiful woman.

2) **Santa Maria di Piedigrotta** at Piazza Piedigrotta 24 was mentioned by Giovanni Boccaccio in 1339. A church founded by fishermen in Mergellina, the building initially faced the grotto, but then was rebuilt to face the city.

3) **Santa Maria La Nova** at Piazza Santa Maria La Nova 44. Charles I of Anjou had this church built with niches full of famous masterpieces of the Renaissance. A cloister courtyard next door is also worth a visit for its stunning frescoes on the walls and even a sculpture by Riccardo Dalisi.

4) **Sant'Anna dei Lombardi** at Piazza Monteoliveto. The Church is tucked along a side road and its most impressive artwork lies in the back at Vasari's refectory that has a ceiling fresco and handcrafted wooden marquetry along the walls.

5) **Gesu Nuovo** at Piazza del Gesu Nuovo contains richly decorated Baroque art and a niche with San Giuseppe Moscati that has silver images of specific body parts. These votive offerings are purchased by worshippers wishing to be healed.

6) **San Gregorio Armeno Church** at Piazza San Gaetano 1 has the weekly miracle of Saint Patricia.

7) **Cappella Sansevero** at Piazza Raimondo De Sangro di Sansevero 16 contains what's considered a "wonder of the world" – the *Veiled Christ*.

8) **Il Duomo** at Via Duomo 147 is also known as the Naples Cathedral.

9) **San Giovanni a Carbonara** at Via San Giovanni a Carbonara 5 has a unique circular Cappella Caracciolo del Sole and has paved Tuscan tiles. Behind the altar is the tomb of Ser Gianni Caracciolo, Joanna II's lover and Grand Seneschal at the court.

10) **Certosa di San Martino** at Largo San Martino 5 is a cloister with beautiful marble columns in a courtyard, opulent gardens, and a richly decorated church. The Certosa also houses several exhibitions that delight adults and children alike, including the *presepe*, European carriages, and medieval ships.

Note, however, that each church opens at its own specific hours. Some are only open in the mornings, others open haphazardly. Most churches tend to open from about 10 a.m. to 12 p.m, close for the afternoon *riposo* or *pausa*, and then re-open from around 4 p.m. to 8 p.m.

Due to the vast riches inside, each church hires a custodian to take care of the grounds. Custodians tend to be elderly retired gentlemen who are kind, well-informed, and enthusiastic about showing tourists the artwork in their church – including gems that might be hidden in back recesses – if only tourists go up to them and ask questions with a sense of wonder and appreciation.

SHOPPING, SHOPPING, SHOPPING

The most upscale shopping is to be had across the street from the Teatro San Carlo inside the impressive **Galleria Umberto I**. Here you'll find a host of brand names at extraordinarily high prices.

Next to the Galleria Umberto I, the street of **Via Toledo** is another shopping haven. At ninety degrees to this you'll find **Via Chiaia** and can descend towards the Bay of Naples, discovering **Via Filangieri** and **Via dei Mille** on the way. Here you'll see jewelry shops and upscale stores such as **Bulgari**. Nearby you can check out the **Emporio Armani** at Piazza dei Martiri 61-62.

On a more affordable scale, but still in the city are the stores along the streets of the **Vomero** district (take the Metro to the Vomero and then make your way down the hill). There's also **Corso Umberto I**, which starts at the central train station in Piazza Garibaldi.

Most Neapolitans prefer to buy their groceries, shoes, clothing, and electronic equipment at the many open markets around the city where incredible deals are to be found. The most famous is located along **Via Pignasecca** where locals haggle for clothes or shoes and seafood vendors display their catch in huge shallow tins.

Another famous market is located in Ercolano near the Herculaneum ruins called **Resina Via Pugliano**. For more information, see their website at www.mercatodiresina.it.

Lastly, the shopping malls (*i Centri Commerciali*) are everywhere. The most entertaining is **Vulcano Buono** at Località Boscofangone, Nola, which was built in the shape of a volcano and has chain stores as well as boutique stores plus a food court with a wine bar and a movie theater. Visit their website at www.vulcanobuono.it.

Don't forget that every year in February and July you'll find deep discounts on all clothing throughout the region – designer skirts for 10 Euro as well as shoes, jackets, and more that are fifty to seventy percent off.

TEN OVERLOOKED SIGHTS IN NAPLES

They are called overlooked because they seldom make it into the travel guides and tend to have fewer tourists, but these gems also won't disappoint because they leave visitors dreaming of mythical lands and legendary heroes. Here is a quick guide that highlights sights mentioned in the previous chapters:

1) **Pizzofalcone**: In myth this is where the siren Parthenope was born. Walking around this area feels like a seedy adventure. The streets behind Piazza del Plebiscito become small; take Via Gennaro Serra then left onto Via Egiziaca a Pizzofalcone as far as you can go, turning left onto the street that houses the Military State Archives. Once you reach the rock itself, there's a fine view of Naples. *(See p. 104.)*

2) **Entrance to Hades**: Meet Carlo Santillo who will guide you with candles and oil lamps through a Roman military tunnel, also known as the Grotta della Sibilla. He'll show you the River Styx and the cave where the sibyl uttered her oracles. *(See p. 17.)*

3) **Temple of Apollo Celebrations**: Come to Lago Averno before sundown during the solstices and equinoxes where a group of nature-minded Italians hold ceremonies to bring together all religions and all cultures. They beat drums and give offerings to nature. The event is free and hosted by Centro Nuova Era. *(See p. 193.)*

4) **The Papyrus Scrolls at the National Library**: Come nose-to-nose with 2,000 year old papyrus scrolls written in Greek and found during the 18th century at the Villa of the Papyri in Herculaneum. If you make an appointment, the librarians take you through the backdoors of one of the most prominent and oldest libraries in Europe until you reach this secluded exhibition. *(See p. 61.)*

5) **The Macabre Dominicans**: Part of the Naples parallel city, the catacombs of San Gaudioso lurk underneath the Santa Maria della Sanità Church. Tours show you the tomb of the African San Gaudioso, a stunning fresco of Saint Catherine, and the artwork of Dominicans who painted their wealthy patrons using skulls and skeletons. *(See p. 87.)*

6) **Santa Chiara Cloister**: Search for the solution to an assassination mystery; somewhere on the grounds, Queen Joanna I's remains were dumped. Still today no marker bears witness to where the remains of the Queen rests. Some say they are located up a flight of stairs behind an ever locked door. The cloister itself is decorated with breathtaking majolica tiles. *(See p. 114.)*

7) **Purgatory**: The Santa Maria delle Anime del Purgatorio ad Arco Church has an underground more macabre than that of the Dominicans. Since the 17th and 18th centuries, innumerable bones of the deceased have been left unburied here. In particular, people leave flowers and cards alongside the bones of Lucia, a girl stricken by tuberculosis a few days before she was to wed a Marquis. *(See p. 82.)*

8) **Sanctuaria Sacra**: Religious shops along the two famed streets of Decumano Maggiore and Via Tribunali sell items necessary for the more than two hundred churches located in downtown Naples. Priestly garb, Eucharist holders, and nick-knacks are everywhere. One of the most charming are the silver body parts. Buy one of these and head down to **Gesu Nuovo Church** where you can leave your healed or in-need-of-healing body part in the side chapel of San Giuseppe Moscati, a physician saint. *(See p. 210.)*

9) **The University of Naples Museums**: Winding up a labyrinth of stairs, passing students and faculty, several science museums display dinosaur fossils, insects, and artifacts from Troy. *(See p. 212.)*

10) **Riccardo Dalisi's Workshops**: Discover this architect, tinsmith, and maker of the Alessi version of the *Napoletana*. Walking along Rua Catalana you can enjoy Dalisi's art between buildings and on street corners. Two workshops are also open, inspired by Dalisi's works. *(See p. 227.)*

TEN OVERLOOKED SIGHTS IN ITALY

In addition to Naples, here I include my quick guide of top ten picks for overlooked sights in the whole of Italy:

1) **The Greek Philosophers City in Velia**: The 5th century Greek philosophers Parmenides and Zeno lived and lectured where these ruins lie. The vast complex has a trail that winds up to a hilltop castle built in medieval times. There's also a Roman theater, a forum, and a Roman villa tucked behind brush. Velia is located in the Cilento National Park where you can camp, hike, and enjoy the beaches. Not far distant are the three dramatic Greek temples at Paestum, remaining from early Greek colonization of the Italian peninsula. *(See p. 35.)*

2) **The Abbey and Cemetery of Monte Cassino**: One of the few remaining territorial abbeys, this monastery is important to scholars because it holds many original codices from the medieval ages and is also where St. Thomas Aquinas lived for a time. Built over a Temple of Apollo in the 6th century A.D., the Nazis tried to take over the region in 1944, but a battalion of Polish forces routed them out. A moving tribute to their heroism can be found at the bottom of the abbey in the form of a large cemetery and memorial.

3) **The Arbëreshë in Cività**: The Albanians are the largest minority in Italy and have been here since the 16th century when they escaped the Ottoman takeover across the Adriatic. Today, hotels are named after Skanderbeg and monuments to Albanian heroes are everywhere in this area. The Arbëreshë have retained an ancient form of Albanian and linguists flock here to study their unique tongue. At Cività, in particular, you can visit the ethnographic museum and walk across a devil's bridge. *(See p. 259.)*

4) **The Etruscan Tour**: These mysterious ancients left bulbous tombs in **Cerveteri**, vibrant fresco tombs in **Tarquinia**, and a 180-meter deep well on the hilltop of **Orvieto**. Start at the **National Etruscan Museum in Rome** and then drive through the countryside to each of these impressive towns. *(See p. 66.)*

5) **The Paper Makers of Amalfi**: The Valley of the Mills is a hiking trail going past the ruins of Amalfi's famous paper mills, which began their production in the 13th century. At the end of the trail, you can picnic next to a beautiful waterfall. *(See p. 154.)*

6) **The Villa of Tiberius at Sperlonga**: Emperor Tiberius had a summer home in Sperlonga while he still ruled Rome. These ruins now contain a mammoth cave and an impressive museum of items that were found inside the villa. A public beach is right next door. Sperlonga is also near Gaeta, where you can visit **Split Rock** (the rock said to have split on the day that Jesus Christ died), **Cicero's Tomb** (the famous Roman senator and writer), or follow signs eighty kilometers into the mountains to see the **Grotte di Pastena**. *(See p. 63.)*

7) **Medieval Physicians of Salerno**: The oldest medical school on the continent also had the largest number of women physicians. They wrote prescriptions for things like wandering uteruses and worms in the ears. Walking toward the medical school means stopping at the macabre **Il Duomo** full of anguished scenes of saints as well as their unburied bones. On the way out of the city, you can follow signs to the **Castello di Arechi**. *(See p. 118 and p. 163.)*

8) **Sailing with Odysseus across Scylla and Charybdis**: Sailing from the Italian mainland to Sicily, a ferry takes you across the **Strait of Messina**, considered to be the original Scylla and Charbybdis where Odysseus passed. From here, my top picks for

travel in Sicily (which is filled with an abundance of gems) are the ancient ruins of **Agrigento**, the ancient philosopher-city of **Siracusa**, and a climb up **Mt. Etna**.

9) **The Archeological Park of Baia**: Three enormous terraces have baffled archeologists for centuries. Nobody knows definitively what purpose these structures served. Located in the Phlegraean Fields or "Fields of Fire," visitors can wander through what looks like baths, steep stairwells, open gymnasium spaces, and three temples, including the Temple of Echoes. *(See p. 19.)*

10) **The Sassi Caves of Matera**: These caves date back 7,000 years, but people inhabited them until the 1950's when the government deemed them dangerous and had the caves evacuated. The picturesque city of Matera cuts into a mountain and you can stay in cave hotels. Mel Gibson also filmed *The Passion of Christ* here.

SELECTED BIBLIOGRAPHY

Avallone, Roberta. *Cucina Napoletana*. Meda: Giunti Demetra, 2006.

Barrett, Anthony A. *Agrippina: Sex, Power and Politics in the Early Empire*. London: Routledge, 1996.

Beard, Mary. *Pompeii: The Life of a Roman Town*. London: Profile Books, 2008.

Beard, Mary. *The Fires of Vesuvius*. Harvard: Belknap Press, 2008.

Bearne, Catherine Mary. *A sister of Marie Antoinette; the life-story of Maria Carolina, Queen of Naples*. Charleston: Nabu Press, 2010. (A reproduction of a book published before 1923.)

Berti, Luciano and Graziella Magherini and Monica Toraldo di Francia. *Artemisia Gentileschi: Our Contemporary*. Florence: Kleine Schnel, 2002.

Bettina, Elizabeth. *It Happened in Italy*. Nashville: Thomas Nelson, Inc., 2011.

Boccaccio, Giovanni. *Famous Women*. Trans. Virginia Brown. Cambridge: Harvard University Press, 2003.

Broad, William. *The Oracle*. New York: Penguin Books, 2006.

Buonoconto, Mario. *A Fantastic Journey In the Light of the Everlasting Lantern: the extraordinary inventions of the Prince of Sansevero*. Trans. into English by Albert Coward. Naples: aloc, 2005.

Capalbo, Carla. *The Food and Wine Guide to Naples and Campania*. London: Pallas Athene, 2005.

Carrington, Hereward. *Eusapia Palladino and her phenomena*. New York: B.W. Dodge & Company, 1909.

Carter, Marina. *Naples, Sorrento & the Amalfi Coast*. Edison, NJ: Hunter Publishing, Inc., 2006.

Chiodi, Antonio Latini and Mario Busso. *Pasta: Passione e Fantasia*. Milano: Gribaudo, 2008.

Cicero, Marcus Tullius and Michael Grant. *Cicero, Selected Works.* New York: Penguin Books, 1971.

Corrado, Vincenzo. *Il Cuoco Galante: Ristampa dell'edizione napoletana del 1793.* Napoli: Grimaldi & C.Editori, 2007.

D'Antonio, Massimo. *Guide of Discovery to the Lands of Fire.* Naples: Massa Editore, 2003.

Davids, Kenneth. *Espresso: Ultimate Coffee.* New York: St. Martin's Griffin, 1993.

De Caro, Stefano and Valeria Sampaolo, eds. *Guide of Ancient Capua.* Trans. Federico Poole and Mark Weir. Santa Maria Capua Vetere: Spointendenza Archeologica Di Napoli e Caserta, 2000.

De Filippo, Eduardo. *Theater Neapolitan Style: Five One-Act Plays.* Trans. Mimi Gisolfi D'Aponte. Massachusetts: Rosemont Publishing & Printing Corp., 2004.

Dudley, Donald R. *The Civilization of Rome.* New York: Penguin Books, 1962.

Fortune, Jane. *Invisible Women: Forgotten Artists of Florence.* Florence: The Florentine Press, 2010.

Garrard, Mary D. *Artemisia Gentileschi: The Image of the Female Hero in Italian Baroque Art.* Princeton: Princeton University Press, 1989.

Giordano, Carlo and Isidoro Kahn. *The Jews in Pompeii, Herculaneum, Stabiae and in the Cities of Campania Felix.* Trans. Wilhelmina F. Jashemski, revised edition Laurentino Garcia y Garcia. Roma: Bardi Editore s.r.l., 2001.

Goldstone, Nancy. *The Lady Queen: The Notorious Reign of Joanna I, Queen of Naples, Jerusalem, and Sicily.* New York: Walker & Company, 2009.

Graham-Dixon, Andrew. *Michelangelo and the Sistine Chapel.* London: Orion Books, 2008.

Green, Monica H., ed. and trans. *The Trotula: An English Translation of the Medieval Compendium of Women's Medicine.* Philadelphia: University of Pennsylvania Press, 2002.

Harris, Robert. *Pompeii.* New York: Random House, 2005.

Hotcher, A.E. *Sophia Living and Loving: Her Own Story.* London: William Morrow & Company, 1979.

Homer. *The Odyssey.* Trans. Robert Fagles. New York: Penguin Books, 1996.

Lancaster, Jordan. *In The Shadow of Vesuvius: A Cultural History of Naples.* London: I.B. Tauris, 2005.

Miller, Naomi. *Heavenly Caves: Reflections on the Garden Grotto.* New York: George Braziller, 1982.

–. *Naples & The Amalfi Coast.* London: Dorling Kindersley Limited, 2011.

Osborne, Richard. *Rossini: His Life and Works.* New York: Oxford University Press, 2007.

Ovid. *Metamorphoses.* Trans. Rolfe Humphries. Bloomington: Indiana University Press, 1983.

Parke, H.W. *Sibyls and Sibylline Prophecy in Classical Antiquity.* Ed. B.C. McGing. London: Routledge, 1988.

Pendergrast, Mark. *Uncommon Grounds: The History of Coffee and How It Transformed Our World.* New York: Basic Books, 2010.

Petronius, Gaius. *The Satyricon.* Trans. P.G. Walsh. Oxford: Oxford University Press, 2009.

Pignataro, Luciano. *I Dolci Napoletani.* Roma: Newton Compton, 2008.

Ricotti, Eugenia Salza Prina. *Ricette Della Cucina Romana A Pompei.* Roma: L'erma di Bretschneider, 1993.

Saviano, Roberto. *Gomorrah: A Personal Journey into the Violent International Empire of Naples' Organized Crime System.* Trans. Virginia Jewiss. New York: Picador, 2006.

Schwartz, Arthur. *Naples at Table: Cooking in Campania.* New York: Harper Collins, 1998.

Sorrentino, Lejla Mancusi. *Manuale del perfetto amatore del Caffè: Storie, racconti e ricette.* Napoli: Intra Moenia, 2003.

Suetonius, Gaius. *The Twelve Caesars.* Trans. Robert Graves. London: Penguin Books, 1957, revised 2007.

Tacitus, Publius Cornelius. *The Complete Works of Tacitus: The Annals. The History. The Life of Gnaeus Julius Agricola. Germany and Its Tribes. A Dialogue on Oratory.* Trans. Alfred John Church and William Jackson Brodribb. Ed. Moses Hadas. New York: Modern Library, 1942.

Tacitus, Publius Cornelius. *The Annals of Imperial Rome.* Trans. Michael Grant. London: Penguin Books, 1956, revised 1977.

Virgil. *The Aeneid.* Trans. David West. London: Penguin Books Ltd., 1991.

Ukers, William H. *All About Coffee.* New York: The Tea and Coffee Trade Journal Company, 1922.

INDEX

Made in the USA
San Bernardino, CA
18 August 2013